FINANCIAL AND ECONOMIC LITERACY

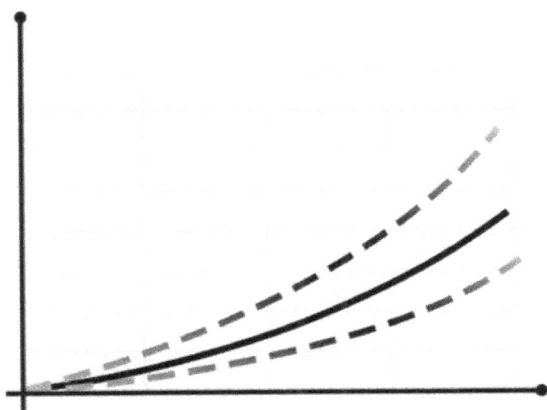

Dan Zhumadilov
Timothy Choi

ISBN: 979-8-218-61898-8 (paperback)
For comments or feedback, please reach out to the authors at
contact@FinEconLit.com.

First Edition: May 2025
Printed in the United States of America

CONTENTS

DISCLAIMER

This book was not written with the intention of providing investing advice. In fact, we spend a significant amount of time explaining why all investing advice should be taken with caution. However, a good deal of the book covers personal finance topics—including investing. The information and examples it covers are intended for educational purposes only. They should not be interpreted as recommendations for making any specific financial or investment decisions.

When analyzing financial and economic trends, this book often provides historical data. It is important to understand that past results are not indicative of future outcomes. Too often, other financial and economic literacy resources will make an extrapolation that long-existing trends will continue into the future. Investment markets and economic conditions are constantly evolving based on an incredibly complex array of factors. There are inherent risks involved in any investment activity or financial decision-making. This book does not account for every potential risk, nor can it anticipate how future circumstances may impact investment performance.

Personal financial situations vary. Readers should consult a qualified financial professional to determine the best approach for their individual needs.

PREFACE

In our rapidly changing world, financial literacy resources are constantly expanding. A wealth of books and workbooks offer a basic overview of financial topics both online and in print, and while many cover an impressive range of topics, they occasionally leave the reader wishing for a more in-depth or data-supported explanation. Conversely, there are many books on economic history and scholarly articles written by academics. These often delve into details that may be excessive for someone seeking a general understanding of economic concepts and financial strategies. Our goal is to bridge the gap between these types of resources.

To help meet this goal, this book has been divided into two parts, "Financial Literacy" and "Economic Literacy," though the division is somewhat arbitrary. Topics covered in one part could have been explored in the other. Nevertheless, we have followed the established convention where "Financial Literacy" typically encompasses personal finance concerns such as saving, investing, managing debt, and spending. On the other hand, the "Economic Literacy" section focuses on factors influencing income, the benefits and costs of higher education, the state of the housing market, the healthcare system, taxation, and government debt. While the lessons from the "Financial Literacy" part may be useful for readers in many countries, the "Economic Literacy" section concentrates primarily on data from the United States, as well as the economic system, policies, and challenges specific to it.

By combining the latest research and practical insights into one cohesive guide, we hope that this book will help readers build a solid foundation of financial and economic knowledge and apply it to their everyday lives. In the realm of economics, we are often confronted with a deluge of statistics, reports, and analyses that (sometimes intentionally) focus on data or interpretations that support a predetermined viewpoint. Cherry-picking results in this way can be worse than not conducting proper research, as it is deliberately misleading rather than a result of ignorance. Therefore, in cases where research has come to contradictory conclusions or where no clear answer exists, we have made sure to indicate that clearly.

We have written this book with two very different types of readers in mind: those left unsatisfied with the depth of coverage in popular financial literacy books and the instructors of financial literacy and economics courses. This text is not intended as the typical, theoretical textbook for readers at educational facilities like high schools and colleges. However, it provides access to a variety of discussions and resources that can supplement and enhance the relevance of classroom treatment of financial literacy and current economic topics.

PART ONE. FINANCIAL LITERACY

CHAPTER ONE

INFLATION

In the summer of 2010, a vanilla ice cream cone at a local McDonald's would have cost you between 50 and 75 cents. Compared to today's prices, that may seem like a steal—except that they were even cheaper (25 to 30 cents) in the late 1990s and early 2000s. In fact, the one-to-two dollars per cone we pay today will seem like a great deal to either our future selves or future generations!

Besides ice cream, most things seem to cost more nowadays than in the past. The graph below depicts the percentage growth in prices for various categories of goods and services over the past three decades. Notably, medical care costs have risen sharply, with the price growth exceeding 250% between 1990 and 2024. Used car prices remained relatively stable until around 2020, after which there was a sudden and significant spike attributed to supply chain disruptions caused by the

COVID-19 pandemic, resulting in a shortage of new vehicles. In contrast, apparel prices have shown minimal growth, staying relatively flat with only modest increases.[1]

Inflation is the rate at which the general level of prices for goods and services rises. Inflation takes into account growth across many categories of goods, including essential items such as food and housing, as well as discretionary spending on things like electronics and entertainment. The overall price level (average of prices for various goods and services; line marked "All Items" on the graph below) has grown by approximately 150% since 1990.

We start our book with this topic because inflation impacts your **purchasing power**—the amount of products and services you can buy with a specific amount of money—and shapes spending and investment choices. By grasping these concepts, you will be better equipped to make smart financial decisions, whether you plan to invest for the long term, understand why grocery prices fluctuate, or make sense of economic policies.

Figure 1. Price growth for select categories of goods and services

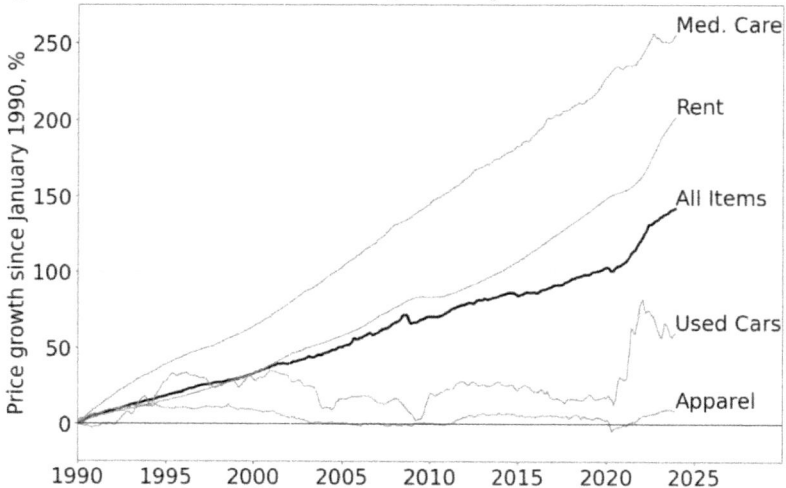

1.1 Brief Historical Overview

Inflation has been a part of our lives for thousands of years and has sometimes surged to very high levels. One of the earliest cases of high inflation in documented history occurred in ancient Babylon after the death of Alexander the Great in 323 BCE. As Alexander died rather unexpectedly and did not leave a designated heir, the struggle for power after his death resulted in very high prices. What caused this inflation? Alexander's successors paid their soldiers using the treasures Alexander brought back from his campaigns to Persia and the further east.[2] The money pouring into the markets increased prices on barley and wool and the resulting inflation lasted for nearly a generation.[3]

In the 1500s, Europe experienced major inflation often referred to as the **Price Revolution**. A significant contributor to the Price Revolution was the widespread practice of monetary debasement during that era. This process involved increasing the proportion of base metals relative to precious metals in coinage. As a result, more coins could be produced from the same quantity of precious metals, effectively expanding the money supply. Advances in mining techniques in Germany led to a substantial rise in silver output from the late fifteenth century through the 1530s, also adding to the amount of money in circulation. The influx of silver from the New World also dramatically increased the European money supply.[4]

The most pronounced instances of **hyperinflation** (monthly inflation rate exceeding 50%) took place during the twentieth century in Europe. The most famous case is that of Germany in the 1920s when their highest monthly inflation rate reached 29,500%.[5] After the end of World War I, Germany had to contend with considerable territorial losses, as mandated by the Treaty of Versailles. The treaty stripped the nation of its overseas colonies and several key territories in Europe. The size of the German army was also limited to prevent it from starting another similar war in the future. Finally, Germany was forced to pay reparations to the Allied nations for the damages they had incurred during the war.[6]

Even before the end of the war, the prices of food, clothing, and fuel in German Empire had already been rising because of the shortages brought on by the war. The German Empire's solution to pay its bills had been to print money and take out loans. Facing even more economic challenges after the war, the authorities of the newly created Weimar Republic continued the policy of money printing to pay for their welfare programs for former soldiers and the poor. Prices skyrocketed, quickly making people's savings worthless.[7]

The economic hardships led to demonstrations, the most significant being the attempted putsch in Munich in November 1923. Although the coup failed and the authorities prosecuted the leaders, the events brought publicity to the organizers—a small, right-wing extremist group called the National Socialist German Workers' Party, commonly known as the Nazi Party. The economic hardships of the 1920s and the events in Munich acted as catalysts for the party's evolution and growth over the next 10 years.[8,9,10,11]

Although the United States did not go through prolonged periods of hyperinflationary times during the twentieth and twenty-first centuries, the American Revolutionary War and the Civil War did bring about hyperinflationary pockets. The Confederate government's unlimited money printing resulted in a monthly price increase of 10% throughout the period from October 1861 to March 1864. As a result, by the war's end, prices in the Confederacy had surged by over 9,000%.[12] The highest inflation rates in the U.S. during the twentieth century capped out at approximately 24% in 1929.

The graph below plots the annual inflation rates in the United States over the past six decades. In the 30 years from 1993 to 2022, the average inflation rate in the United States was about 2.5% per year. In the same period, only about 40 countries (one-fifth of all the countries in the world) had inflation rates between 1.5 and 2.5%. For nearly half of the world's countries, the average inflation rate in the same 30-year period was 5% or higher. With the exceptions of the years 2022 and 1990, single-year inflation in the U.S. has not exceeded 5% since the high inflation decade of 1972–1982.[a,13]

To smooth the data and infer overall trends more easily, we'll also plot a 30-year rolling average. For example, for 2023, we'll calculate the average inflation rates in 1994, 1995, and so on until 2023.[b] As you can see, the rolling average values show that long-term inflation rates have not exceeded 6% in recent decades.

---

[a] In 1980, the annual inflation rate reached 13.5%, the highest it had been since 1947.
[b] There is no strict rule on how many years should be used to calculate averages. We could have picked two, three, 10, or 15 years.

Figure 2. Annual and average inflation rates over the past six decades

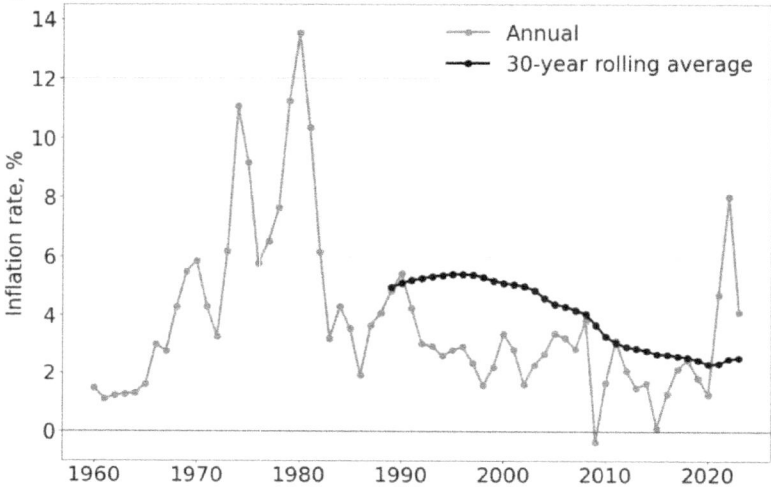

1.2 Causes

An intuitive explanation for inflation can be described by a scenario in which too much money is circulating in the economy relative to the amount of goods and services available. Note how, so far, all the historical examples of inflation we have considered were said to result from excessive "money printing."

A rapidly increasing money supply is one of the potential causes behind what economists call **demand-pull inflation**. Demand-pull inflation occurs when the **aggregate demand** (the total demand for goods and services) rises, but **production capacity** (the maximum amount of output companies can produce) remains the same. The increase in aggregate demand sets off a chain of events. Facing higher demand and increased labor costs, firms can charge higher prices. They may also start hiring more people to meet this growing demand. In turn, the increased demand for labor pushes wages up, subsequently raising household incomes and consumption.

Another potential cause of inflation is the **cost-push inflation**, which occurs when the **aggregate supply** (the total supply of goods and services) decreases. One potential reason for this phenomenon is supply chain disruptions. Shortages of raw materials drive up production costs, and to cover these expanding costs firms are forced to charge higher prices for the goods and services they produce.

Consider the market for cars during the COVID-19 pandemic. After quarantine mandates took effect, some car manufacturers stopped production, and others saw their workforce shrink as employees either chose different jobs or experienced health issues. This effect was not felt instantly—in fact, many were able to buy cars with great interest rates in the beginning stages of the pandemic. However, as the economy made its way out of the pandemic, the sudden rise in demand for cars—both new and used—along with the previous supply issues caused car prices to increase dramatically. Since millions had been quarantined and many had saved up by forgoing holiday trips, dining out less, and spending less on "outdoors entertainment," those who could afford to spend had extra money to offset the higher car prices.

Not all economists agree with the cost-push explanation of inflation. A key critique is related to inflation's impact on consumers' budgets. For example, if cars become more expensive because of an increase in car production costs, consumers must allocate more of their budgets to purchasing them. Consequently, they have less disposable income to spend on other goods and services. This can lead to reduced demand in other sectors, and, ultimately, to lower prices in those sectors. Thus, the lower prices in other sectors should balance out the higher car prices, keeping overall inflation at bay.[14] Critics of the cost-push explanation would likely blame the inflation of the early 2020s on higher aggregate demand caused by the stimulus the government provided during the COVID-19 pandemic.

Another possible cause of inflation is the expectation of rising prices. For instance, if firms anticipate a rise in production costs (perhaps due to constant news about inflation), they may start charging higher prices in advance to cover them. This reaction can lead to higher prices, making the expectation of inflation a self-fulfilling prophecy.

An interesting potential effect of price increases driven by such expectations is the growth in profits of firms that raise prices without yet facing higher input costs. In 2022, as news of companies making record profits spread, many started questioning whether the rising prices were due to "corporate greed" (corporations raising prices because they can rather than because they need to) rather than due to the demand-pull or cost-push factors that were quoted by economists. The term **greedflation** (a portmanteau of "greed" and "inflation") began to appear in the news. While some economists argued that rising prices were simply the result of demand and supply dynamics, the public remained unconvinced.[a,15,16,17,18]

So far, research has not reached a unanimous conclusion on whether greed was really one of the reasons behind the inflation in the early 2020s. A 2023 study analyzed the financial statements of 1,350 companies and found that many large international firms significantly increased prices during the global inflation period, leading to higher profit margins.[19] Research by the Kansas City Fed arrived at a similar

---

[a] In 2023, an Illinois jury ruled that major egg producers had conspired to limit the supply of eggs in the U.S. to raise prices. This conspiracy occurred between 2004 and 2008, but with egg prices rising in the 2020s (in 2022, egg prices increased by 60%), the ruling was seen as evidence that "greedflation" is indeed possible.

observation, showing that markup growth contributed more than 50% to inflation in 2021, a much higher contribution compared to the previous decade. However, the authors noted that the increase in markups was likely not due to greed but due to the expectation of rising costs. [20] In contrast, a study published in 2023 focusing on 6,000 publicly traded companies found virtually zero correlation between price increases and markups in the early 2020s. The authors further noted that even though corporate profits peaked in 2022 and started decreasing afterward, inflation remained high in 2023. This seemingly provided additional evidence for the lack of a relationship between the two. [21,22]

1.3 Effects

Living through a period of rapidly growing prices can have lasting, sometimes life-long effects. A 2022 study investigated how the oil crises of the 1970s and the resulting four-fold increase in gas prices affected people who were teenagers at the time. The study found that people who experienced these shocks in their formative years associated driving with high costs and, hence, today, drive less than those who are older or younger than them. [23]

Rising prices are a painful topic of conversation for many and are frequently reported on by news outlets. In 2022, a year when annual inflation reached 8%, the highest value in 40 years, the Wall Street Journal published over 6,000 articles that mentioned the term "inflation" on their website. For comparison, the Journal published a similar number of articles mentioning "elections" in 2020, a year of presidential election in the United States. [24]

Economic factors, including inflation, also drive votes. According to the poll of likely voters in the presidential elections of 2024, economic issues (inflation, economic growth, housing, and unemployment) were the most pressing issues in the elections. In 2024, a survey of U.S. adults by the Pew Research Center found that 62% of Americans considered inflation to be a "very big problem." This is higher than the share of people who thought the same about healthcare affordability (60%), partisan cooperation (57%), drug addiction (55%), and gun violence (53%).[25]

We measure inflation using a variety of metrics. One common one is the **Consumer Price Index** (CPI). This is a measure that examines the average prices of a basket of consumer goods and services such as housing, food, transportation, healthcare, and entertainment. Not everything goes into the CPI. The basket is supposed to represent "typical" consumer purchases. Using the basket of goods, inflation is calculated as the percentage change in the CPI over a certain period, often one year. For instance, if the CPI was 100 last year and it's 103 this year, we would say that inflation for the year is 3%.

The standard base "year" for most categories of goods and services tracked is the period between 1982 and 1984. We know that a basket of goods that cost $100 in 1982 cost more than $300 in 2023.[26] This means that in 40 years we have witnessed a cumulative inflation rate of more than 200%.

Even modest rates of inflation can lead to significant price increases over time. For example, a 3% inflation rate may seem small in a single year, but compounded over several decades, it can lead to a substantial increase in the cost of living. Just as interest earns additional interest in a bank account, each year's inflation rate builds upon the increased price level of the preceding year.

To visualize this, imagine a cart full of goods from a supermarket worth $100 in 1982. With a consistent inflation rate of 3% per year, the same basket of goods would cost roughly $134 a decade later, by the end of 1991. By 2022, the original $100 basket of goods would cost over $326. That is more than triple the original cost, all due to a seemingly modest annual inflation rate of 3%.

Table 1. Effects of a 3% inflation rate

Time	Cost of a basket of goods
Beginning of Year 1	$100
End of Year 1	$100 + 3% = $103
End of Year 2	$103 + 3% = $106.09
End of Year 3	$106.09 + 3% = $109.27
...	
End of Year 9	$126.68 + 3% = $130.48
End of Year 10	$130.48 + 3% = $134.39

1.4 Nominal versus Real

The concepts of **nominal** and **real dollars** are used to distinguish between the current or reported value of money and its value adjusted for inflation. Nominal dollars refer to the actual, current dollar amounts without any adjustment (i.e., the price you see in stores). Real dollars consider the effects of inflation on the purchasing power of money.

Say your annual income is $40,000, and it remains unchanged over a period of five years. In nominal terms, you're still earning the same amount of money as you did five years ago. However, if the prices of the things you typically buy rose during those five years, your purchasing power has decreased, resulting in a decrease in your **real income**. In other words, while your **nominal income** has remained constant, the real value of that income has declined over time as inflation erodes its purchasing power.

When reporting real dollars, we often take one specific year as a benchmark and adjust all other values to that base year. Most of the dollar amounts you will see in this book are reported in 2023 dollars. This means that if you're reading this book in, say, 2030, the base comparison reference is seven years prior.

1.5 Target Level

A certain level of inflation is considered healthy for an economy. **Central banks** (institutions overseeing and regulating monetary policy) like the **European Central Bank** (ECB) and the **Federal Reserve System** (Fed), often aim for an inflation rate of around 2%. Why 2%? Simply because this value is not too low and not too high.

High inflation erodes the purchasing power of money. When prices rise rapidly, the same amount of money can buy fewer goods and services over time. This can diminish the standard of living for individuals and reduce the purchasing power of their income. High inflation also introduces uncertainty into the economy, since it erodes the reliability of long-term contracts and undermines economic stability, making it harder for businesses and households to plan for the future. Thus, businesses face difficulties in forecasting costs, setting prices, and making investment decisions. When businesses and governments must allocate more money for day-to-day operations, they are unable to hire new employees and may even have to lay off current workers.

To combat a rapid rise in prices, the government can utilize monetary and fiscal policy to "cool down" the market. In this case, the Fed could raise interest rates as a monetary policy tool to incentivize potential buyers to save money (and earn interest) rather than taking out loans with higher interest rates (driven by the interest rate increase from the Fed). Concurrently, the U.S. Congress could act by passing a law aimed at adjusting people's paycheck sizes, by increasing the tax rate, or by doing away with certain tax deductions. Congress could also limit companies by setting a price ceiling on goods and services sold.

How exactly does the Fed "set" interest rates? In short, the Fed determines at what rates banks lend money to each other.

Then, using that rate, banks and credit card companies determine what to charge businesses and consumers. Here's a more detailed explanation. The amount of money a bank holds (its **reserves**) varies by day. When banks need additional reserves, they can borrow them from other banks in the **federal funds market**. The federal funds rate can fluctuate depending on the demand and supply of reserves in this market. The Fed steers the federal funds rate by adjusting "administered rates" (rates not determined by the market) like interest on reserve balances, the overnight reverse repurchase agreement rate, and the discount rate. **Interest on reserve balances** (IORB) is the interest paid on money that banks hold in their reserve balance accounts at the Federal Reserve bank. It's the lowest rate, at which a bank would be willing to lend out its funds—why would a bank lend its money to someone at a lower rate when it can deposit it at the Fed and earn the IORB rate? The Fed utilizes the **overnight reverse repurchase agreement** (ON RRP) rate in a similar manner for institutions that operate in the federal funds market but are unable to earn interest on their reserve balances. The IORB and the ON RRP rates, thus, provide a floor (lower limit) on the federal funds market. The Fed can also lend money and charge the discount rate on that money. The discount rate sets a ceiling (upper limit) on the federal funds market—why would a bank borrow money from someone at a higher rate when it can borrow it from the Fed at the discount rate?[27,28,29,30]

How does the rate set by the Fed affect you? Banks generate revenue by charging higher interest rates than what they pay on deposits and other funding sources. When the Fed lowers the federal funds rate, borrowing becomes cheaper for banks, allowing them to charge lower rates to their customers. The interest rate banks charge their most creditworthy customers (those least likely to default on loans) is called the **prime rate**.

You can find the average of these prime rates on the Wall Street Journal's website. Banks and credit card companies often use this average prime rate to calculate the interest on your credit card balance. Thus, if the federal funds rate goes down, it usually decreases the prime rate, which, in turn, decreases the amount financial institutions charge you for your loans. The exact interest rate you pay will depend on additional factors, such as your credit score, but it's frequently based on the prime rate published in the Wall Street Journal.

Although rare, overall price levels in the economy may also fall over time, leading to a phenomenon referred to as **deflation**. While seemingly a good thing for consumers (who doesn't like lower prices?), deflation can be harmful to the economy. The anticipation of lower future prices incentivizes individuals to delay their purchases which can lead to a decline in consumer spending. Because consumer spending is a significant driver of economic growth, its reduction can negatively affect businesses through decreased revenue, potentially leading to reduced production, lower economic growth, and layoffs.

1.6 Secondary Effects

Depending on the direction of inflation, there are interesting scenarios where the change in prices has varying effects on borrowers and lenders. Let's say you borrow $500 to buy a new phone. You agree to pay back this loan in one year (we'll assume that you aren't charged any interest). If there is no inflation you will be paying back the same value that you borrowed when the loan is due. However, suppose that, due to a rise in fuel prices, the same phone costs slightly higher six months after you purchased yours. With inflation, the phone now costs over $500 for someone buying it now, while you still must pay back only the original $500. But the company receiving your $500 at the end of your loan won't be able to buy as much with it as it did a year prior. You're paying back less "value" than you borrowed, which is good for you as a borrower.

Although you may have "won" the inflation battle with your phone purchase, the rise in prices may still have affected you negatively. That is, if you're earning $40,000 a year and there is 2% inflation, you will need to be earning $40,800 the next year to have the same purchasing power. If your income doesn't increase with inflation (i.e., you don't get a raise), then even though inflation might be good for you as a borrower, it will be bad for you as a consumer because the "value" or "purchasing power" of your income is going down.

On the other hand, lenders benefit from deflation or a lower-than-expected inflation rate since the value of the dollar you lent out increases. If you lent out $100 at an interest rate of 5%, due exactly a year from now, in nominal terms, you would receive $105 when the loan is due. If the inflation rate at the time of the loan was expected to be 3% for the life of the loan, your real return would net you about $2 at the end of the loan.[a] However, if instead of the projected 3% rate, the inflation rate turned out to be 1%, your real return would be approximately $4.

---

[a] $\frac{1.05}{1.03} \approx 1.019$, that is, a 2% return on the loan.

CHAPTER TWO

SAVING AND INVESTING

One important consequence of inflation is how it affects our investment choices. As prices increase over time, the purchasing power of cash diminishes. This means that if you merely keep savings in cash, the value of your money will slowly decrease due to loss of purchasing power. To safeguard against this "silent theft," it becomes essential to invest your savings wisely.

There are various investment options available to you, each with its own set of characteristics, potential returns, and risks. You can put your money in a bank account where it will earn interest and be insured up to a certain amount. You can also lend it to the U.S. government.

Another investment instrument is stocks. According to the Federal Reserve, over 58% of U.S. households owned stocks in 2022. Although not all stocks behave the same, owning a stock in a company gives you proportional ownership in the company—depending on how many stocks you own. For example, if you own one stock of Netflix, that means you own about 1/400,000,000 of Netflix. Companies that issue stocks have "gone public," meaning that they have registered with the **Securities and Exchange Commission** (SEC) and plan to or have already issued stocks, for example, through an **Initial Public Offering** (IPO). Some stocks even allow you to vote on certain company measures, with your vote weighed by how many stocks you own. Before we get into the details of investment options, we first will go over why investment decisions matter.

2.1 Investment Benchmarks

For a long time, Donald Trump's critics have claimed that his success as a businessman was overstated. As Trump himself admitted, his career started with a loan he received from his father. Trump's critics often suggested that Trump could have made more money if he invested the money he received from his father into an index fund that tracked the S&P 500 index. In a 2021 article, Forbes estimated that Donald Trump had been quite successful at outperforming the index for most of his life. However, according to the article, this changed in March 2021 when Trump's real estate empire, concentrated in office buildings and hotels, struggled to recover amid the pandemic lockdowns. At that point, the nearly 40-years of business decisions that Trump had made were outpaced by the S&P 500's performance.[a,1,2]

What is the S&P 500 index exactly? How can someone invest in it and then outperform some of the most famous businessmen

---

[a] According to the Forbes estimates in May of 2024, Donald Trump's most recent net worth stands at $7.5 billion, thanks to the value of his shares in his social media venture. That amount is about double what Trump would have been worth if he simply invested the money he received from his father in the S&P 500 index.

in the country? In short, it's possible thanks to the hard work of the CEOs of America's 500 largest companies and the power of compound interest.

An **index fund** is a type of investment fund designed to replicate the performance of a specific financial benchmark. One example of such a benchmark is the Standard and Poor's 500, also known as the **S&P 500 index**, which monitors the performance of 500 publicly traded companies in the U.S. These companies are chosen based on various criteria, one of which is their market capitalization. **Market capitalization** is commonly interpreted as the market's perception of a company's value. It's calculated by multiplying the total number of a company's outstanding shares by its current market price per share.

While there are over 4,000 domestic companies listed on US stock exchanges, the companies included in the S&P 500 index represent over 80% of the U.S. stock market's estimated market capitalization.[3] Out of the 503 individual stocks on the list, 10 stocks (representing nine companies, with Alphabet being represented by two classes of shares) make up about 30% of the market capitalization in the index. Because of their large weight, the performance of these nine companies can have a significant impact on the index's overall performance. Seven out of the nine companies are either classified as working in the Information Technology sector (companies like Apple and Microsoft) or heavily rely on Information Technology to power their business and operations (companies like Meta and Alphabet). Thus, events affecting the IT sector (for example, the introduction of ChatGPT or inquiry regarding privacy issues by the U.S. Congress) can have a disproportionate impact on the S&P 500 index. Choosing stocks that grow higher than this index over extended periods of time is what some refer to when talking about "beating the market."

The origins of index funds can be traced to the 1970s, when multiple companies decided to establish funds that would serve as benchmarks for the performance of their in-house investors. These companies got the idea from academics who, for about a decade prior, had been theorizing about a fund that would earn "average" returns. The ingenuity of the idea was that by sacrificing the chance of earning higher-than-average returns, the investors would be "assured" that they wouldn't do much worse than average. The biggest benefit of establishing such a fund would have been nearly non-existent advisory costs: there would be no need to spend money on advisors who promised to beat the market, but only on advisors who could follow it.[4]

How much can you expect to earn by investing in the S&P 500 index? Nobody really knows. What we can do, however, is look at the historical trends and assume that the future performance will be similar. This is a big assumption and one you should be careful about making.

Let's look at the long-term performance of the S&P 500. To smooth out year-to-year volatility and focus on long-term trends, we'll plot 30-year averages. On the graph below, a solid black point for 2020 corresponds to the average of S&P 500 returns over the period between 1991 and 2020. We see that if you put your money in a fund that tracked the S&P 500 index for 30 years at any point between 1930 and 1990, on average, you would have made about 11% every year.[a] Does this mean that people who invest their money in such a fund today will, on average, earn 11% a year for the next 30 years? The trend

---

[a] Note that we cannot observe the performance of our 30-year-old investments for years after 1994 simply because there has not been 30 years since 1994 as of writing of this book.

we just observed has been present for so long that some people feel comfortable making such a statement.[a]

Figure 3. S&P 500 returns

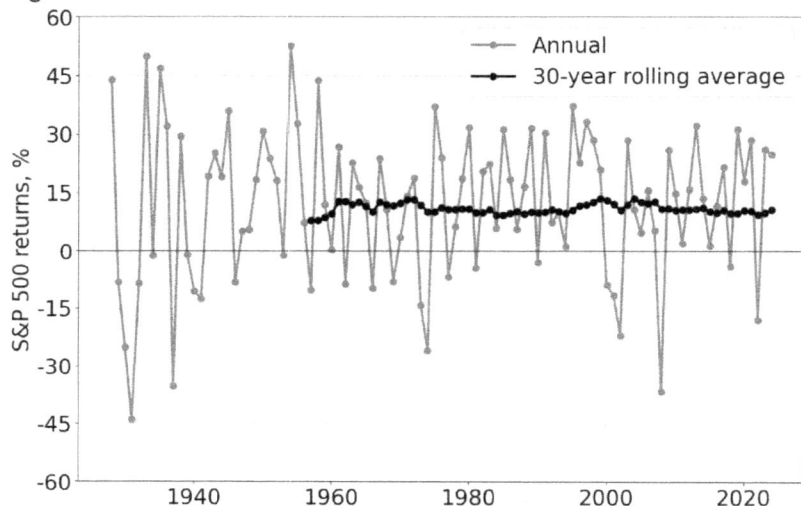

There are multiple ways for you to invest in the companies in the S&P 500 index. Some of them are more laborious than others. You can:

- Invest in an S&P 500 index mutual fund. Examples of such funds include Vanguard 500 Index Fund Admiral Shares

---

[a] To calculate averages for growth rates across years in this book, we use geometric averages instead of arithmetic averages. The geometric average is preferred for growth rates because it accounts for the compounding effect of consecutive periods of growth or decline. If you earn 10% in one year but lose 10% in the following year, the arithmetic average suggests that you broke even. However, this is not the case. If you invested $100, you would have $110 at the end of the first year due to the 10% gain. In the subsequent year, with a 10% loss, you would end up with $99 (10% of $110 is $11, leaving you with $110 - $11 = $99).

with **ticker symbol** VFIAX.[a] Other examples include Fidelity 500 Index Fund (ticker symbol FXAIX) and Schwab S&P 500 Index Fund (SWPPX). Vanguard, Fidelity, and Schwab are some of the largest and most well-known investment firms in the United States, offering a wide range of financial services. If you know someone who has an investment account, it's likely they use one of these major companies.

- Invest in an S&P 500 **exchange traded fund** (ETF). Compared to mutual funds, which are traded only once at the end of the day, ETFs can be traded throughout the day. Examples of such ETFs include Vanguard S&P 500 ETF (VOO), iShares Core S&P 500 ETF (IVV), and SPDR S&P 500 ETF (SPY).
- Invest in every one of the 500 companies individually. Undoubtedly, this would be a very labor-intensive task.

Since mutual funds and ETFs do all this work for you, they will charge you a small fee. For example, as of 2024, the fee ("expense ratio") of the Fidelity 500 Index Fund is 0.015% or $1.50 for every $10,000 invested.

You can further diversify your investments by allocating your money to a fund that invests in companies not only within the U.S. but also internationally. You must know, however, that the performance of U.S. companies is considered exceptional in the world. Thus, the return on such an (international) investment will likely be lower. The median real stock market appreciation rate for 39 countries around the world between 1921 and 1996 was 0.8% per year. In the same period, the U.S. stock market grew by 4.3% per year.[5]

---

[a] Ticker symbol is an abbreviation used to uniquely identify companies in the stock market.

The founder of the Vanguard Group, John C. Bogle, also agrees that including non-U.S. companies in your portfolio may be unwise. According to Bogle, if the investor lives in the United States and earns and spends money in U.S. dollars, there is little motivation to take currency risks (risks on fluctuations in exchange rates between different currencies can impact the value of investments denominated in foreign currencies). Besides, Bogle notes, half of the revenues and profits of U.S. companies come from other countries anyway.[6]

Over the past five decades, investing in the S&P 500 index has shown to be a lucrative option even compared to gold, which is traditionally perceived a "safe" investment. While gold has long been considered as a "safe haven asset" during times of economic uncertainty, its returns have been relatively modest over the long term. Despite occasional market volatility, the S&P 500 has historically shown resilience and the ability to recover from downturns, making it an attractive choice for investors seeking substantial long-term returns.

Figure 4. Value of $100 invested in 1969 in the S&P 500 compared to gold

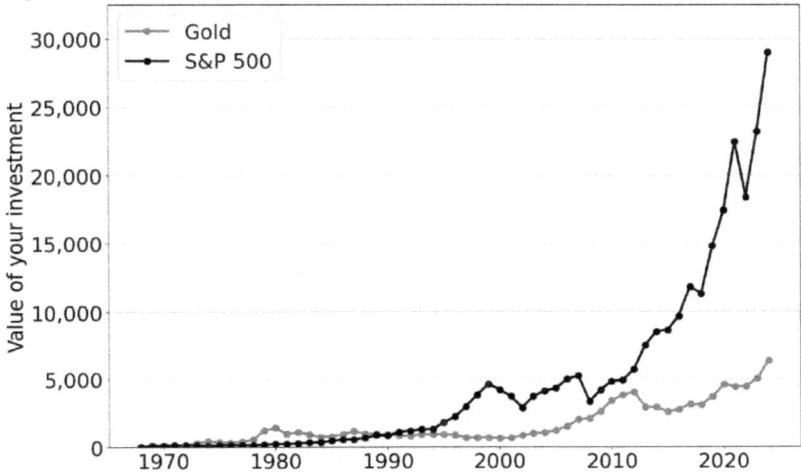

Still, the financial markets are constantly evolving, and what was true yesterday may not hold true tomorrow. While historical data may suggest that some investment options have outperformed others, readers should be aware that higher returns often come with higher risk and volatility. Certain asset classes or investment strategies may have yielded impressive returns in the past, but the future is inherently unpredictable. Economic conditions, market trends, and unforeseen events can quickly turn once-promising investments into potential pitfalls.

Difficulty in outperforming the market

It's a very difficult task for even professional investors to outperform the market. Over any five-year period, only 20% of equity funds outperform the S&P 500 index. For a 20-year period, the percentage of funds that can do so drops to less than seven.[7] Out of 355 funds that existed in 1970, 62% had gone bankrupt by 2005. Out of the 132 surviving funds, only two outperformed the S&P 500 by more than 2%.[8] Generally speaking, the longer the investment horizon, the smaller the number of funds that outperform the market.

John Bogle, the founder of Vanguard, analyzed the consistency of funds' performance in the early 2000s.[a] He divided funds into five performance categories based on their 2011–2016 returns: "Highest," "High," "Medium," "Low," and "Lowest." From 2011 to 2016, only 15% of firms remained in their initial performance categories. Nearly half of the Highest-performance firms moved to the Low and Lowest categories, while 10% of them either closed or merged with other firms. At the same time, 35% of the Lowest-performance firms moved to Highest and High categories.

Even Warren Buffett, one of the most successful investors in history, has found it difficult to outperform the market in recent decades. Buffett's company, Berkshire Hathaway, publishes annual letters to the shareholders written by Buffett on its website. An informative insight into the performance of the company, the letters also consist of Buffett's investment philosophy, his views on the economy, and his thoughts on various business and investment-related topics. The most intriguing part of each letter is a table, usually appearing on the second page, showing the performance of Berkshire Hathaway relative to the S&P 500 index. And the results published in 2025 for the years 1965 to 2024 look impressive. Berkshire, on average, made 20% returns a year, while the S&P 500 gained on average, "only" 10% every year. Over the entire period, Berkshire earned 5,502,284% while the S&P 500 grew by 39,054%. The year-by-year comparison looks impressive as well. In 1976, when the market rose by 23.6%, shares of

---

[a] Vanguard is particularly famous in the industry for being the first company to bring low-cost and diversified investment opportunities to individual investors in 1976. Today, adherents of index fund investing often call themselves Bogleheads (after the founder, John C. Bogle).

Berkshire jumped by 129.3%! You can see the reported numbers on the graph below.

Figure 5. Performance of Berkshire Hathaway compared to the S&P 500

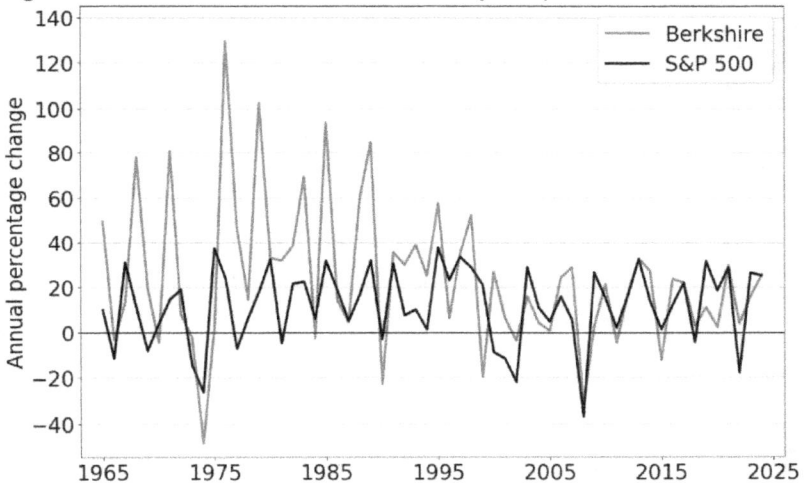

To smooth out the data, we use five-year rolling averages. On the graph below, we see that while the performance of the S&P 500 index is not as great as that of Berkshire, it is somewhat consistent. That is, the five-year performance of the S&P 500 index has rarely been negative and has mostly hovered around 10%. The graph also shows the reduction in Berkshire's performance in recent years, implying that the 5 million percent returns are largely due to the company's success more than two decades prior.[a] In Buffett's defense, he admits that beating the market is a hard task and investing in the S&P 500 may be the "best thing to do" for most people.[9]

In fact, in December 2007, Buffett made a bet with hedge fund Protégé Partners on whether the hedge fund could outperform

---

[a] Though, to be fair, this could be only a temporary trend.

the S&P 500. Protégé selected five "funds-of-funds" that, in turn, owned interest in more than 200 other hedge funds. The result? Four of the five funds-of-funds underperformed the market, and one was liquidated a year before the bet was over.[a]

Figure 6. Berkshire Hathaway and the S&P 500 index, five-year averages

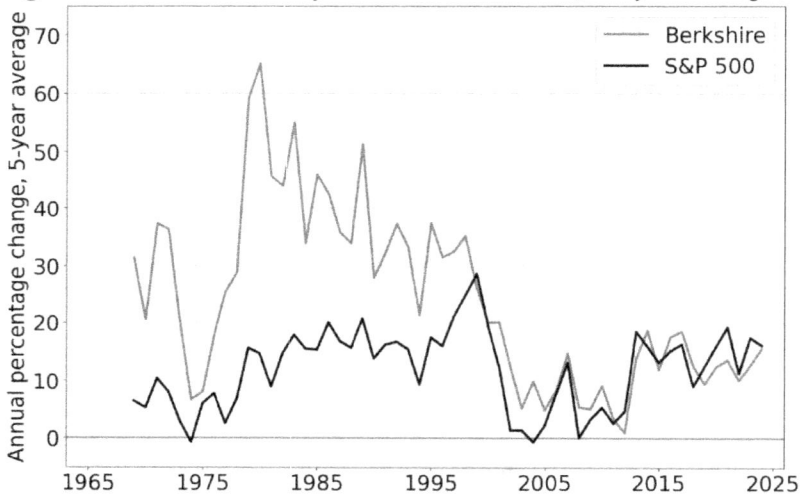

If the returns on investments in the S&P 500 index are only modest compared to what a professional investor can achieve, how can it make you as successful an investor as Donald Trump or Warren Buffett? The answer lies in the mathematics behind the concept of compound interest.

Compound interest
Compound interest is the process by which the interest you earn on an investment then earns interest itself. It's a powerful

---

[a] It should be noted that the problem with professional advisors is not just that they may choose losing bets, but that the fees they charge may make it not worthwhile to use their help even when they manage to outperform the market.

concept because it allows for the exponential growth of your investment over time. We have already seen the effect of compound interest on the example of inflation eroding the purchasing power of your savings. We can also consider an example related to returns on investment.

Say you invest $10,000 at a 5% annual interest rate. After the first year, you would earn $500 in interest, bringing your total to $10,500. However, in the second year, you would earn 5% on $10,500, not just your original amount. This means you would earn $525 in interest in the second year. This continues year after year, with the interest you earn earning more interest itself.

We'll now apply this concept to investing in the stock market, specifically in an index fund that tracks the S&P 500. Consider a fund that has an average return rate of 11% per year—the average annual return for 30-year investments in the past few decades. However, we'll account for inflation, which we'll assume is 5% per year.[a] (This is a little high compared to the values in recent decades. Using a larger value here will help us be conservative in our estimates to ensure we don't overstate returns to our investments.) Thus, the **real rate of return** (the return rate after accounting for inflation) we'll expect is approximately 6%.[b]

The graph below shows how much your $10,000 would grow depending on the number of years and the real interest rate. If you make a one-time deposit of $10,000 and leave it to grow for 30 years, the value of the investment could reach approximately $57,000.[c] If left for 40 years, these $10,000

---

[a] An upper bound for 30-year periods in recent decades.

[b] More precisely, it's $\frac{1.11}{1.05} \approx 1.057$, that is, 5.7%.

[c] $10,000 * (1 + 0.06)^{30} \approx 57,435$.

could turn into $102,857. The possibility of a tenfold return by simply investing in the American economy is incredible.

Figure 7. Growth of $10,000 under various (inflation-adjusted) interest rates

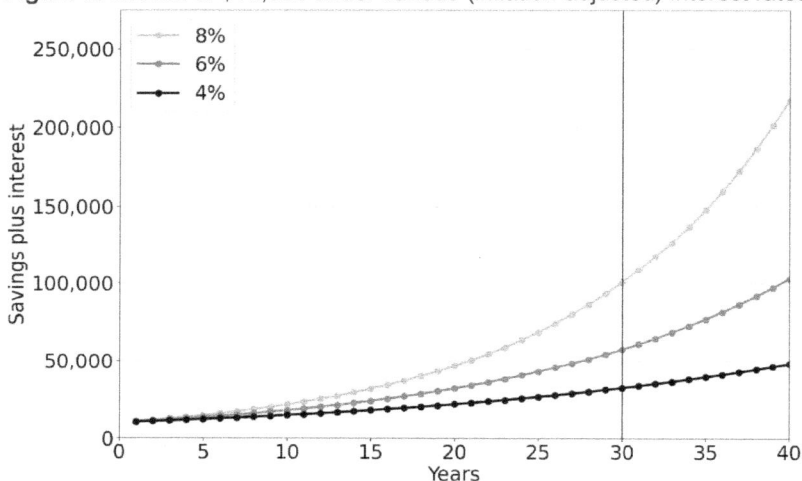

Saving early allows you to take advantage of the power of compounding. The longer your money remains invested, the more time it has to grow. The previous graph showed that even with a "low" real interest rate of 4%, a $10,000 investment could grow to $32,000 in 30 years. As the common saying goes, "Time in the market beats timing the market."

But what if you happen to invest in a year when markets are overvalued? What if, as soon as you invest your $10,000, the S&P 500 drops and doesn't recover for a year or two? Such a scenario took place in the year 2000. If you invested your money in a fund that tracked the S&P 500 in 2000, you would have lost 9% in your first year. Then, you would have lost 11% in 2001 and 22% in 2002. Although some of the losses would have been recovered in the years that followed, the housing market crash and the **Great Recession** (the severe world-wide economic downturn that occurred between 2007 and 2009) would have reduced your gains with a 37% loss in 2008. Given recent volatility and large movements in markets, how do you know that the year you're investing in is not another "year 2000"?

If you are worried about entering the market at its peak, you can try a strategy called **dollar-cost averaging**. Dollar-cost averaging means investing the same amount at regular intervals regardless of whether the market is going up or down. Thus, you will buy more when prices are low, and you will buy less when prices are high.

Some may say there is no point in dollar-cost averaging because markets are always going up. This is a great point to make, provided you add a caveat that markets grow over the long term. Markets, however, don't always go up in a linear fashion over the long term. While historical data generally shows upward trends, there have been periods of market downturns (like the early 2000s) and extended sideways movements. Trying to predict market movements accurately is challenging even for seasoned investors. Regardless of your investment plans (whether they are long- or short-term), you should employ a good strategy that best fits your risk tolerance.

Now that we have considered the potential return on our one-time $10,000 investment, we should notice that such an investment would be very difficult for many Americans. In 2023, the median personal annual income in the United States was about $42,000.[10] That is, half of the U.S. population earned less than $42,000 a year. Setting aside $10,000 with such a salary after paying for necessities like rent, food, transportation, and medical expenses is not easy. Instead, let's analyze a slightly more realistic example: saving small amounts every year.

In lieu of investing $10,000 once, suppose you were to deposit 5% (about $2,000) per year for 30 years using the same assumptions as before. In this case, the value of your investment after 30 years would be $167,000. Thus, by investing $60,000 ($2,000 per year for 30 years), you could enjoy $107,000 earned through interest accumulation.

Figure 8. Growth of $2,000-deposits with (inflation-adjusted) interest rates

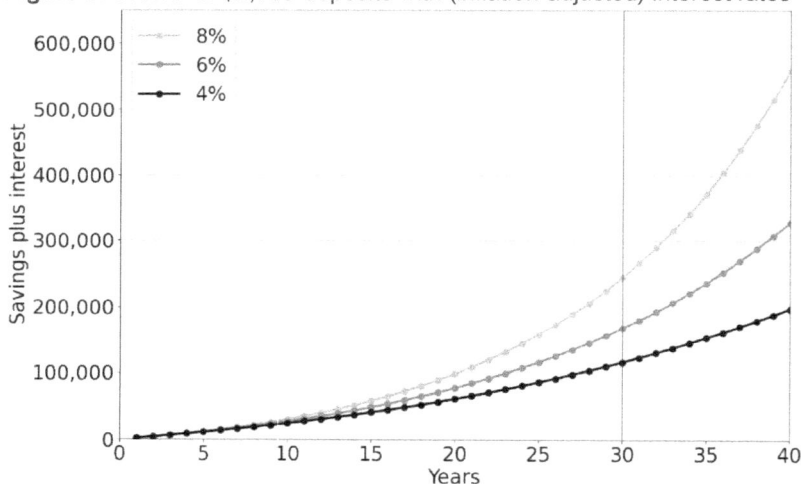

Note that all these calculations are idealized and simplified for the sake of explanation. The return rates and inflation rates are average values and will vary from year to year. Investing in the stock market always comes with risks, and it's possible that you won't achieve the expected return rate. In our calculations, we used inflation rates that would be relatively high compared to historical trends and assumed that the returns to the S&P 500 would be stable and similar to what we have observed in the past decades. We also did not allow for fees associated with investment accounts, such as account maintenance fees or fund expense ratios that can reduce your net returns. Lastly, while this explanation focuses on investing in an index fund tracking the S&P 500, it's always wise to diversify your investments to reduce risk by considering investing in bonds or putting some money into a bank deposit as well. Diversification is especially important for people on the cusp of retirement. Older individuals typically don't have the luxury of waiting out market downturns as they approach their retirement years, so preserving capital becomes a higher priority. As such, bonds are often seen as safer investments. Investing a portion of one's portfolio in bonds can provide income stability and act as a cushion against potential stock market volatility. Additionally, some individuals nearing retirement may choose to allocate a portion of their savings to bank deposits. While the interest rates on these investments may be lower, they also offer a lower risk of your investments losing value. In the following sections, we'll consider different investment options, their return rates, and the risks associated with them.

2.2 Investing in Stocks

Compounding interest is powerful, indexes such as the S&P 500 are a great way to invest, and outperforming the market is difficult. What about picking individual stocks? How can we narrow down the choices, and how do we filter out the "good" companies from the "bad" ones?

As we mentioned before, owning a company stock essentially means becoming a partial owner of that business. You can buy a stock at one price and, hopefully, make money by selling it at a higher price. You can also profit from a stock's decline through a process called **short selling**. This involves borrowing shares of a stock you believe will decrease in value, selling them, and buying them at a lower price later.

Investing in stocks can be remarkably profitable. Just look at the list of some of the best performing stocks of different eras in the table below.

Table 2. High-performing stocks

Stock and ticker symbol	Era	Return
Cisco Systems (CSCO)	1990s	69,222.90%
Hasbro (HAS)	1980s	32,901.22%
Jack Henry & Associates (JKHY)	1990s	24,387.92%
Qualcomm (QCOM)	1990s	17,236.56%
Nike (NKE)	1990s	15,189.92%
Nike (NKE)	1980s	11,200.00%
Best Buy (BBY)	1990s	9,550.54%
Microsoft (MSFT)	1990s	9,533.20%
Charles Schwab (SCHW)	1990s	8,715.03%
Bio-Techne (TECH)	1990s	7,558.94%
Monster Beverage (MNST)	2000s	7,074.89%
Applied Materials (AMAT)	1990s	6,830.86%
Home Depot (HD)	1980s	5,913.56%
Amgen (AMGN)	1990s	5,753.99%
Oracle (ORCL)	1990s	4,603.61%
Walmart (WMT)	1980s	4,490.00%
Caesars Entertainment (CZR)	2010s	4,487.69%
Netflix (NFLX)	2010s	3,979.61%
Jabil Circuit (JBL)	1990s	3,927.73%
Domino's Pizza (DPZ)	2010s	3,916.82%
Micron Technology (MU)	1990s	3,864.71%
Home Depot (HD)	1990s	3,812.26%
Deckers Outdoor (DECK)	2000s	3,775.05%
Electronic Arts (EA)	1990s	3,740.28%
Paychex (PAYX)	1990s	3,685.90%

Another benefit of owning a stock is the potential to receive dividends from the company, typically on a quarterly basis. **Dividends** are a distribution of a company's earnings to its shareholders, usually in the form of cash or equivalent stock reinvestment. There are no legal requirements for companies to pay dividends. However, they can be an indicator of a company doing well. According to a report by one asset management company, payment of dividends is closely associated with the company's performance. The results of the report are presented in the graph below and show that the companies that performed the best were often those that paid the highest dividends (top 20% in terms of dividends paid).[11]

Figure 9. Returns on the S&P 500 and stocks paying dividends

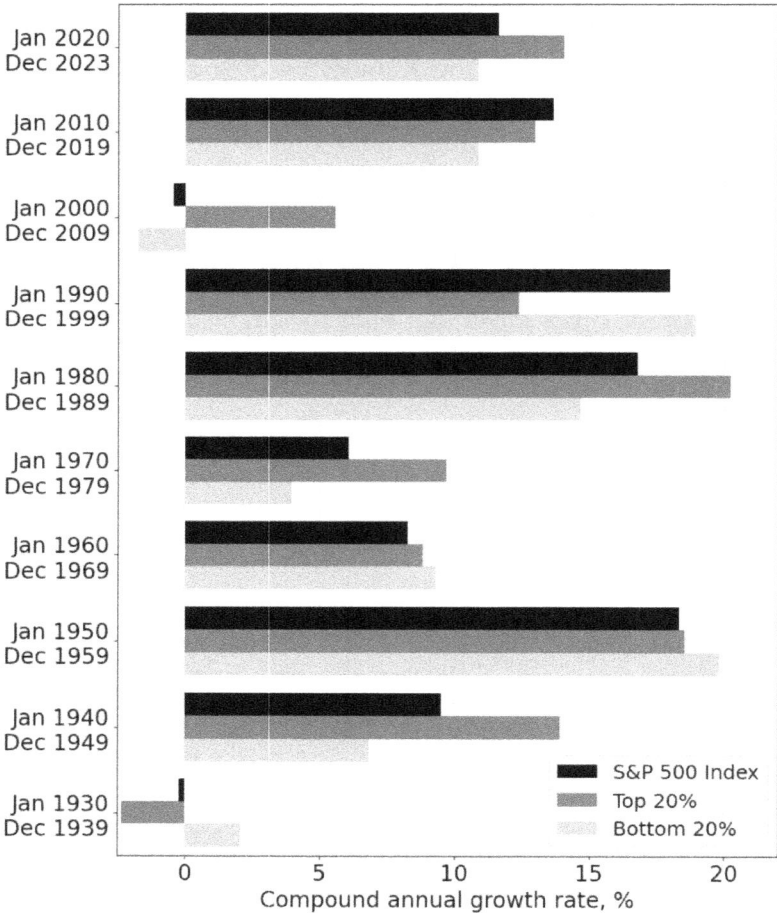

Finally, investing in stocks is attractive because of potential tax advantages. Just as you pay taxes on your salary, you must also pay taxes on any profits made from trading stocks. These profits are called capital gains. **Capital gains tax** calculations vary based on the holding period and the investor's income level. Short-term capital gains (applicable to stocks held for one year or less) are taxed similarly to your ordinary income. Long-term capital gains, for assets held longer than a year, benefit from more favorable tax treatment. For example, in 2024, individuals with taxable incomes below $47,025 (single filing status) paid no tax on long-term capital gains. On the other hand, when you sell a stock for less than its original price, the amount you lose is known as a capital loss. If your capital losses exceed your capital gains, you can use a portion of those losses (up to $3,000 in 2024; up to $1,500 if married filing separately) to decrease your taxable income. Consult a tax professional to discuss which strategy may be best for your financial situation.[12,13]

Value investing

Benjamin Graham's book *The Intelligent Investor* is considered a must-read for anyone interested in the world of investing. Published in 1949, it has remained a timeless classic and an essential resource for individuals seeking to learn about this field. Graham is often referred to as the "father of value investing," and his book presents a wealth of knowledge and insights that are still highly relevant today.[a,14] Warren Buffett, who was a student of Graham at Columbia Business School, calls *The Intelligent Investor* the "best book about investing ever written."[15]

In the book, Graham provides numerous case studies and examples to illustrate his principles and strategies. For example, he suggests two paths that a defensive investor (a person who is mostly interested in preserving money rather than gaining high returns) should follow in setting up their portfolio. The first

---

[a] Another good (and a more recently published) resource on value investing is *Value Investing: From Graham to Buffett and Beyond* by Greenwald, Kahn, Bellissimo, Cooper, and Santos.

includes buying every stock in the **Dow Jones Industrial Average**, an index of 30 companies. The other approach includes selecting individual companies to invest in based on a list of criteria.[a] Some of these criteria are:

- *Adequate size*: According to Graham, defensive investors should invest in larger, well-established companies because they are safer investments.

- *Strong financial condition*: The company should have assets that are at least twice the amount of their current liabilities.

- *Earnings stability*: The company should have a good earnings record over multiple years.

- *Uninterrupted dividend record*: If a company has earned profits in a given time period, it can distribute part of the profits to shareholders in the form of dividends. Graham dedicates an entire chapter to the often-occurring debate between shareholders and management regarding dividends. While investors often want generous dividends, the management often insists on keeping the money and, instead, reinvesting it into projects that will strengthen the company. Graham insists that either the dividend payments should be significant or the management should be able to show that such investments are paying off.[b]

- *Moderate price-to-earnings (P/E) ratio:* The **P/E ratio** is a metric used to evaluate the relative value of a company's stock by comparing its market price per share to its earnings per share. Earnings-per-share can be calculated over an

---

[a] Graham also provides a similar list for enterprising investors (those who will "devote a fair amount of [their] attention and efforts" toward obtaining better-than-average investment results). According to Graham, this list is "rather similar" to the one presented for defensive investors but is not as restrictive.

[b] Berkshire Hathaway interestingly does not pay dividends because the management thinks that they can "turn every dollar [they] retain into more than a dollar of market value."

extended period of time to smooth out individual quarterly volatility in earnings. A high P/E ratio isn't inherently good or bad, but it can reflect strong future growth expectations. As such, it might give investors reason to believe the company will earn more money in the future. It could also indicate that the stock is overvalued, meaning it's priced higher than its actual worth based on current earnings.[a]

Now, we'll consider the above criteria for the example of deciding whether to invest in Meta in 2022. That year, it seemed that things were not going well for Meta investors. In the early 2020s, the inflation rate increased in the U.S., and the Federal Reserve concurrently raised interest rates to curb the inflation. The intended goal was to make borrowing money more expensive, which in turn would reduce consumer and business spending. This strategy worked and the rate of inflation slowly started to decline towards the target 2% value. While this was great news for many, the slowing expansion of businesses meant trouble for companies like Meta, which rely on advertising as a major source of revenue.

In 2021, Apple started requiring apps running on their devices to ask users for permission to track their data. This seemingly consumer-friendly policy came at a cost to companies like Meta, which regularly use data to serve targeted ads and, hence, make money.

Around the same time, the company rebranded itself from Facebook to Meta, focusing on the metaverse and virtual reality rather than the social networks it owned. Returns on this enormous investment had not materialized by the end of 2022. This pivot with an uncertain return timeline, at a time when TikTok had been driving the market share away from Meta's

---

[a] Note that a P/E ratio can also be calculated for the entire market or a specific group of companies, such as those included in the S&P 500 index, to provide a measure of the overall valuation of the market or the selected companies.

products, led to negative implications for Meta's performance and, hence, investors' sentiment. [16] By the end of 2022, the stock price of Meta had dropped significantly from nearly $380 in 2021 to $90 in October of 2022, reaching its lowest point since 2015.

Starting in 2023, however, the situation for Meta's stock price reversed entirely, with the price reaching and passing the previous peak.

Could we have expected this reversal based on Graham's framework? Meta undoubtedly satisfies the criteria of "adequate size" and "earnings stability." It's one of the largest companies in the world in terms of market capitalization. Furthermore, unlike many companies in the technology sector, Meta became profitable within the first five years of its existence and has been consistently profitable since then.

Let's now observe the company's P/E ratio. The graph below shows the stock price and the P/E ratio for Meta between January 2020 and December 2023.[a] The first thing to notice is that the P/E ratio in this period was very volatile. It fluctuated between 10 and 40 with a median value of 26. In contrast, high P/E ratios aren't atypical for the technology industry. In 2023, profitable companies in the same industry as Meta had an average P/E ratio of nearly 150.[17] The high P/E ratios in this industry are often attributed to high growth potential, as disruptive technologies developed at these companies can lead to significant growth. By these measures, one might consider the price of the Meta stock to be undervalued.

---

[a] As is common in many resources reporting financial data, we plot the P/E ratios based on the earnings over the previous 12-month period. However, in his book, Graham suggests looking at earnings over three previous years.

Figure 10. Price and P/E ratio of Meta stock

As an exercise, let's go back to 2022 and look at where Meta was in February of that year. The P/E ratio for Meta stock had just fallen to a value of 15, along with the decline in the stock price. During this time, news articles about its unfavorable stock performance seem plenty. Will the stock continue to fall, or has it bottomed out? Is it possible that TikTok will become the next big thing and replace Meta as the leader in the social media domain? As an investor, you may also be questioning the rebranding move, the resources spent on the "metaverse," and the confidence in the CEO.

At this moment, would you have invested in Meta stocks? If you had, you would then have seen an excruciating eight months of the stock price dropping from $198 to $89. However, if you had held on to your stocks throughout 2023, you would have ended up with a 50% gain on your investment. That's a pretty good return!

Of course, your investment decision must consider many more factors than those we have listed. *The Intelligent Investor* mentions multiple, like how experienced a company's management is, whether the company has shown consistent earnings growth, and whether the stock has a moderate price compared to the company's assets.

Use of models and technical analysis

What does it mean to use a model to beat the market? In short, it means finding patterns that investors could use to make better deals.

Some have questioned whether ordinary investors can outperform markets using various "models." In his 1973 book *A Random Walk Down Wall Street*, economist Burton Malkiel claimed that **technical analysis** (which is based on the belief that past trading data like price movements can be studied to identify patterns and trends that can predict future stock price movements) didn't work. Malkiel argued that the market is efficient, and stock prices already reflect all available information, making it impossible to consistently outperform the market by studying past price movements and trends.[a,18] This argument was somewhat controversial as it contradicted the fundamental premise of technical analysis.

Other academics have also questioned the validity of technical analysis rules.[b] A 1995 study tested the profitability of "one of the most, if not the most" reliable patterns called

---

[a] When stating this, Malkiel, apparently, did not have literature to support his claims. When economist Robert Shiller asked him for sources on his findings, Malkiel didn't have an immediate answer.

[b] There were likely a lot of studies done by hedge funds. But the results were never shared publicly.

"head and shoulders." Head and shoulders is a pattern that consists of three peaks on a price graph with the middle peak (head) being taller than the two around it (shoulders). The study found that the rule had some predictive power for the German mark and Japanese yen, but not for the Canadian dollar, Swiss franc, French franc, or pound. The authors noted that if you tried trading in all six currencies concurrently, profits could be significant. Nevertheless, the fact that this pattern worked for only two of the six currencies considered raises the question of whether the "most reliable" pattern is reliable at all.[a,19,20]

Let's examine a related example. There is a popular belief that Tuesday is the best day to book an airline ticket. Since 2017, this phenomenon has been confirmed by one study and debunked by another.[21] Suppose for a minute, that it's true and that if you're planning to purchase an airline ticket, you should do so on a Tuesday evening. If this secret tactic becomes known to everyone, the airlines will see a surge in purchases on Tuesdays. Since, for whatever reason, they are charging less for the tickets on this day, they will also witness a dip in their revenue. Given this scenario, the airlines will start charging more on Tuesdays. It becomes an ongoing game of cat and mouse, with the airlines constantly trying to maximize revenue and the consumers constantly trying to outsmart the system and find the best deals. Thus, we end up in a situation where there is no best day of the week to book airline tickets.

Speaking of days of the week, the existence of a day-of-the-week effect for the stock market has been explored by researchers for over half a century. A study published in 1973

---

[a] Alan Greenspan, a former Chair of the Federal Reserve, recollects asking the management of JP Morgan how they were able to make money on foreign exchange trading (buying and selling currencies of different countries) when the research suggested that it was not possible to predict the exchange rate movements. The management replied that the money was not made from models that predicted the exchange rates, but from taking a cut from all the trades facilitated by them.

documents that the Standard & Poor's Composite Stock Index (predecessor of the modern S&P 500 index, which tracked only 90 stocks) was more likely to advance on a Friday than on a Monday.[22] A 1980 and a 1981 study found that returns were generally lower on Mondays.[23,24] However, a 2002 review found that this "weekend effect" has disappeared since then.[25]

It's possible that the day-of-the-week effect may be the result of random variations in stock prices rather than a systematic pattern. Perhaps the studies that find it are "lucky" enough to be focusing on the periods when a day-of-the-week effect exists, but the effect wouldn't hold up if they examined a longer or different time period. It's also possible that such an effect comes and goes as investors learn about its presence and try to utilize it. If a pattern exists where stock returns tend to be higher on certain days of the week, such as Friday, and lower on others, investors may try to take advantage of it by buying stocks at the beginning of the week and selling them at the end. This behavior could reinforce the pattern and make it more pronounced. However, as more investors become aware of the pattern and start to act on it, the effect may start to diminish or disappear altogether.

Now, consider an example of the relationship between a stock's P/E ratio and its subsequent 10-year return. This can be represented by the graph below. The data on the graph is imaginary, simulated to illustrate a simple relationship. Nonetheless, the relationship closely mirrors that observed in the real world: "years with low price-earnings ratios have been followed by high returns, and years with high price-earnings ratios have been followed by low or negative returns."[26] That is, there is a negative relationship between the P/E ratio and the subsequent annual return for the S&P 500 index (a higher P/E ratio is correlated with lower future returns).

Figure 11. Simulated relationship between P/E ratios and returns

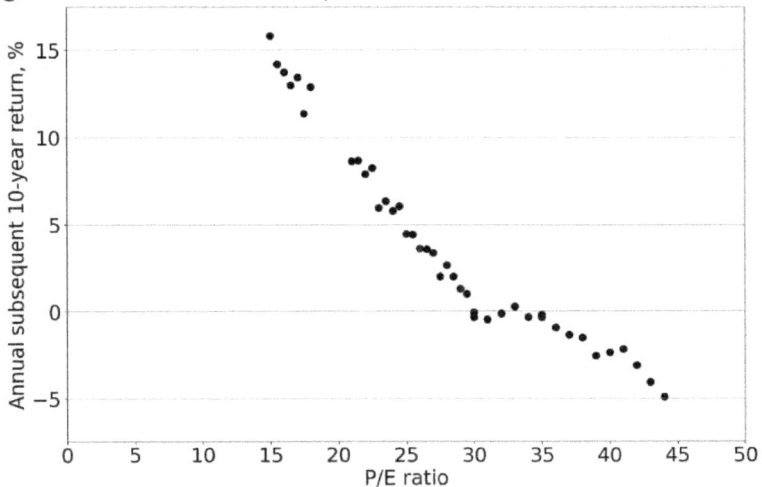

A simple analysis approach is to draw a straight line through all the points—an analysis method referred to as **linear regression**. You can see this line in gray on the graph below. The line has a downward slope (higher values on the horizontal axis are associated with lower values on the vertical axis), so it captures the general relationship between the P/E ratio and the subsequent returns well. How do we know where to draw this line? Why didn't we draw it more to the right or the left? Why didn't we make it steeper? The statistical method of building linear regression lines ensures that the line we draw has minimal error among all points: it calculates the difference between the actual return values and the predicted return values.

Given the linear regression line, we can make predictions about stocks with P/E ratios we have not seen before. Note how (by design) no companies in the data had a P/E ratio of 20. However, we can make a prediction that a hypothetical company with a P/E ratio of 20 will, on average, have an annual return of about 9%. While intuitive, the single regression line can also give misleading results. Specifically, if we look at the predictions for a P/E ratio between 30 and 35, our model suggests growth rates somewhere between -1% and 3%, even though the data suggest that the growth rate should be 0%.

Figure 12. Models of relationships between P/E ratios and returns

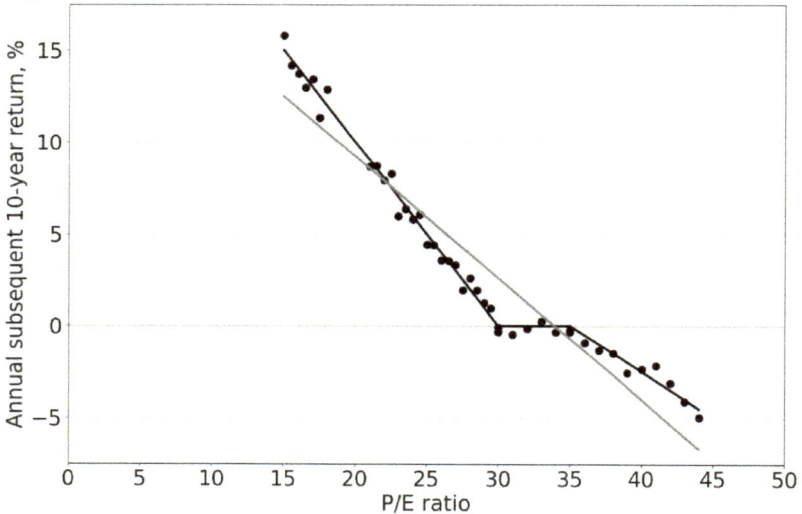

We can make the predictions even more accurately by creating three distinct line segments, shown as the black line on the graph above. In this setup, the zigzag line accounts for the "kinks" in the data, which exist around P/E ratio values of 30 and 35. Overall, the new line seems to be an even better "fit" for the data, and as such, we can make more accurate growth rate forecasts.

But what if the relationship was even more complicated? Instead of a straight line, what if the data called for a curve? Could there be differences between various industries and among various company sizes? Definitely! Can we explain these differences with economic theory? We certainly could try. Or we could employ a computer to do all the work—finding patterns, correlations, and even new methods of analysis.

In his book *The Man Who Solved the Market: How Jim Simons Launched the Quant Revolution,* Gregory Zuckerman documents Jim Simons's journey in establishing Renaissance Technologies, one of the most successful hedge funds in recent history, with an annual average return of 72% between 1994 and 2014.

According to Zuckerman, the models used by Simons and his colleagues didn't ask why the markets behaved the way they did. Rather, they were simply fed the data and looked for patterns that could help make money, however complicated they might be. Such models are often said to belong to the field of **machine learning**, a method of data analysis in which models are designed to discover patterns, relationships, and insights from data automatically. These models can then generalize and make predictions or decisions on unseen data. However, even sophisticated models do not guarantee that you will beat the market.

Effect of economic news and timing the market
We can rationally expect important events to influence stock markets. Positive events such as strong corporate earnings reports can boost investor confidence and drive stock prices up. On the other hand, negative events like natural disasters can create volatility and lead to declining stock prices. However, it's not uncommon to see news articles covering negative stock market movements "despite strong economic data." In the same manner, journalists often report positive stock movements happening despite events that, seemingly, should have sent stock prices down. In both cases, one must only think about the incentives in each scenario to come to a natural conclusion:

perhaps, fear or deviation from the norm sells papers and clicks. Ultimately, economic news, good or bad, has the potential to affect consumers' sentiment and the market.

A 1971 analysis of New York Times article headlines found that the S&P Composite Index showed a "large" gain on only 10% of days following major events. Most of the time, however, the markets moved by less than 1%. News on inflation and real economic output seemed to have no effect, while unexpected moves in monetary policy had significant ones.[27] In line with previous findings, a 2003 study showed that investors are slow at reacting to bad news, and when they do react, they tend to overreact, resulting in high trading volumes and a reversal in price movements.[28] Similarly, a 2011 study found that trading by investors in different regions is heavily affected by the way the same information is covered by local media outlets.[29]

On an average day, market movements tend to be relatively modest. However, there are select days that significantly impact returns. In fact, approximately 95% of the gains between 1963 and 1993 occurred on just 90 days scattered throughout those three decades. Merely 1% of all trading days during that period represented most of the overall gains. Attempting to time the market and pinpoint these days is a difficult task. On average, you can anticipate encountering only three such days per year!

Additionally, people are very bad at knowing when the market is under- or overvalued. As such, confidence in the stock market (measured through surveys) is known to fluctuate, with the highest levels right before the market crashes.[30]

What does this all mean for you as an investor? It's hard to believe that an average person can effectively utilize the news to make meaningful gains in the financial markets. Consider the following example of how fast professionals react to economic news. A book by Michael Lewis, *Flash Boys: A Wall Street*

Revolt, focuses on the efforts of financial institutions to cut down data transfer speeds, as even milliseconds can be important in having an advantage. In completeness, it's not necessary to be the first one to react to major news. Market selloffs can last for hours or even days. And we have already established that not selling low through such times and having a long-term view can be beneficial.

Insider information

Insider information refers to important, non-public facts about a business that are known only to its employees or individuals closely associated with it. Trading stocks of a company while using significant access to privileged information is called insider trading and is illegal.[31]

In 1989, Peter Lynch, who successfully ran Fidelity's Magellan Fund between 1977 and 1990, published a book called *One Up On Wall Street*. In the book, he shared some heuristics he used in his career to identify companies worth investing in. One such heuristic says that the best indicator of a company doing great is when its own employees buy its stock. At a minimum, this indicates that the company is not about to become bankrupt. This line of thinking certainly may be true, because employees have access to private information about the inner workings, performance, and prospects of the company.

At the same time, however, it's rare that workers have full information about all aspects of a business, especially for large and complex organizations. Employees' stock purchases may signal confidence, but they may not always have a comprehensive view of the risks, competitive threats, or strategic challenges facing the firm. Consider the example of Enron, an energy company that seemingly was doing extremely well in the market until its quick demise. Many employees of Enron must have believed that they knew their company well.

At the end of the year 2000, more than half of Enron's 401(k) plan (worth at the time more than two billion dollars) was invested into the company's own stock. By November 2001, the stock price had fallen by 94% compared to the previous year, wiping out the retirement savings of many. The losses for some employees amounted to hundreds of thousands of dollars.[32,33]

Employment is not the only way to come across non-public information that can affect stock performance. Lawmakers and government regulators who oversee certain industries may gain access to information that could aid profitable market speculation through their committee work or policy planning. Taking advantage of this became illegal in 2012 when Barack Obama signed the Stop Trading on Congressional Knowledge (STOCK) Act designed to combat insider trading by the members of Congress and other government employees. It prohibited the members of Congress from trading stocks using "any nonpublic information derived from the individual's position." Despite the legislation, multiple U.S. senators drew negative attention in 2020 when they sold stocks worth millions of dollars on the cusp of the COVID-19 pandemic outbreak in the United States.[34]

One of them was Senator Richard Burr, who, on February 13th of 2020, sold 95% of his holdings in his Individual Retirement Account in the wake of the government-mandated shutdowns of business and public spaces.[35] On the same day, after a short call with Burr, his brother-in-law sold between $97,000 and $280,000 worth of shares in six companies—including companies whose stock prices fell sharply in the next few weeks.[36] A month later, it became known that the Department of Justice, in coordination with the Securities and Exchange Commission, had started a review of stock sales made by public officials, including Burr, in the wake of the pandemic's spread in the U.S. While the investigations have not led to any action being taken against the politicians involved, they reignited the public's attention to the potential for insider trading among our elected officials.[a][37]

An analysis conducted by the New York Times revealed that 97 congressional members or their relatives traded financial assets in industries where they potentially wielded influence between 2019 and 2022.[38] For example, in 2019, a stark incident of insider trading came to light when Representative Chris Collins admitted to providing his son with insider information about an unsuccessful drug trial at Innate Immunotherapeutics. Collins, who sat on the company's board of directors and was one of its largest shareholders, helped his son and others avoid $800,000 in stock losses. He was sentenced to 26 months in prison before being pardoned by President Donald Trump in 2020.[39,40,41,42]

On multiple occasions after the passage of the STOCK Act, members of Congress have proposed legislation aimed at prohibiting themselves from trading stocks altogether. In January of 2023, Senator Josh Hawley introduced the Preventing Elected Leaders from Owning Securities and Investments (PELOSI) Act, which aimed to prohibit members of Congress and their spouses from holding or trading individual stocks.[b] A few months after the introduction of the PELOSI Act, Senator Jeff Merkley introduced the Ending Trading and Holdings in Congressional Stocks (ETHICS) Act, another bill to ban stock trades by members of Congress.[43] As of 2024, neither bill has become law.

---

[a] It does not help Burr's image that he was one of the only three Senators who voted against the STOCK Act.

[b] The bill's name is a playful jab at Nancy Pelosi, the Speaker of the House of Representatives, and is a reference to her husband's successful investing and the speculative role Pelosi's position might play in aiding those investments.

Can investors gain an advantage by monitoring the trading activity of elected officials?

For a long time, economists have been intrigued by how legislators could utilize their knowledge to beat the market. A 2011 article in *The Quarterly Journal of Economics* analyzed the stock prices of companies around the world that stood to benefit from the coups backed by the Central Intelligence Agency (CIA) across the twentieth century.[44] Often, these companies were multinational corporations previously expropriated by "unfriendly" regimes, and the overthrow of such regimes could have benefited the stock prices of these businesses. Predictably, the researchers found that the share prices of these companies did increase with successful coups. What is more interesting is that the share prices rose even higher on the days these coups were authorized. The authors attribute these increases to leaks of classified information to asset traders. They provide multiple examples of early CIA leadership being connected to Wall Street, in general, and to companies affected by the coups, specifically. Although the results were clear, the authors were unable to trace who was involved in the trades.

Another team of researchers found that, in the 1990s, members of the U.S. Senate and the U.S. House of Representatives outperformed the stock market by 12% and 6%, respectively. However, a similar study looking at trades made between 2004 and 2008 found no evidence of a congressional trading advantage. Lastly, a 2022 study found "no evidence of stock picking prowess" among U.S. Senators and House members between 2012 and 2020. [45,46,47,48]

Despite high-profile cases that occasionally make headlines, it's crucial to note that economists have not reached a consensus on whether members of Congress systematically exploit their insider knowledge and influence for personal gain in the stock market. We place emphasis on the word "systematically." Those who do trade based on insider knowledge might do so sporadically, making it difficult to identify clear patterns. Some Congress members who trade may lose money, offsetting gains made by others and complicating statistical analyses. There is a clear conflict of interest when lawmakers are able to trade stocks in industries they directly regulate or influence through legislation. However, there is little compelling evidence that tracking the trades of elected officials provides a meaningful benefit to investors' portfolios.

Political parties
The question of whether the American economy thrives more under a Democratic or Republican administration has long been a subject of debate and speculation. In the lead-up to the 2016 presidential election, former Secretary of State and presidential candidate Hillary Clinton asserted that the U.S. economy tends to fare better under Democratic presidents. Additionally, she argued that recessions are more prone to happen during Republican presidential administrations. It's natural for observers and analysts to seek correlations between party affiliations and economic outcomes. But do we have any evidence supporting either side?

Data on political affiliations and recessions provides a mixed view. Indeed, 10 of the 12 recessions that occurred between 1948 and 2020 started with a Republican president in office.[a] However, Democrats controlled the House in nine of the recessions and the Senate in eight.[49,50]

---

[a] For various reasons, when considering economic trends and policies, economists tend to focus on the period of history after World War II. Some of these reasons include data availability, relative economic stability, and the new role of the United States as a global economic leader. This era also saw significant advancements in technology and the establishment of key economic institutions and policies.

So, are recessions caused by Republican presidents, Democratic Congresses, or a combination of the two? Which political party has historically been better for the economy?

Table 3. Parties in power during the recessions since World War II[51]

Recession start	President (party in parentheses)	Senate Majority	House Majority
Feb 2020	Donald J. Trump (R)	Republicans	Democrats
Dec 2007	George W. Bush (R)	Democrats	Democrats
Mar 2001	George W. Bush (R)	Republicans	Republicans
Jul 1990	George H. W. Bush (R)	Democrats	Democrats
Jul 1981	Ronald Reagan (R)	Democrats	Democrats
Jan 1980	James Carter (D)	Democrats	Democrats
Nov 1973	Richard Nixon (R)	Democrats	Democrats
Dec 1969	Richard Nixon (R)	Democrats	Democrats
Apr 1960	John F. Kennedy (D)	Democrats	Democrats
Aug 1957	Dwight D. Eisenhower (R)	Democrats	Democrats
Jul 1953	Dwight D. Eisenhower (R)	Republicans	Republicans
Nov 1948	Harry S. Truman (D)	Republicans	Republicans

Multiple attempts have been made to test whether the U.S. experiences differential economic outcomes depending on which political party is in charge. For example, research by Vanguard claims that portfolios consisting of 60% stocks and 40% bonds showed no difference in returns between Democratic and Republican presidents when focusing on data since 1860. [52] Studies focusing on more recent periods, however, have found that real (i.e., adjusted for inflation) GDP (**gross domestic product**; the monetary value of final goods and services produced in a given period of time) grows more under Democratic presidents.[53]

A 2016 study found "robust" evidence that the U.S. economy performs better under Democratic presidents than Republican ones across multiple criteria.[a] For example, real GDP growth is, on average, 1.79 percentage points higher (5% versus 3.21%) under the Democrats. However, the gap cannot be explained by initial economic conditions, trends, or measurable differences in fiscal or monetary policy between the parties.[b] Instead, the data show that Democrats have benefited from more favorable oil shocks, stronger growth in defense spending (wars are important "shocks" that boost government spending and lead to growth spurts) during some periods, and higher productivity growth on average during their administrations. They may also have benefited from stronger foreign economic growth which could have positive impacts on the domestic economy. These factors are estimated to account for up to two-thirds of the total Democratic growth edge over Republicans. While intriguing, some portion of the growth difference remains unexplained.[54]

What about the effect of the election results on the stock markets? Are markets more optimistic about Democratic or Republican presidents? If one party is better for the economy (or, at least, the stock market), surely Wall Street analysts have already identified which party that is. Let's look at the growth rate of the S&P 500's closing values around presidential election days. The growth rate, in this case, is defined as:

$$Rate = \frac{Value, 1\ business\ day\ after\ -\ Value, 1\ business\ day\ before}{Value, 1\ business\ day\ before} * 100$$

The elections of a Democratic and a Republican president in the past two elections both led to significant rise in the S&P 500 index. However, the index's growth rate was much lower

---

[a] In the context of economic studies, the term "robust" generally means that the results hold up even if the underlying assumptions of the analysis are changed (within a reasonable range).

[b] This is not to infer that monetary policy is swayed by the party in power.

during previous elections. Unfortunately, the small sample size (nine Democratic and 11 Republican presidents in this period) means that we cannot conclude with certainty that the difference in growth rates we are observing (-0.11% for Democrats and 0.75% for Republicans—values too close to zero in both cases) is not just due to chance.[a] There have not been enough elections for us to safely rule (bad) luck out of the equation, not to mention that parties' policies and views do change over time.

Table 4. Market reactions to presidential election results

Election year	President (party in parentheses)	S&P 500 two-day growth rate, %
2024	Donald J. Trump (R)	3.79
2020	Joe Biden (D)	4.02
2016	Donald J. Trump (R)	1.49
2012	Barack Obama (D)	-1.60
2008	Barack Obama (D)	-1.40
2004	George W. Bush (R)	1.12
2000	George W. Bush (R)	-1.60
1996	Bill Clinton (D)	2.53
1992	Bill Clinton (D)	-1.33
1988	George H. W. Bush (R)	-0.22
1984	Ronald Reagan (R)	0.35
1980	Ronald Reagan (R)	3.03
1976	James Carter (D)	-0.95
1972	Richard Nixon (R)	-0.76
1968	Richard Nixon (R)	0.20
1964	Lyndon B. Johnson (D)	0.33
1960	John F. Kennedy (D)	0.82
1956	Dwight D. Eisenhower (R)	0.28
1952	Dwight D. Eisenhower (R)	0.62
1948	Harry S. Truman (D)	-3.45

---

[a] Imagine you're tossing two coins, and you want to see if one coin lands on heads more often than the other. You toss each coin 10 times. One coin lands on heads seven times, and the other lands on heads five times. Would you say that the first coin is more likely to land on heads?

Behavioral aspects

Let's say you purchase stocks in a company, but the stock price immediately drops. You hold onto it, believing it's just a temporary setback, possibly due to investors undervaluing the stock. After all, you originally considered it a sound investment based on the company's financial statements and analyst opinions, which seemed positive. However, the low price persists and keeps decreasing each month. You come across a report suggesting that the stock was overvalued when you bought it, and the company's overall prospects aren't looking good. Despite your disagreement, you have decided to review the company's latest financial statements, which reveal unfavorable trends. Experiencing discomfort because of this new information is what psychologists define as **cognitive dissonance**.

How do you handle this discomfort? You have a few options. You could choose to ignore reports that cause you stress. Alternatively, you might try to alter your memory by convincing yourself that you did notice red flags but believed the positive aspects outweighed them. Another approach could be to forget about these losses and focus solely on the investments that have generated profits.

There is no "right" response here, as humans aren't cold, calculating machines. Even those who perceive themselves to be very rational are often victims of various biases that can distort their decision-making or affect how they retain information. In fact, psychologists suggest that such behaviors are common when individuals face cognitive dissonance.

In the 1990s, a new subfield of economics called **behavioral economics** emerged, as more economists acknowledged that psychological factors, beyond mere numerical analysis, could influence how individuals allocate limited resources to fulfill their needs. The birth of this field is commonly attributed to the works of Daniel Kahneman and Amos Tversky in the late 1970s. Through a series of experiments, they demonstrated that decision-making is not solely driven by rational calculations but is also impacted by cognitive biases and mental heuristics.[55] This research led to the integration of psychology into the realms of economics and finance, giving rise to behavioral economics and behavioral finance, respectively. The significance of this work was so profound that Kahneman, alongside experimental economist Vernon L. Smith, was awarded the Nobel Memorial Prize in Economic Sciences in 2002.[a]

Are there any interesting psychological factors that have been found to affect investing behavior? A 1993 study found that the weather in New York City affects the trading patterns on Wall Street.[56] In general, people in a good mood have a more positive outlook on things. Happy people are more optimistic about the probability of good events.[57] A good mood also brings about a positive outlook on other people, consumer goods, life satisfaction, and past events. According to the study, cloudy days see lower returns compared to sunny days because gloomy weather affects traders' moods differently.[58]

However, one concern with studies that find "intriguing" results is that the authors may have used data that was (perhaps unintentionally) bound to find a "statistically significant" effect. Would we still see the effect of cloudy weather if we used data from a different period? What if we used data from cities other than New York? Are there other researchers who have already studied the effect of weather on trading activity but did not find any "significant" results?

Researchers who tried to test the results of the 1993 study with new data failed to come to an agreement. A paper published in

---

[a] Tversky had passed away six years prior, and the Nobel is not awarded posthumously.

1997 found that the weather effect is present in some periods and absent in others.[59] However, a study published in 2003 looking at the data across 25 different cities concluded that "sunshine is highly significantly correlated with daily stock returns."[60] With all these confusing conclusions, for an individual investor, it's probably a good idea not to rely too heavily on sunny weather to help with stock market forecasts.

Advisors and experts

Consider Bob, a college student trying to make some side money by selling his art online. He spends six hours drawing a very detailed painting which he tries to sell online at a price of $70. Alice, a college student working part-time at the university library for $10/hour, finds Bob's painting lovely but is appalled by the price. "I would have to work an entire day to afford this!" she exclaims. Would Bob sell it for anything less? Even if the supplies cost him only $20 (let's say he got his canvas at a discounted price and has some paint left that he can use for other projects), his hourly wage turns out to be less than Alice's. That begs the question: why doesn't he work at the same library?

One possibility is that the process of painting brings Bob some level of satisfaction that is not measured by the price of the art. Although he may eventually end up with a net return of $50 on his work ($70 minus the $20 cost of supplies), he has also gained what economists call **utility**: some amount of enjoyment obtained while painting. Similarly, Alice could have painted the art herself. However, she would have needed to sacrifice a day's worth of earnings.

The opportunity cost of time is crucial for many, especially when considering investment options. Spending hundreds and thousands of hours over the years reading 10-K and 10-Q reports (annual and quarterly reports showing a company's performance) may give you a slight edge over a person who is solely focused on tracking the S&P 500 index. However, doing so comes at a huge opportunity cost, preventing you from doing other activities that you enjoy. Since managing our investment portfolios may be time-consuming, perhaps we could delegate this work to a professional in exchange for a fee. Will their advice be worth the fee?

It turns out that not all financial advisors have your best interests in mind. A 2012 study found that financial advisors tend to make recommendations that maximize their fees and "have no problem discouraging clients from investing more in their current strategies if this is not in the interest of the advisor."[61] Financial advisors often help clients buy what is currently "hot" (for example, cryptocurrencies in 2021) and sell what is not. And they may advise you to do so at the worst possible time. During the Great Recession, brokers and financial planners were selling their clients' stocks, even though cheaper stock prices should have encouraged them to buy.[62]

When working with a financial advisor, you must ensure that your advisor is bound by **fiduciary duty**: that is, they are legally obligated to offer advice that is in the best interest of your finances. Not everyone who calls themselves a financial advisor is required by law to do so. You should be especially careful if your advisor is paid based on the financial products they sell you, as that will motivate them to prioritize their own commissions over your best interests.[63,64]

In early 1999, Amazon's stock price fell by nearly 50%. This fall caught the eye of a senior editor at Barron's, a weekly magazine covering financial markets, who ran a cover story titled "Amazon.bomb." Across four pages, the article meticulously outlined various problems facing Amazon, from slowing book sales (Amazon was founded as an online marketplace for books) to threats from competitors like Walmart to concerns over the company's cash flow and sustainability. It also took a jab at Amazon investors, who were called out for being "oblivious to considerations such as profits." Finally, the article concluded by expressing hope that one day the investors would "wise up." [65] Yet, over the following 25 years, Amazon's stock price has increased more than 60-fold, making it one of the greatest success stories in business history. In 2018, nearly half of all online retail sales dollars in the U.S. were spent on Amazon. The company's closest competitor, eBay, accounted for less than 7%. [66] This example shows just how difficult it is for even experienced analysts to predict the long-term prospects of a business. Even professionals with deep industry knowledge and analytical skills often fail to correctly identify which companies will revolutionize their markets and which will fade into obscurity.

One such professional is Jim Cramer, the host of the finance television program "Mad Money." In March of 2008 (the middle of the Great Recession), Cramer famously declared that it was "silly" to pull money out of investment bank Bear Stearns. In the previous year, the bank's stock price had fallen from more than $180 to $60. On March 16, 2008, Bear Sterns was acquired by JP Morgan Chase for just two dollars a share. [67,68,69] More recently, on January 3, 2022, Cramer tweeted "Netflix! BUY!" when the tech giant's stock traded at more than $540 per share. In the next four months, the stock price plummeted to $180, and it only returned to the $540 mark two years later. These are only a few prominent examples—Cramer's forecasting mishaps were so numerous that they became a part of popular culture and, in 2023, inspired the creation of the "Inverse Cramer Tracker ETF, which was aimed to deliver the opposite returns of whatever stocks Jim Cramer recommended."[a,70]

---

[a] ETFs or exchange-traded funds are instruments allowing you to invest in a "basket" of stocks or bonds.

Academics also often make erroneous predictions, just as Kevin Hassett and James K. Glassman did in 1999. The two (one an economist, the other a journalist) published a book titled *Dow 36,000: The New Strategy for Profiting From the Coming Rise in the Stock Market*, which argued that the stocks were undervalued despite what "the so-called market experts" were saying.[71] The market P/E ratio that year was above 35, the highest it had ever been to that date.[72] Hassett and Glassman, however, claimed that the Dow Jones Industrial Average would soon reach 36,000—triple its value in 1999. Shortly after the book's publication date, the **dot-com bubble** (the period from the mid-1990s to the early 2000s, when the stock prices of internet companies grew significantly, fueled by speculative investments) ended. The Dow slowly lost about 30% over the next four years. Although Glassman and Hassett's claim of Dow 36,000 did eventually become true, it wasn't until two decades after their book was published.

We'll conclude this series of forecasting mistakes with an example of a celebrity making a somewhat correct economic prediction. On January 12th, 2022, political commentator and televangelist Pat Robertson was asked on "The 700 Club" television program "what the Lord showed [him] regarding 2022." Robertson responded, "I believe that the Lord showed me we were going to have a financial collapse. There is going to be a time when the financial authorities in the world cannot meet the debt obligations."[73] Three months later, Sri Lanka declared that it was suspending payment on most foreign debt. In June, Russia defaulted on its foreign debt. In December, Ghana suspended payments on most of its external debts.[74] By the end of the year, the S&P 500 had lost 20%—not quite a collapse, but a significant decline, nonetheless.

However, more likely than not, this was a case of a broken clock being finally right. Robertson had a rich history of making bizarre forecasts. In 2006, he predicted that a tsunami would devastate the Pacific Northwest (it didn't happen); in 2020, he predicted that Donald Trump would be re-elected as President of the United States. Robertson also predicted the end of the world. Twice. First, in 1982, and then, in 2007.[75] In 2011, Robertson, among a few other people who incorrectly predicted the end of the world based on "numerical evidence," was awarded a satiric Ig Nobel Prize in mathematics for "teaching the world to be careful when making mathematical assumptions and calculations."

These errors in forecasts highlight the difficulty of making general predictions in market movements. Often, we hear experts provide forecasts and the reasoning behind them, but we rarely verify the accuracy of their predictions in the future. Such assessments should be done across a large number of forecasts to ensure that the experts weren't just lucky to have made one correct prediction.

With this issue in mind, Philip Tetlock, the co-organizer of the Good Judgment Project, collaborated with the Intelligence Advanced Research Projects Activity (an organization within the Office of the Director of National Intelligence) to assess the forecasting abilities of experts from various fields. The process required asking experts to estimate the likelihood of various events, with Tetlock identifying the most successful individuals at the end. While occasional forecasting errors are inevitable for anyone, Tetlock discovered that some people can be consistently good at forecasting events.[a]

Unfortunately, the predictions of celebrity experts are rarely assessed for their accuracy in the same rigorous manner. This lack of accountability allows these high-profile pundits to continue making bold claims without facing consequences or

---

[a] A good read on Tetlock's findings is his book *Superforecasting: The Art and Science of Prediction*.

scrutiny for their errors. Moreover, the media's tendency to amplify dramatic predictions further exacerbates this problem, giving more attention to sensational forecasts rather than more measured, evidence-based assessments.

All in all, it may be worth listening to and weighing the views of financial experts and being informed of their advice. But before you make any decisions based on that advice, it's a good idea to check their track record and see if other credible experts agree with them.

2.3 Risk and Uncertainty

You may have heard it before: when investing, one should diversify. But why? Let's try to take an intuitive approach by considering two unrelated companies, Chrysler and Netflix. The former solely produces internal combustion engine (ICE) cars, while the latter focuses on streaming services. Given that you have some amount of money saved to invest, which company should you choose to invest in?

Unless you're an expert in this industry and have considerable knowledge about the "ins and outs" of the two companies, it could be argued that investing half of your money in Chrysler and the other into Netflix would mitigate the most amount of risk. Let's say that there is a 50/50 chance of your investment growing or shrinking if you invest all of your money into Chrysler.[a] We'll assume the same thing can be said if you invest all of your money into Netflix.

Now, what if you invested half of your money into Chrysler and the other half in Netflix? The diagram below shows the potential outcomes of splitting your investment between the two. Arrows on the outside of the diagram indicate growth

---

[a] Assuming you think the market for ICE cars has a 50% chance of growing (which would lead to higher stock prices for Chrysler).

(arrow pointing upward) or decline (arrow pointing downward) in stock prices. Cells on the inside of the diagram show what will happen to your investments in different scenarios.

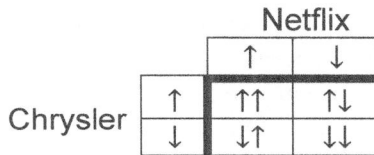

	Netflix	
	↑	↓
Chrysler ↑	↑↑	↑↓
↓	↓↑	↓↓

In this case, we see that there is a 25% chance of both Chrysler and Netflix doing well (indicated by two arrows pointing upward), a 25% chance of Chrysler doing well and Netflix not doing well, a 25% chance of Chrysler not doing well and Netflix doing well, and a 25% chance of both companies not doing well. Comparing the diversification outcome with the non-diversification possibilities (i.e., investing all of your money in one stock), we see that you would have a lower risk of your investment shrinking if you diversify.

Table 5. Investment outcomes

Investment	Possible Outcome
All of your money in Chrysler	50% chance of growth, 50% chance of decline
All of your money in Netflix	50% chance of growth, 50% chance of decline
Half of your money in Chrysler Half of your money in Netflix	25% chance of growth, 50% chance of no change, 25% chance of decline

Investing in related industries, such as Chrysler and Tesla, may also affect risk. As the two types of cars manufactured by these companies are substitutes for one another (most people will only buy one car, and not both), an increase in demand for ICE cars may have negative impacts on the market for electric vehicles (EVs). Conversely, an increase in the sales of EVs may come at a cost of negative impacts on the market for ICE cars. Meanwhile, a total decrease in the demand for all types of cars may negatively impact both!

The simple scenarios described here assume that you believe each stock has a 50/50 chance of growing or decreasing in value. Although such an assumption may be unrealistic, it shows that risk can be mitigated when diversifying. Furthermore, risk mitigation is one of the main reasons why mutual funds are so prevalent in the market and indexes such as the S&P 500 are often utilized.

Options

Suppose you're hired by Delta Airlines as a purchasing specialist, a job title that entails buying all the necessary goods and services required by Delta to conduct its business. In addition to smaller purchases such as napkins and baggage tags, you also need to place orders for airplane fuel, the price of which is known to vary widely year-to-year, and even month-to-month. Although small variations in fuel price are expected and can be dealt with, large ups and downs force Delta to institute "fuel surcharges" for their customers, which negatively impact the demand for travel. As a purchasing specialist, how should you mitigate the large variance in fuel prices (and, in turn, make flight ticket pricing more predictable)?

Figure 13. Historical jet fuel prices

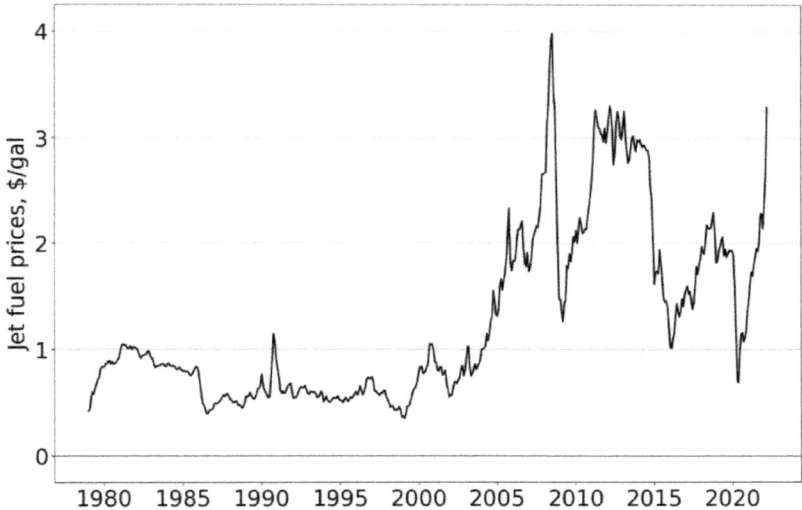

Enter options. An **option** is a financial contract offering the owner of the contract the right, but not the obligation, to buy or sell an asset over a specified period. In our example with Delta Airlines, you could recommend that the airline buy an option that provides Delta the right but not the obligation to buy jet fuel at a pre-determined price.

Let's consider an example from the stock market. Say you invested all of your money into GameStop stock and fear a large decrease in the company's stock price. In this case, you could purchase an option that gives you the right, but not the obligation, to sell your GameStop stocks at a predetermined price. Such options act like an insurance policy, and thus aren't free, but usually cost substantially less than the good (jet fuel) or stock (GameStop) you want to "insure" against large price swings.

The two main types of options in the financial markets are called puts and calls. A **put** option allows the holder of the option to sell the stock or a good at a certain specified price within a certain specified window. In the previous example with GameStop, the option you would purchase to insure against a significant decrease in the price of this stock would be a put. In other words, you would pay another party for the legal right to sell GameStop stock at a predetermined price.

On the other hand, if you're concerned about large increases in jet fuel prices, you would purchase a **call** option, which allows the holder of the option to buy goods (for example, jet fuel) at a certain specified price within a certain specified window. In this case, the purchasing specialist would pay another party for the legal right to purchase jet fuel at a predetermined price.

Notice that puts and calls are utilized in different scenarios, with the former being used as insurance against a large decrease and the latter as insurance against a large increase. As a result, owning a put option is useless if the price of the good or stock increases, while owning a call option is useless if the price of the good or stock decreases. To visualize this, let's return to our example with Delta Airlines.

According to Delta, the airline used approximately four billion gallons of jet fuel in 2023. Using an average price per gallon of $2.50, a total cost of $10 billion would have been spent on fuel. For the upcoming year, the company thinks that the average jet fuel price will increase by 15%, from $2.50/gal to $2.875/gal, meaning that the company is expected to spend $11.5 billion on fuel, up $1.5 billion from a year prior. Because Delta is so confident in its projections of average prices rising to $2.875/gal, it decides to purchase call options in the marketplace for jet fuel.

As proof of concept, let's suppose the airline purchases one call option for 10 cents, which gives Delta the right to purchase one gallon of jet fuel at an agreed-upon price of $2.65 within the next year (365 days from the contract date). Given the current price of $2.50, the option is useless to Delta until the market price per gallon increases above $2.65. In other words, Delta wouldn't exercise the call option and buy a gallon of jet fuel for $2.65 from the broker when they can buy it for less on the market.

However, if the market price of fuel has increased to $3 within a year of purchasing the call option, Delta should exercise the option and buy the gallon of jet fuel for the predetermined price of $2.65 (rather than the three dollars the company would have paid in the market). Doing so would save Delta $3 − ($2.65 + $0.10) = $0.25 per gallon.

Although saving a quarter may not seem like much, with four billion gallons used in 2023, Delta would have saved one billion dollars by properly utilizing a call option. If, however, jet fuel prices didn't rise as Delta expected and the company bought call options, the company would have lost $400 million (10 cents × four billion gallons).

Table 6. Put and call options

You own	Stock price falls	Stock price rises
A put	Exercise the contract, sell the stock. You're out the contract fee.	Don't exercise the contract. You're out the contract fee.
A call	Don't exercise the contract. You're out the contract fee.	Exercise the contract, buy the stock. You're out the contract fee.

So, when should you purchase or sell puts and calls? In the case of using these options like insurance, it's clear—you can buy puts if you're insuring against a price decrease, a call if you're insuring against a price increase, or both if you want to insure a price range. Since future prices remain unpredictable, it may be in the investor's interest to purchase both puts and calls for a given stock (or good) to ensure a window of prices.

Things get a bit more complicated (and much, much, riskier!) when you're the seller of these contracts: that is, people and businesses pay you a **premium** (i.e., the cost of a put/call) to take on the risk brought by options. If you sell a put option, you're giving another party the legal right to sell you a stock (or good) at a predetermined price within a predetermined window of time for a fee. Suppose you sell a put option for a stock, allowing the buyer to sell the stock to you at an agreed-upon price of $100. For this risk, you charge the buyer $10. If the stock price remains over $100, you face no additional risk and have made $10 following the expiration of your put. However, the largest amount of money you can lose is up to $90, if the value of the stock reaches $0 but you're still legally required to buy it for $100. For put sellers, we say that there is "limited risk," up to the amount of the underlying asset's strike price.

If you sell a call option, you're giving another party the legal right to buy a stock (or good) from you at a predetermined price within a predetermined window of time for a fee. In this instance, you face (theoretically) unlimited risk. Let's say you have sold the right for someone to buy a stock from you for $100, and for the risk, you charge the person $15. If the price of the stock doesn't go over $100 by the expiration of your call, you will make a profit of $15. However, if the stock's price exceeds $115, your losses may be exorbitant. What if the stock price skyrockets and ends up at $1,000? You would have lost $885. What about $10,000? $9,885. Theoretically, there is no limit. If you're thinking about selling call options, it's in your best interest to protect yourself by buying a call option as well.

Figure 14. AMC and GameStop stock prices

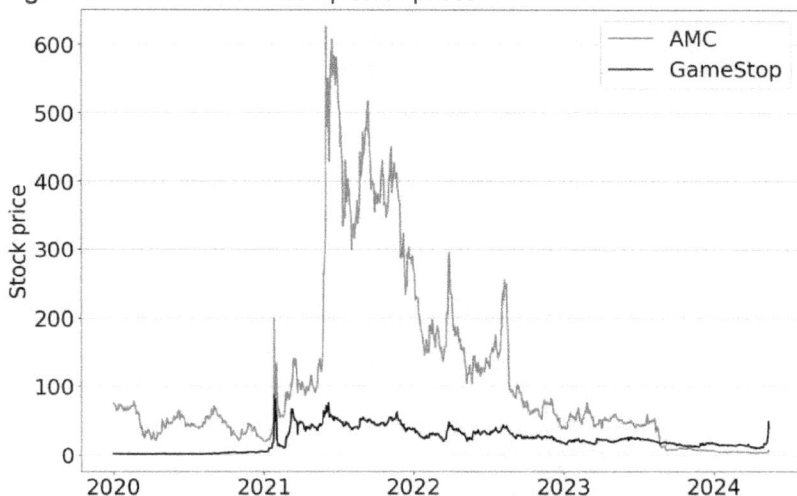

In early 2021, GameStop Corp's stock price skyrocketed over 20-fold from an initial price of $4 over the first few weeks of the year. Shortly after, AMC Entertainment Holdings' stock also saw its price grow exponentially, seemingly following the footsteps of GameStop weeks prior. Although both stocks saw sharp decreases in their prices paired with large volatility, the price trend tended to approach its pre-2021 prices.[a] So, what happened? Why did the price suddenly skyrocket?

Leading up to 2021, both AMC and GME's prices were on a downward trend, with the latter having failed to find a buyer for the company a few years earlier as they struggled with video game sales. Due to their lackluster outlook, professional investors were purchasing "short" options—a scenario where the buyers borrow a stock and sell it at the current price, betting that when the time comes due for the borrower to return the

***

[a] However, during mid-2024, GME's stock prices went through a similar increase once again.

borrowed stock, they can buy it for a lower price in the market. In this way, they were hoping to profit from the companies' (stock price) downfall. As more professional investors saw and took a risk with this opportunity, GME became one of the most widely shorted stocks.

At the same time, retail investors (i.e., non-professional, "average Americans") were becoming more knowledgeable in online investing, with apps like Robinhood and Webull providing millions of Americans access to trading from the comfort of their homes. Furthermore, the COVID-19 pandemic meant more people were staying indoors, and social media platforms such as Twitter, Facebook, and Reddit became ever so relevant to many. These scenarios all played a role in the sudden rise of GME and AMC's stock prices, with the final strike being attributed to a public discussion on a Reddit forum known as "WallStreetBets." Retail investors who had tuned in to the forum were discussing the large short positions made by professional investors, and that if many "average Americans" suddenly started buying these stocks (thereby driving up the price), it would deal a large financial blow to the professionals—since they had bet that the stocks' prices would fall. Whether driven by the potential of money, feelings of inclusion, or something else, we now know that the retail investors were successful, albeit for a short period of time. Due to the high volatility and demand, one of the major mobile investing apps, Robinhood, even restricted trading of GME stocks for a few days. The high volatility in prices has led to a new term, **memestocks**, describing stocks with a share price that is more dependent on their popularity and speculation than the company's underlying assets.

While it may seem easier than ever to invest in all sorts of financial products, it's important to trade only what you can afford to lose. Proper risk management is crucial. Diversifying your investments is equally so. It's wise not to invest all your money in stocks; instead, you should keep some in traditionally safer options like bank deposits. Remember that large price swings aren't uncommon in the stock market, and if a stock price drops significantly, it may take decades for it to reach its previous peak level.

2.4 Less Volatile Investment Opportunities

Research has shown that, except for a small portion of the population, most individuals don't enjoy risk—whether in the stock market, in the natural environment, or even when it comes to choosing what restaurant to dine at. This distaste for volatility is made clearer when we look at all the different types of insurance policies that exist today—health, vision, dental, life, home, auto, travel, business, and even hand insurance for certain professions such as surgeons and musicians! In investing, less risky opportunities may seem attractive if you're just getting started or perhaps don't have much time to dedicate to the process.

For investors seeking opportunities with less risk and volatility than the overall market, bank deposits and Treasury bills provide stable, predictable returns.

Certificates of deposit

Bank deposits, such as savings accounts and **certificates of deposit** (CDs), allow investors to earn interest on funds held at a bank. The interest rate paid is usually very modest, but the money you keep in your savings account is insured by the Federal Deposit Insurance Corporation (FDIC). As of 2024, the

FDIC insures $250,000 per depositor, per insured bank, for each account ownership category.[a]

The FDIC was created during the Great Depression as a measure to restore people's confidence in the banking system of the United States. In the decade prior to the Great Depression (before October 29, 1929), nearly 600 banks failed every year. After the collapse of the U.S. stock market in 1929, banks suffered losses because borrowers could not repay their loans. Concurrently, many individuals correctly feared that their money would be at risk and rushed to the banks to withdraw their money (a process known as a "run on the banks"). Most customers were not able to do so, as banks didn't have enough cash and the FDIC had not been created. Nearly 2,300 banks failed in 1931. An estimated 4,000 banks failed in the first three months of 1933. To deal with the issue, the newly elected President Franklin D. Roosevelt signed the Banking Act on June 16, 1933, creating the Federal Deposit Insurance Corporation.[76] Today, the United States experiences less than 10 bank failures per year.[b,77]

The graph below shows the annual return rates on two five-year investment options, the S&P 500 and a 60-month CDs. CDs usually offer higher rates than ordinary savings accounts, but, in return, require you to keep money in the bank for a set amount of time. Investing your money in an S&P 500 fund in 2010 for five years, on average, would have earned you nearly 16% yearly (before subtracting the management fees). Parking your money in a CD for the same period would have only

---

[a] Some ownership categories are single accounts (checking accounts, savings accounts), certain retirement accounts (Individual Retirement Accounts, 401k accounts), and government accounts.

[b] A notable exception is the period during and immediately after the Great Recession. Between 2008 and 2014, on average, there were 70 bank failures per year. Still, this is only a tenth of the bank failures that happened in the 1920s.

earned you 3% per year. However, that money would have been insured by the FDIC up to the $250,000 limit.

Figure 15. S&P 500 vs CD

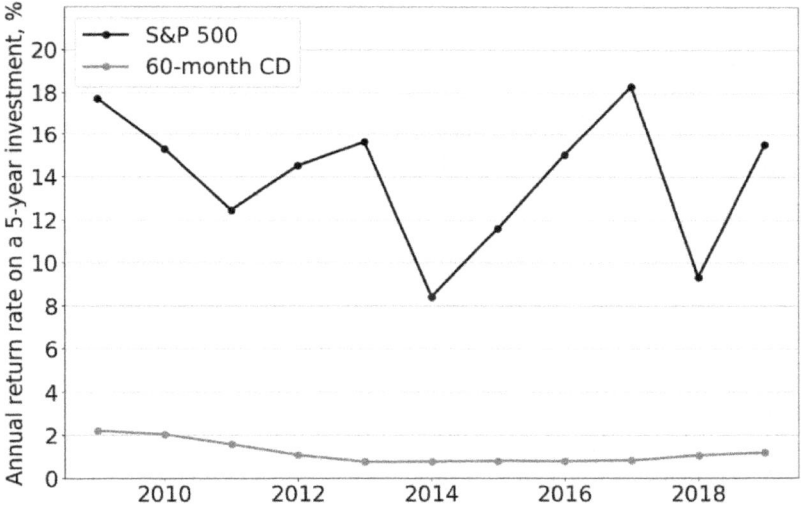

Treasury securities

In 2023, the U.S. government collected $4.4 trillion in revenue. Most of the funds came from personal income taxes ($2.18 trillion) and taxes collected to fund Social Security and Medicare ($1.61 trillion). Other large sources of revenue included corporate income taxes ($420 billion) and customs duties ($80 billion). The U.S. government uses this money on programs with the purpose of supporting the economy and the people of the United States. In fiscal year 2023, estimated federal spending was $6.1 trillion, representing 24% of the nation's GDP. Yes, the government spent $1.7 trillion more than it collected, meaning that it ran a **budget deficit**. The last time the U.S. government ran a budget surplus (when revenue exceeded spending) was in the late 1990s. We'll talk more about the budget deficit at the end of the book.

To finance a deficit, the federal government resorts to borrowing money by selling United States Treasury securities. You can essentially loan your money to them by purchasing one of these securities, which include Treasury bills, Treasury notes, Treasury bonds, Treasury inflation-protected securities (TIPS), floating rate notes (FRNs), and U.S. savings bonds. They are backed by the full faith and credit of the U.S. government and purchased directly from them. For many, even outside of the U.S., this is enough of a guarantee that your money will be returned at the maturity date (the date when you receive your investment back, along with any unpaid interest).

Treasury bills, notes, and bonds have different maturity dates, with bills maturing in under a year, notes maturing anywhere between two and 10 years, and bonds maturing in 20 or 30 years. The principal value of TIPS (the amount of money returned at maturity) adjusts based on changes in the Consumer Price Index, providing protection against rising prices. When TIPS mature (in five, 10, or 30 years), you get either the increased (inflation-adjusted) amount or the original amount, whichever is greater. Floating rate notes (FRNs) mature in two years and have an interest rate that can change over time. Unlike the other instruments mentioned, savings bonds aren't transferable, meaning you cannot buy or sell them on the secondary market. But you can typically buy savings bonds for as little as $25, while other instruments require a minimum investment of $100.[78]

Ultimately, the decision of whether to invest in the stock market or put your money in a savings account or Treasury bills depends on your personal financial goals and risk tolerance. A person planning to retire in the next couple of years will probably prefer safer investment options, whereas younger individuals may be more willing to take on greater risk in their investments in order to potentially earn higher returns over a longer investment horizon.[a] Younger people generally have more time to ride out market downturns and recover from potential losses, whereas someone who is close to retirement may not have this luxury.

2.5 Preparing for Retirement

A high salary alone is often not enough to live a comfortable retired life. Even with a median income of $3.2 million, nearly 16% of NFL players declare bankruptcy within 12 years of retirement. After running out of money, they must navigate their future carefully, as the average yearly pension of NFL players stands at "just" $30,000.[79]

Understanding the various income and savings programs available for retirees in the U.S. is crucial to planning for a financially secure future. It is important to start early, make informed decisions, and perhaps even seek the advice of a financial advisor. Let's explore some of these programs, including their history, examples, and benefits.

Social security

The **Social Security** program, established in 1935 as part of the New Deal legislation under President Franklin D. Roosevelt, is a federal program that provides a source of income for individuals who are retired, disabled, or survivors of deceased workers. About 85% of all money raised through Social Security taxes goes to a fund that pays benefits to current retirees and families of workers who have died. The remaining 15% goes to a fund that supports people with disabilities and

---

[a] Similar statements are also often made in a context that encourages young individuals to bet on individual companies—a significantly riskier endeavor.

their families. Currently, there are 50 million retirees in the United States receiving Social Security benefits, and for six million of these recipients, the Social Security payments constitute more than 90% of their income.

When you work, you pay taxes into the Social Security system that provides benefits to current retirees. Then, at the time of your retirement (at the age of 67 if you were born in 1960 or later) or in the unfortunate case you become disabled, you, your spouse, and your dependent children may be eligible to receive monthly benefits.[a,80] This intergenerational approach aims to create a sustainable system where the workforce continuously supports the retired population.

The problems start when the money being collected from the workforce is not enough to support the retirees. High unemployment rates, reduced wages, increasing costs, or a sluggish economy can result in decreased tax revenues and strain the program's ability to fulfill its obligations. Increasing life expectancy also poses a challenge. While people living longer lives is a great achievement of society, it also puts a strain on the Social Security system as it must support a growing number of beneficiaries.

All these issues are not hypothetical and are prompting conversations about the future of the program. Social Security already experienced issues with potential insolvency in the 1980s. These prompted significant reforms to the program's funding in 1983, including a delay in cost-of-living adjustments, suspension of benefits to certain nonresident aliens, acceleration of already enacted payroll tax increases, and increases in retirement age.[81] For nearly 40 years since 1983, the Social Security program ran a surplus (collected more money than it spent) until 2021, when the total costs finally

---

[a] You're eligible for reduced payments as early as age 62. If you choose to begin receiving benefits five years early, your benefits would be reduced by about 30%.

exceeded the total income, forcing the program to use the reserves it had accumulated by then. According to the 2023 projections, the program can run as-is for another 10 years, after which the payments will have to be reduced.[a,82]

The U.S. government will likely maintain the program but adjust its funding and expenses, similar to the changes made in the 1980s. They may increase Social Security taxes deducted from workers' paychecks, raise the full retirement age, or implement a combination of both strategies. Raising taxes would generate more revenue for the program, while increasing the retirement age would result in fewer people receiving benefits at any given time, thus reducing costs. These scenarios are speculative, but it's reasonable to expect substantial changes to Social Security by 2033 and whenever the program faces financial problems.

Defined benefit plan

A **Defined benefit plan** (DBP) is an employer-provided pension plan, often referred to as a "traditional" pension plan, in which the employer commits to paying a specified benefit to eligible employees, typically based on criteria such as years of service and age. These benefits are generally paid throughout the entirety of the beneficiary's retirement, continuing until their death. The American Express Company, originally an express mail business but now known for its financial services, established the first corporate pension plan in 1875. It was designed for disabled workers who reached the age of 60 after completing at least 20 years of service with the company. Similar pension plans gradually expanded across the country,

---

[a] To be clear, the first projections about the need for reduced payments in 2033 were created more than a decade ago. However no significant action has been taken to address the program's upcoming money shortage as of 2024.

encompassing industries such as railroads, banking, and, later, manufacturing.

Pensions are not without risk, as some companies fail to make their pension payments—many due to financial difficulties, often leading to reduced payments. A notable example occurred in 1963 when automobile manufacturer Studebaker closed an assembly line in Indiana. About 7,000 workers received no more than 15% of their pension's value, with nearly 3,000 of those workers receiving nothing at all. To address the public concern, on September 2, 1974, President Gerald Ford signed into law the Employee Retirement Income Security Act (ERISA), which established minimum standards for private sector pension plans.

The number of active participants in defined benefit plans reached its peak in the 1980s and has since declined by half. Presently, only 15 million Americans participate in DBPs, while 85 million participate in defined contribution plans (DCPs).[83]

The disappearance of pension plans is sometimes said to have contributed to a rise in "job hopping," as the incentive to stay longer with one company is marginally reduced. In recent years, a narrative has emerged surrounding the frequent job changes of young professionals. Within this narrative, older generations often perceive these individuals as lacking commitment or dedication to their careers and derogatorily label them as "job hoppers." The younger generation argues that their motivations for switching jobs stem from seeking better pay, meaningful work, diverse experiences, and a healthy work-life balance.

However, job hopping is not a new phenomenon. In fact, baby boomers, on average, held eight jobs by the age of 28, making them just as prone to changing jobs as millennials are now. For baby boomers, switching jobs nearly every year resulted in an average annual pay increase of 6.5%.[84]

Defined contribution plan

Defined contribution plans, including 401(k), 403(b), and other similar plans, are retirement savings accounts that enable employees to contribute a portion of their pre-tax earnings. Employees have the flexibility to choose the amount they wish to contribute, and employers may offer a matching contribution. The contributed funds are then invested, often in a selection of mutual funds, bonds, or stocks, and they grow tax-free until withdrawal during retirement.[a] If your employer has a program like a 401(k) where they agree to match your contributions, it's usually a wise decision to contribute enough earnings to receive the full match. It is, essentially, free money!

Compared to defined benefit plans, defined contribution plans offer predictable costs. Employers simply direct a portion of employees' salaries to the fund, which employees can carry with them when changing jobs. The amount retirees receive depends on the performance of the funds. In contrast, defined benefit plans may require employers to make additional payments in the event of investment losses to fulfill the promised benefit to their workers.

After contributing to your 401(k) account, if you need to take money out before you reach the age of 59½, you will generally be required to pay a 10% tax on the withdrawn amount. However, there are some situations where you may not have to pay this penalty. For example, you may be exempt from it if you're unemployed for a long time and need to use the money to pay for health insurance premiums, or if you need it to cover higher education expenses.[85]

---

[a] Note the "until withdrawal" part. You cannot avoid paying taxes on your savings—you can only defer them.

Individual retirement accounts (IRAs)

Introduced in 1974 with the Employee Retirement Income Security Act, an **individual retirement account** is a tax-advantaged account that individuals can use to save and invest for retirement. While plans like 401(k) are employer-sponsored, anyone with a taxable income can open an IRA.

There are two primary types of IRAs: traditional and Roth. The money you put into a traditional IRA, along with any earnings it generates, won't be taxed until you withdraw it during retirement. You're also allowed to deduct your contributions from your taxable income, potentially reducing your current taxes.[86,87]

With a Roth IRA, you contribute money that has already been taxed, so you don't have to pay taxes on it when you withdraw it in retirement. This can be helpful if you think your tax rate will be higher when you retire or if you want to minimize future tax obligations. Therefore, when deciding whether to contribute to a Roth IRA, consider your current and expected future tax brackets.

You cannot contribute to a Roth IRA if you make more than a certain amount. However, the backdoor Roth IRA strategy allows you to contribute to a Roth IRA by first contributing to a traditional IRA and then converting it to a Roth IRA. You should consult a tax professional to discuss which strategy may be best for your financial situation and goals.

Life insurance

Life insurance provides financial security for loved ones upon the policyholder's death. Hence, it's often chosen by people as an investment option for retirement, ensuring their beneficiaries receive financial support even after they are gone. However, life insurance often underperforms as an investment due to low returns and high fees. Two main types of life insurance are term life insurance and permanent life insurance. Term life insurance offers coverage for only a set period (typically between 10 and 30 years). During this period, you agree to pay a premium, while the insurance company promises to pay out a specific death benefit to the beneficiaries (typically, your family).[88]

Permanent life insurance is usually more expensive and provides lifelong coverage (as long as you pay the premiums). Part of your premiums are directed towards a reserve called "cash value." The money in this reserve can grow tax-deferred and can be used for borrowing money against it, paying premiums, or even withdrawn.[89]

The primary goal of life insurance is to provide money for your beneficiaries when you pass away. It's not a great long-term investment tool. In the short run, you can get tremendous returns on your investment if you get a payout but don't live long enough to have paid a lot in premiums. As you pay more in premiums, however, the rate of returns decreases. It's not entirely clear how low it gets. Some estimates suggest that, combined with high fees compared to traditional investment options, the rate of return on life insurance as an investment is under 4% per year.[90]

CHAPTER THREE

SPENDING

Despite being known for our consumerism, Americans show a higher-than-average savings rate compared to OECD countries, saving about 10% of our disposable incomes.[1] This rate tends to increase during recessions, indicating people's prudency in the face of hard times (either because of uncertainty or compensating for already lost incomes). This was especially evident during the first months of the COVID-19 pandemic in 2020 when the savings rate in the United States skyrocketed to more than 30%. Yet, we regularly find ourselves in debt. Of the more than 260 million adults in the U.S., more than 80% have at least one credit card, and more than 40% of accounts carried a balance from one month to the next (that is, they didn't pay off the full debt by the due date).[2] For homeowners, only 40% are mortgage-free.[3] The two other largest balances of debt Americans hold are auto loans and student loans (about $1.6 trillion each). In this chapter, we examine some crucial considerations around spending.

3.1 Credit Cards

Credit cards, when promptly repaid, can be a beneficial means to earn rewards and establish a credit history. Young adults are often encouraged to get their first credit cards early so they can build credit history. A good credit history is valuable because it demonstrates an individual's ability to repay debt and can facilitate borrowing substantial amounts, such as a mortgage for a house.

Many financial literacy books and websites focus on credit card debt. However, Americans, on average, are pretty good at using their credit cards responsibly. Only 0.8% of credit card accounts are 90 or more days past due on their payments. The average credit card debt was also a manageable amount of $6,500, only a sixth of median personal income.[a] In 2023, the average FICO Score 8 (there are multiple iterations of the FICO credit score with a FICO Score 10 released in 2020) reached 718, the highest it has been since its introduction in 2009.[4,5,6]

Multiple reasons likely contributed to this. First, even despite the turmoil caused by the COVID-19 pandemic, the economy has been doing relatively well since the Great Recession. Prior to 2020, the unemployment rate reached the lowest level it has been since 2010, and in 2022, it sank back to its 2019 level. Second, the number of adults in the share of the population (especially those older than 65) has been steadily increasing. Older people tend to be better at maintaining good credit scores, whether because they hold higher-paying jobs or because they have witnessed the financial struggles of others and have learned from those experiences. Overall, more consumers are "willing and able to pay their bills" now than in the past.[7] Most Americans are also aware of their credit score. While only 58%

---

[a] At the same time, an average auto loan balance is nearly $24,000 and an average student loan balance is $39,000.

of individuals between the ages of 18 and 24 claim to know their credit score roughly or exactly, that number jumps to nearly 80% for people 25 years or older.

Choosing the right credit card can feel overwhelming, but it doesn't have to be. Start by checking your credit score, as this will determine which cards you're eligible for. If you don't have any credit history, consider starting with a secured credit card. These cards require a deposit that acts as your credit limit, helping you build credit over time.

One of the biggest perks of credit cards is the rewards, like cashback and travel points. Today, there are plenty of online resources that compare different credit cards, making it easier to find one that fits your lifestyle. However, be careful of the annual fees on some cards. It's important to ensure that the benefits outweigh the costs. For instance, if a card offers 3% cashback on groceries but has a $100 annual fee, you will need to spend at least $3,333 on groceries to break even. Tracking your expenses can help you be aware of how much you spend on different categories of goods. That, in turn, will help you choose a card that maximizes your savings and rewards.

While trying to take advantage of various benefits, be mindful of "spaving." **Spaving** (a portmanteau of "spending" and "saving") refers to the psychological trick we often play on ourselves when we justify unnecessary purchases by focusing on the money we are supposedly saving rather than the money we are actually spending.

A **balance transfer** is a financial strategy that involves moving debt from one credit card to another, typically to take advantage of a lower interest rate. The primary purpose of this maneuver is to save money on interest charges and potentially pay off debt more quickly. It can be an effective tool for managing credit card debt and reducing overall interest costs.

For example, you can apply for a new credit card that offers a low or 0% introductory interest on balance transfers. If your application is approved, you can then transfer your existing credit card balance to this new card. The goal is to pay off the transferred balance during the promotional period, taking advantage of the lower interest rate.

We have seen how interest can positively affect your savings over long periods of time. But this compounding effect doesn't just apply to savings—it also happens with debts, like student loans or credit card debt. Many people deal with simple interest on their student loans, meaning it doesn't compound. However, some student loans, especially private ones, use compounding interest. Let's look at how fast compounding interest can make your debt grow. Typically, credit card companies convey how much interest you will have to pay by telling you the **annual percentage rate** (APR) of the card. For some credit cards, you accumulate interest every day in the amount of daily periodic rate (DPR), which is the APR divided by 360 or 365.[8] Because the interest accumulates daily based on the amount from the previous day, the amount of interest accumulated at the end of the year will be larger than DPR times 365.[9] Thus, even though the interest is often stated in terms of APR, the actual "effective" interest may be higher.

Suppose you didn't repay all the balance last month and have $2,500 remaining to pay. Your credit card accumulates interest daily with an APR of 15%.

- If you keep paying the minimum allowed payment (say, $50) every 30 days, how long will it take for you to repay your debt?
- Will the amount you paid be much larger than $2,500?

On day one, you will owe $2,500 plus DPR times $2,500. That is,

$$\$2{,}500 + \left(\frac{15\%}{365} \ of \ \$2{,}500 \right) \approx \$2{,}501.03$$

Only $1.03 in interest!

However, on day two, the interest will be calculated not on the original $2,500 but on the $2,501 and three cents from day one. So, $2,502.06. A dollar and three cents again. A naïve way to calculate how much you would owe in a year if you decided not to pay anything would be to just multiply $1.03 by 365, which is $375.95. The accurate amount, considering the compound interest, is $404.50.[a]

- If you keep paying $50 every 30 days, you will repay your debt in 2,340 days—more than six years.
- In total, you will pay $3,925.96. That is almost 60% more than what you originally owed.

If, instead, you decided to pay an additional $10 every month, you would have repaid your debt in only 1,741 days (a year and a half faster) and paid only $3,539.95. As demonstrated, minimum payments aren't the best way for the borrower to repay the debt. The longer you wait to repay it, the more interest you accumulate. Thus, it's very important to repay any debt as soon as possible.

While credit cards can have their advantages, it's important to acknowledge the potential dangers associated with unchecked credit card spending. Credit cards make purchasing goods and services easier by allowing individuals to postpone payment. Even simply swiping a card can provide a sense of pleasure due to the conditioning effect stemming from past positive experiences associated with using it and the products purchased. A 2021 study published in *Scientific Reports*, compared the spending behavior of people using cash and credit

---

[a] Note that this is more than 15% of $2,500, which is $375.

cards. The report notes that the use of credit cards differently affects the striatum, a specific area in the brain "involved in processing reward." The authors explicitly refrain from claiming that consumers get addicted to credit cards, but they do note that the mechanism is similar to the one identified in addiction studies.[10]

It's important to note that you don't need to use credit cards if you aren't comfortable using them. You could even become a homeowner without having a good credit history. For example, you may try to use one of the various mortgage programs catered to individuals with minimal or no credit history, including programs from the Federal Housing Administration, the Department of Veterans Affairs, and the U.S. Department of Agriculture. Each of these loans has different minimum credit score requirements and benefits. To qualify for these programs, however, you still need to provide comprehensive documentation that demonstrates your financial reliability to lenders. This documentation can include proof of on-time payments for rent and utilities, stable income that is relatively high compared to potential monthly mortgage payments, savings that can cover at least a year of mortgage payments, and a significant down payment.[11]

There are two popular debt repayment methods that are often described in the financial literacy realm. The "debt avalanche" method involves paying off the debt with the highest interest rate first. This way, you can save money on interest payments in the long run and accelerate your journey towards becoming debt-free. The "debt snowball" method prioritizes paying off the smallest debt first, regardless of the interest rates. Consequently, although you may end up paying more interest compared to the debt avalanche method, this approach is more likely to provide motivation through the achievement of small debt repayment victories.

Another way to deal with debt is refinancing, which is replacing a current loan with a new one that typically has better terms. The improved terms can include lower interest rates, lower monthly payments, or debt consolidation (replacing multiple loans with just one). The point of refinancing is to address your specific needs, and sometimes, addressing these needs can come at a cost. For example, you may be able to reduce your monthly payments if it's proving difficult for you to keep up with multiple ones. However, this may come at the cost of "compensating" for the lower payments by having to make them for a longer period of time. That, in turn, can increase the overall cost of your debt. The process of refinancing can also affect your credit score since you are applying for a new loan and that can lead to an inquiry on your credit report. (Generally speaking, an inquiry negatively impacts your credit score.[a,12])

Interest is not the only cost you may need to pay on top of your principal (the amount you borrowed). There are a myriad of fees that can make loans more expensive. Sometimes, it can even seem as if companies attract you with a lower advertised interest rate and then offset it by charging you numerous fees. Origination fees are those charged at the start of the loan for lending you the money. The typical justification for these is that they are needed to cover work associated with the lending process, like preparing documents. These fees can range from 1% for mortgage and student loans to 8% for personal loans.[13] Similarly, loan application fees are supposed to cover the costs of reviewing your application. This is typically a flat amount

---

[a] Dave Ramsey, the host of The Ramsey Show radio program focusing on finance, calls debt consolidation "dangerous" as it focuses on treating only the symptoms rather than the causes of debt, which, according to him, are overspending and undersaving. That is why, Ramsey notes, in 78% of cases, "after someone consolidates his credit-card debt, the debt grows back."

(rather than a percentage of the loan) and can be as high as $500.[14]

By now, you know that earlier debt repayment typically means that you will pay less in interest. Lenders recognize this too, and hence, some of them charge a prepayment penalty. Some states prohibit prepayment penalties on certain types of loans. According to credit reporting company Experian, Massachusetts doesn't allow prepayment penalties on mortgages older than three years. Similarly, 36 states prohibit prepayment penalties on auto loans 61 months or older.[15]

On the other hand, not making a payment on time can lead to a late payment fee as well as a hit to your credit score. In fact, credit card companies earn more than $14 billion a year on late fees.[16]

3.2 Harmful Habits: Gambling

Gambling addiction is a serious mental health matter best addressed by professionals. The American Psychiatric Association lists multiple criteria for gambling disorder, like "repeated unsuccessful efforts to control, cut back on or stop gambling" and "risking or losing a close relationship, a job, or a school or job opportunity because of gambling."[17] Experts estimate that approximately 1% of US adults (two million people) meet the criteria for a severe gambling problem each year. Another five million people meet at least one of the criteria.[a,18]

It's not entirely clear why some people continue to gamble after continuously losing money. Pathological gamblers are likely aware that "the house always wins." People generally feel

---

[a] If you or someone you know thinks they might have a gambling addiction (or other mental health and/or substance problem), you can reach out to the Substance Abuse and Mental Health Services Administration's free and confidential helpline at 1-800-662-HELP or 1-800-662-4357.

good when winning. Some gambling addicts, however, enjoy the process of gambling itself and the uncertainty involved.[19]

We explore the topic of gambling to provide insight into how risky behaviors can lead to debt and financial instability.

Casinos: the house always wins

Casinos are designed to make a profit, and they accomplish this by offering games that give the house an inherent mathematical advantage. Most of the games you find at a casino, from blackjack to roulette to slot machines, are structured in a way that favors the casino over the player in the long run.

Roulette is a game of chance where you bet on the outcome of a ball spinning on a wheel with numbers. You can bet on the number, grouping of numbers (odd or even), and color (red or black). The wheel has two main variations: European (with numbers ranging from zero to 36) and American (which includes an additional "00" slot). The payout depends on how unlikely the outcome is. If you guess the number correctly, you get your money back, plus 35 times the amount you bet on top of it. If you guess the color correctly, you get back twice the amount you bet.

Interestingly, some people have tried to develop strategies to beat the casino's mathematical edge. In some cases, like with blackjack, groups of players have reported being able to gain a statistical advantage through techniques like card counting.

The Martingale betting strategy is one such technique, which is based on the idea of doubling your bet after every loss, with the goal of recovering your previous losses and making a profit. The strategy encourages the player to "chase losses" (in the hopes of getting even following a loss).[a] Here's an example:

---

[a] Chasing losses is one of the criteria for diagnosing gambling disorder.

- You start by placing a bet of $5 on black.
- If you lose, you double your bet to $10 on the next spin.
- If you lose again, you double your bet to $20.
- You continue doubling your bet after each loss until you eventually win.

Table 7. The Martingale betting strategy

Bet	Win or Lose	Your balance
$5	Lose	-$5
$10	Lose	-$15
$20	Lose	-$35
$40	Win	$80 − ($40+$35) = $5

Thus, eventually, you will win and recoup all your losses, plus a profit equal to your original bet. It sounds logical, but it fails to account for a few important factors:

- The Martingale system assumes you have unlimited bankroll. In reality, most players have a limited amount of money with which they are willing to gamble. A long losing streak can deplete your bankroll before you have a chance to recoup your losses. Consider the example above with a five dollar first bet.[a] A streak of eight losses will make you lose more than $1,200 (and, hence, require you to bet at least that amount to make your money back).
- Casinos often have table limits. Thus, you may not be able to make the bet that would enable you to recoup your losses.
- The probability of winning is smaller than the probability of losing. If you bet on red, you have 18 red spots that would let you win. There are, however, 18 black spots plus at least one "zero" spot, which aren't considered as having color.

Many betting systems rely on the gambler's fallacy: the idea that a win is more likely to occur after a series of losses. In

---

[a] Often, five dollars is the minimum bet you can make.

reality, each spin is statistically independent, and past outcomes have no influence on future outcomes. The ball and the wheel are inanimate objects which don't have memory. Yet, casinos often report numbers that have not appeared in a while, as if to suggest that the next number will be one of those. At the same time, they report numbers that have shown up frequently in the last few spins, implying that these numbers are currently lucky.

Lottery tickets: overwhelming odds (against the player!)

Another costly habit that is considered a form of gambling addiction is overspending on lottery tickets. Occasionally buying a lottery ticket isn't an issue. Winning small amounts (which is quite achievable) is an exciting experience. Winning a jackpot, however, is nearly impossible. Thus, overspending on lottery tickets can cause a financial strain with no promise of a reward. Unlike casinos, which are confined to special locations, lottery tickets are as easily available as alcohol and tobacco.

It's crucial to understand that the probability of winning a lottery is extremely low. Take the example of Powerball. In order to win the main prize in Powerball, you have to correctly select five white balls ranging in value from one to 69 in any order and one red ball, ranging in value from one to 26. The total number of combinations we can generate is 292,201,338. In other words, your chance of guessing the winning numbers for the Powerball jackpot is one in 292 million.

To put things into perspective, below are a few events that are more likely to occur than winning the Powerball jackpot.

Table 8. Likelihood of various events. [20,21,22,23,24,25,26]

Event	Likelihood
Admission into an Ivy League school	1 / 20
A baby born in the world being born in the U.S.	1 / 36
A man developing breast cancer in a lifetime	1 / 833
A high school basketball player making it to the NBA	1 / 9,000
Being struck by lightning in a given year	1 / 1,222,000
Dying of a shark attack in a lifetime	1 / 4,332,817
Powerball jackpot	*1 / 292,000,000*

Other forms of gambling

As we have seen with casino games and lotteries, traditional forms of gambling continue to attract millions of players hoping to strike it rich. However, the gambling industry is rapidly evolving, with new options emerging that blur the lines between gambling and other activities.

Today, the video game industry has embraced "loot boxes," making the thrill of gambling more accessible than ever. These virtual items operate on the principle of unpredictability, enticing players with the allure of valuable in-game enhancements. The contents of these prize crates are randomized, creating an element of uncertainty akin to gambling.

There is limited worldwide regulation surrounding loot boxes. In line with regulations introduced in China, Apple now requires apps utilizing loot box mechanisms to publish the probabilities of receiving each item type to customers.[27,28] The Netherlands and Belgium banned games using loot box mechanics (some developers simply made the loot boxes unavailable in these countries to comply with new regulations).[29] In Australia, starting in September 2024, the sale of games containing gambling-like content to those under 18 was prohibited. Additionally, computer games with in-game purchases tied to chance, such as paid loot boxes, were classified with a minimum rating of M, indicating they were not recommended for children under 15.[30] Despite these measures, loot boxes continue to remain largely unregulated.

What sets sports betting apart from casino games or lotteries is its compelling disguise as a game of skill. For many, sports betting feels different from other forms of gambling. Fans follow teams religiously, analyze player statistics, and track the historical performance of their favorite teams. For some, this engagement creates a belief that their insights and knowledge give them an edge in predicting the outcomes of games.

In 1992, Congress passed the Professional and Amateur Sports Protection Act, which banned government-sponsored or authorized sports-related gambling. This effectively banned sports betting in most states, except for states that had previously allowed sports betting (Nevada) or sports lotteries (Oregon and Delaware). The reasoning behind the ban included concerns over the effect of sports gambling on the integrity of amateur and professional sports. However, the Judiciary Committee was especially concerned over the effect of legalized gambling on young people. Out of eight million compulsive gamblers at the time, one million were under the age of 20.[31] In 2018, the Supreme Court struck down the Act, allowing states to legalize sports betting. As of 2024, it's now legalized in 38 states.[32]

Many sports betting companies provide incentives to garner people's interest, with the intention of creating "lifelong customers." The goal is to provide a gamified app on your phone that they can use to continuously provide personalized ads and get you spending more. Sign-up bonuses, deposit match bonuses, and "risk-free" bets are all commonly used tactics to get customers hooked.

Remember—nothing is free, companies are driven by profits, and the odds are stacked against the players. Recent studies have observed a decrease in savings and stock investments alongside an increase in bankruptcies in states that have legalized sports betting.[33] Despite the perception of control, the reality of sports betting is that outcomes are often highly unpredictable. Overspending on sports betting can have serious financial consequences, and the emotional aspect can further complicate one's ability to make rational financial decisions.

3.3 Scams

While young people often believe they are less likely to fall victim to fraud than their elders, the numbers reveal a more complex story. Among individuals aged 20–29 who reported scams to the Federal Trade Commission, 44% disclosed losing money to fraud. Conversely, among individuals aged 70–79 who reported scams, "only" 25% reported fraud-related financial losses. However, while individuals aged 20–29 generally lose less than $500, those aged 80 and above encounter losses three times that amount.[34] In this section, we'll look at forms and signs of common scams. Let's start the discussion with examples of two major scams that happened in recent history on opposite sides of the world.

Two historical examples

In 1991, after nearly a decade of economic struggles and violent suppressions of numerous popular protests across its member states, the Soviet Union was finally dissolved. Soviet people were already experiencing some aspects of capitalist ideas (like unprofitable enterprises potentially facing bankruptcy) in the years prior because of perestroika, a series of reforms aimed at addressing the stagnation in the Soviet Union's economy. Nevertheless, with the collapse of the Soviet Union, its people were barraged with the spoils of capitalism, such as an influx of multinational corporations and consumer goods. Television channels began running ads for exotic brands such as Colgate, Electrolux, LG, Minute Maid, Nivea, Orbit, Pantene, Pfizer, and many others. In 1998, Mikhail Gorbachev, the last leader of the Soviet Union, even appeared in a Pizza Hut commercial.

This was also the time when former Soviet citizens were first introduced to financial markets. One organization that offered "vouchers" was MMM, which promised significant returns in a short period of time. MMM was especially notable for its catchy series of ads employing the fictional character of Lyona (short form of Leonid) Golubkov, who represented an average Russian man. According to the TV commercials, by investing in MMM, Lyona was able to buy his wife new boots and even considered buying her the ultimate item of luxury, a new fur coat.

An estimated 10 to 15 million people purchased MMM vouchers, which, for a short period of time, indeed showed significant returns. However, beneath the surface, MMM was nothing more than a **Ponzi scheme**—a business model that focused on recruiting participants and redistributing the money from new recruits to the rest of the group, rather than selling legitimate products or services. [35] Therefore, MMM was destined for failure as soon as the inflow of new participants started to slow down and the number of withdrawals increased due to people attempting to cash out.

In August of 1994, the shares of MMM fell from a high of 115,000 rubles to 1,000 rubles within three weeks. [36] Blaming the government for the company's crash, victims of the scheme started collecting signatures, hoping to gather the one million required to hold a nationwide vote of no-confidence that would have obliged the government to step down. [37] Sergei Mavrodi, the mastermind behind the whole operation, managed to get elected to Gosduma, one of the chambers of the Russian parliament, which, for a while, gave him immunity from prosecution.[38] The victims didn't receive their money back.

Many attribute the success of MMM to the financial illiteracy of citizens in the former Soviet countries, which undoubtedly aided the spread of the scheme. However, many of the investors were aware of the impending collapse and were simply hoping to cash out before it happened.[39] For many, it was a way to protect what little savings they had from rising prices. In 1993, inflation reached a whopping 874%. The next year (the year of MMM's collapse), prices grew by 307%.[40]

It's important to note that experience with financial markets doesn't guarantee immunity from such fraudulent schemes. While former Soviet citizens were exploring the financial markets for the first time, another Ponzi scheme was slowly reaching its collapse in the Midtown Manhattan neighborhood of New York City, mere blocks from Wall Street, the undisputed financial center of the world.

During the 1990s, Harry Markopolos was working as an options trader in Boston. One day, his bosses assigned him the task of preventing his company's clients from switching to their rival based in New York. However, when he attempted to uncover how the competitor, Bernard Madoff's company, achieved extraordinary returns, Markopolos could not find a reasonable answer. Rather, he came to the realization that Madoff's whole operation must be a scam—a sentiment that Markopolos' bosses could not believe. After all, Madoff had been a renowned figure on Wall Street for over three decades, at one point serving as the chairman of Nasdaq.[41] How could such a person be a fraud? Madoff's hedge fund continued its operations until December of 2008, when Bernard Madoff was arrested by the FBI for running a Ponzi scheme, which is now considered to be the largest in history.[42]

According to investigative journalist Richard Behar, Madoff's operations were a scam from almost the beginning, since "a year or two after he opened his office in 1960."[43] Instead of engaging in actual securities trading, Madoff and his team simply invented performance numbers. An entire floor of the company was dedicated to printing trade reports. On paper. Investors could neither communicate with that floor via email nor check their accounts online. Since the reports included trades that never happened, they were backdated to maintain the illusion of successful operations.

How could such a scam have persisted for so long? Why didn't the improbable returns raise suspicions? According to Behar, they did. However, no one wanted to report these concerns to regulators for fear that the regulators might "start looking into [their] offices." As in the case of MMM, it's likely that some investors were aware of the red flags but had little reason to complain while the scheme was still operational. After all, the scheme was generating profits not just for Madoff's company but for the investors as well. Some of Madoff's investors reportedly received returns of up to 600%. Although this money was not coming from successful trading, but rather from the accounts of other investors, many were happy with the profits. By the time of his arrest, Madoff managed $65 billion that belonged to thousands of investors, including individuals, municipal governments, and college endowments.[44]

Ponzi, pyramids, and MLMs

Ponzi schemes are often grouped together with **pyramid schemes**. Like pyramid schemes, Ponzi schemes (named after the 1920s swindler Charles Ponzi) pay old investors with money they raise from new investors. A Ponzi scheme is typically presented as a legitimate business which yields very high returns. The money usually goes to the originator of the scheme, who then distributes it to others. Pyramid schemes, however, involve a more hierarchical structure, where recruiting new members benefits the recruiters directly. Pyramid schemes rely on an unsustainable model of exponential growth that results from each participant recruiting a set number of new members. Consider the illustration below. We have the founder of the scheme at the top of the pyramid, who recruits the first five members. Each of these five members will recruit another five members. In just two cycles, the total number of members has exceeded 30. By the third cycle, we'll have over 150 members. By the ninth, over 2.4 million people will be involved. Such growth requires recruiting a vastly larger pool of new individuals, which realistically is not possible.

Figure 16. Members in the first three levels of a pyramid scheme

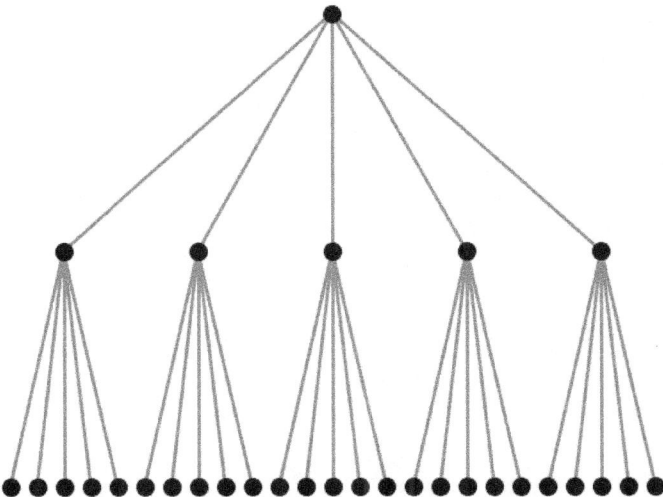

Multi-level marketing (MLM) businesses are enterprises that incentivize their members to recruit others within their network to sell products. In an MLM structure, each member is encouraged to build their own "downline" by recruiting individuals who will, in turn, recruit more. While MLMs operate on a similar recruitment model as pyramid schemes, the key distinction lies in the product or service being sold. A legitimate MLM business focuses on the sale of tangible products or services, where the revenue primarily comes from product sales. Truth is, it's hard to distinguish between MLMs and pyramid schemes, as the line between them can be quite blurry. This ambiguity has led to numerous legal battles and investigations over the years. While some MLM companies have shut down, others have managed to clear their names or reach compromises with regulatory bodies.

However, even legitimate MLMs often present significant financial challenges for participants. A 2018 study conducted by the AARP Foundation shed light on the economic realities of working for MLMs. The findings were stark: approximately 75% of survey respondents reported either making no money or actually losing money through their MLM participation. Only a small fraction, around 7% of participants, managed to earn $10,000 or more.[45]

Here are some of the signs of a pyramid scheme:

- An emphasis on the recruitment of new members as a main way to earn money. Remember that legitimate MLMs allow you to make money by simply selling their products.
- Questionable product quality or value. Pyramid schemes often "sell" products or services that are overpriced, of low quality, or have little to no genuine market demand.
- Use of high-pressure sales tactics and appeals to emotion. Recruiters might emphasize how joining the scheme could help you support your family, pay for your children's

education, or care for aging parents. They might even shame you for your current financial situation, implying that not joining means you aren't ambitious or don't care about your family's future. They might also create a sense of urgency by saying you will miss out on the opportunity of a lifetime if you don't sign a contract immediately. Legitimate business opportunities typically allow time for due diligence and don't rely on emotional manipulation.

- Promise of easy money. This claim contradicts the reality of legitimate sales work, which typically requires significant effort and skill. If a company presenting itself as a legitimate MLM promises easy earnings, it's, at best, misleading you about the nature of sales work. At worst, such promises of easy money could be indicative of a pyramid scheme.[46,47,48]

Foreign money exchange scams

In this scheme, the victim is contacted via email by an individual claiming to be an official from a foreign government or a member of royalty. This person offers a significant reward if you assist in transferring (even more significant) funds out of their country. However, the victim is first asked to pay money transfer fees that are promised to be compensated. Needless to say, the victim sees neither the compensation nor the promised reward.

This is one of the oldest, least prevalent, and least successful scams. Only 0.1% of reports of this scam included a monetary loss. Nevertheless, it's also one of the most expensive scam types, with a median loss exceeding $7,000 in 2023. Because of its structure, this is considered a type of advance fee scam. More generally, advance fee scams involve solicitation of an upfront payment for receiving money, services (like help in debt elimination), or expensive products.

Some signs of such scams include:

- Poor grammar. Many of these scams originate from non-English-speaking countries and contain noticeable grammar and spelling errors.[a]
- Urgency. The scammer may emphasize the need for quick action, pressuring you to make decisions without thinking.
- Appeals to emotion. The scammer often crafts a heart-wrenching story designed to evoke sympathy. The email may contain a story of an ill parent in desperate need of expensive medical treatment, an unjust arrest requiring legal fees, or a political persecution threatening the sender's life.
- Unsolicited contact from a representative of a foreign government or royalty. Legitimate international financial transactions of such a level take place across proper channels and don't require the involvement of unknown private citizens.[49,50]

Investment scams

Investment scams promise victims high returns from putting their money into projects, companies, or other opportunities. One of the oldest types of scams in the stock market is the "pump and dump." This scheme involves fraudsters spreading false or misleading information to create a buying frenzy and inflate the price of a stock. They then sell their own shares at an inflated price. This often causes the stock price to drop, resulting in financial losses for other investors.

---

[a] Another popular explanation for the poor grammar in such scam emails is that it's intentional. This theory suggests that by using obvious grammatical errors and implausible stories, scammers can quickly identify the most gullible or vulnerable targets. Those who respond despite these red flags are more likely to fall for the scam and follow through with sending money.

Today, running a pump-and-dump scheme has become easier thanks to social media. You don't have to be a financial professional to promote yourself as one. Financial "influencers" often promote their private messaging channels, where they announce stocks for their followers to invest in. These often involve **penny stocks** (companies with low market capitalization, sometimes, also defined as stocks traded at or below five dollars).

One of the dangers of investment scams is how long it may take for a victim to realize they've been scammed. Victims can receive reports that their investments are doing well, encouraging them to "hold" (or even invest more) in the hopes of even higher returns. Unfortunately, when victims eventually decide to withdraw their funds or collect their profits, they encounter significant obstacles. The trouble begins when they try to access their money, only to face delays, excuses, or outright refusal from the scammers. The scammers involved may employ various tactics to stall withdrawals, such as claiming technical issues, regulatory hurdles, or unexpected fees that need to be paid before funds can be released.

With the explosion in popularity of cryptocurrencies like Bitcoin, scammers have taken advantage of this trend to lure victims into fraudulent investment schemes related to cryptocurrencies. These scams promise extraordinary returns, which, thanks to Bitcoin's success, seem plausible to the victims. In 2023, payments made through cryptocurrencies led to 48,000 fraud reports totaling $1.4 billion in losses.[51]

The following are some of the common signs of investment scams:

- Investment returns that are too good to be true. In the chapter on investing, we learned that extraordinary returns are extremely rare. The promise of high returns (especially if they fail to mention investment risks) should raise suspicions.

- Lack of transparency and vague descriptions. Scammers might use complex jargon to confuse you or claim the details are too technical to explain. Legitimate investments come with detailed and clearly explained documentation.
- Promise of hot tips and insider information. Using insider information for trading is illegal. Moreover, it's likely that you won't receive any genuine insider information at all. Instead, scammers often provide tips on stocks they already own in an attempt to artificially drive up the price.[52]
- Testimonials and success stories. Scammers often use persuasive testimonials or success stories to lure potential victims. For example, they might share a story about how their relative turned a small investment into millions. Legitimate investments focus on factual information and potential risks, not on unverifiable anecdotes of extraordinary success.

Romance scams

Investment scams can also manifest as romance scams. These can start on a dating app or with an unexpected text message from an unfamiliar person clearly intended for someone else. You respond to inform them of the mistaken number, and they respond with an apology while introducing themselves. Engaging in a back-and-forth conversation, you unknowingly develop a romantic relationship with this individual without ever meeting them in person.

As time passes, your newfound partner introduces the topic of cryptocurrencies or other investments, sharing their successful money-making experiences. Intrigued, you decide to explore investing in cryptocurrencies yourself. Your new partner recommends a platform seemingly associated with a reputable financial institution. Without hesitation, you invest some money and witness promising returns. However, when you attempt to withdraw your funds, you encounter unexpected delays. Eventually, you uncover the harsh truth that the platform you invested in has no affiliation with any legitimate financial institution, and the entire "relationship" was nothing more than a fraud. In 2023, the median loss for romance scams was $3,600, making it the third most expensive type of scam behind foreign money exchange and investment scams.

When navigating online relationships, it's important to remain coolheaded and alert to warning signs that may indicate a potential romance scam, even if you feel a strong connection with a newly found partner.

Some of the signs of romance scams are:

- Your dating app "match" appears to be exceptionally attractive or extremely successful. When creating a profile of a fictional person, scammers often utilize pictures of models or stock photos to make their fake persona more appealing. Consequently, they will avoid video calls or meeting in person.
- Displaying an eagerness to quickly shift communication to another platform (such as a messaging app or email). This way, if the scammer's dating profile gets banned, they still have a way to contact their victims.
- Stories of misfortune that hint at a need for financial assistance. Scammers typically don't ask for money immediately. Instead, they slowly introduce stories of hardship to build sympathy. Common stories include medical emergencies and legal troubles.
- Stories of extraordinary achievements in the financial markets. While some scammers use tales of hardship, others take the opposite approach by boasting about extraordinary financial achievements.[53,54]

Courses with no educational benefits

In the current digital age, a myriad of "modern" businesses have become accessible to anyone at their fingertips. They're often promoted on social media as lucrative opportunities for making money. You may have heard about dropshipping, which involves setting up an online store and selling products without keeping the inventory (customers' orders are sent to another company for fulfillment). Affiliate marketing involves promoting products or services on behalf of others and earning a commission for each successful referral. Trading stocks, foreign currencies, and cryptocurrencies are also often portrayed as an easy way to earn thousands, if not millions, of dollars.

There is an equally large number of people offering courses teaching you how to start these businesses. Video-sharing platforms like YouTube and TikTok have empowered individuals to share their own experiences in running such startups. Platforms like Udemy allow anyone to create online courses that teach anything from web development to photography to counting cards in blackjack.

Beware of fraudulent courses that claim to unlock the secrets of successful stock trading or other valuable skills. These courses often make grand promises of guaranteed financial success, enticing individuals with dreams of quick riches and financial independence. However, many of these fraudulent courses lack substance and fail to deliver on their extravagant promises.

A simple rule that we can all be aware of is: if it seems too good to be true, then it probably is!

3.4 Role of a Personal Budget

Before starting this section, we want to remind the reader that it's not our intention to tell you what you should or should not spend your money on. Instead, we simply aim to highlight that adopting certain good financial habits can benefit your financial well-being.

Establishing and adhering to a budget—a plan outlining your anticipated spending for a given period—is a great way to organize your financial life. The purpose of setting a budget and regularly assessing your adherence to it is to help minimize unnecessary expenses. The primary benefit of budgeting stems from the ability to prioritize and restrict spending on categories that are considered less important. Additionally, reviewing your expenditures at the end of each week or month can reveal areas where you may have unknowingly exceeded your intended spending. Thus, another value of budgeting lies in conducting an audit of your expenses.

Budgets can be created in different formats, but fundamentally, they are spreadsheets that allow you to record your expenses and provide an overview of your spending. Additionally, you can include all sources of income, such as after-tax salary and interest earned on savings. By incorporating a "planned" category, you can compare your actual expenses and income with the initial plans to identify any deviations.

One widely popular budgeting approach frequently mentioned in financial literacy resources is the 50/30/20 budget. According to this guideline, you allocate 50% of your income towards "needs" (groceries, rent, utilities, health insurance), 30% towards "wants," and then dedicate 20% to savings (emergency fund, retirement savings) and debt repayment. Although the percentages may seem arbitrary, the structure and existence of a plan by itself may help you get on top of your budget.

As we learned from our students, one common example of advice on reducing "wants" is the advice to stop spending money on coffee from Starbucks and make it at home instead.[a] We also learned that this advice often gets dismissed by young people because the savings don't seem significant enough. However, using our knowledge of compound interest, we know that investing $5 instead of buying a cup of coffee at Starbucks can lead to savings of tens of thousands of dollars in the long run. Besides coffee, other items listed as sources of overspending by financial literacy resources include app subscriptions, sweet treats, buying lunch at work instead of bringing it with you, buying name-brand items instead of the generics, and buying a new car instead of a used one.[b,55]

How do you know if you're overspending on something? This is a difficult question to answer. Every person's "needs" and "wants" are unique. Nevertheless, we can start by looking at how much other people are spending. The second column in the table below shows the distribution of average expenditures across 14 major spending categories.[c,56] If you notice that the share of your expenditures is significantly larger than the number provided in the table below, it may be a sign that you're overspending on that category. The third column shows how much a person spending $40,000 a year would spend on each category.

---

[a] Turns out, avoiding spending money on Starbucks coffee is often part of on-campus orientation for new undergrads!

[b] A statistic that is frequently quoted from a 2010 report by Edmunds states that a new car loses 9% of its value as soon as you drive it off the lot. That is, a pre-owned car with minimal mileage in great condition would cost 9% less than a similar new car.

[c] Cash contributions include child support payments, care of students away from home, and contributions to religious, educational, charitable, or political organizations.

Table 9. Average expenditures across different categories

Spending Category	Percent	Share of $40,000
Housing	32.9	$13,160
Transportation	17.0	$6,800
Food	12.9	$5,160
Personal insurance and pensions	12.4	$4,960
Healthcare	8.0	$3,200
Entertainment	4.7	$1,880
Cash contributions	3.1	$1,240
Apparel and services	2.6	$1,040
Education	2.1	$840
Miscellaneous	1.5	$600
Personal care products and services	1.2	$480
Alcoholic beverages	0.8	$320
Tobacco and smoking products	0.5	$200
Reading	0.2	$80

Surprisingly, little research has been done on the effectiveness of budgets as a money-saving technique. Common sense suggests that setting a budget is helpful. However, until recently, we weren't sure exactly how much setting a budget could actually help in saving money.

A 2023 study looked into precisely this. The authors examined the expenses of individuals who used Money Dashboard (MDB), a personal finance app based in the UK. By leveraging MDB's access to users' expense data from at least three months prior to app installation, they were able to observe a reduction in spending for various categories. Specifically, installing a budget-tracking app like MDB led to a decrease of 17–33% in dining and drinking expenses, 9–15% in grocery expenses, and 6–20% in fuel expenses.

While we do know that installing a budget-tracking app can lead to a decrease in spending, we cannot claim that this decrease is thanks to the app because of the potential issue of selection bias. That is, people who install these apps are likely to be those who were already planning to cut down on expenses. Chances are they were going to cut back on spending whether they set a budget for themselves or not. Also, the decision to install an app may have been preceded by a period of increased spending. Thus, their decrease in spending after installing the app may have been simply a return to "normal."

Recognizing this, the authors embarked on a collaborative experiment in partnership with Vancity, a Canadian credit union. They were able to recruit 226 members of Vancity, who were randomly assigned to either a "control group" or a "treatment group." The participants in the treatment group were encouraged to establish a budget outlining their projected expenses for the upcoming month. People in the control group didn't receive such encouragement. The result? Those in the treatment group spent 20% less than those in the control group.[57]

3.5 Family Matters

In this section, we'll highlight the significance of financial considerations, even when making decisions that seem to be outside the realm of financial planning, such as selecting a life partner. In line with the spirit of this book, the purpose of this section is not to dictate what you should do but to demonstrate the importance of finances in every aspect of life.

About nine in 10 Americans say that love is a very important reason to get married, and only a quarter say the same about financial stability.[58] While love is the main driver for marriage, arguments about money are a leading predictor of divorce.[a,59] According to a survey commissioned by a debt settlement company, National Debt Relief, more than half of Americans believe that a partner who is in debt is a major reason for considering divorce.[60] Nearly a third of Americans keep a

---

[a] Financial arguments, of course, can be both the cause and the effect of other issues that can lead to a divorce.

financial secret from their partner. Of those who do keep secrets, 40% have made a secret purchase and 18% have significant credit card debt.[61]

Bad financial decisions made together with your partner can haunt you, even in the case of a divorce or widowhood. Most often, this applies to cosigned debt (when you sign documents to get a loan or a credit card together to guarantee payments). In some states, creditors can even contact members of the deceased's family to clear the debt. These states (known as community property states) include Arizona, California, Idaho, Louisiana, Nevada, New Mexico, Texas, Washington, and Wisconsin and see nearly everything as jointly owned, unless it was acquired before marriage.[62] The rules on inheriting debt can be tricky and differ across states, so it's best to contact a lawyer and ask for a consultation.[63]

Although marriage is not a requirement to have children, it often does lead to larger family sizes. Raising a child is costly. In 2015, families with a before-tax income of less than $59,200 spent nearly $10,000 per child. At the same time, families with a before-tax income above $107,400 spent nearly twice as much.[64]

Despite some claims that Americans enjoy an unprecedented degree of **intergenerational mobility** (children being able to enjoy high incomes regardless of their parents' background), research suggests that these claims aren't strictly true. Thus, bad financial decisions made by parents can perpetuate cycles of poverty and limit economic mobility across generations. We explore intergenerational mobility more in the second part of this book.

Interestingly, having a financially responsible partner can also have an unexpected negative effect. In many couples, one person typically assumes the primary role in managing the family's finances. As time passes, this individual, the "household CFO," gains more experience and practice in managing money. Thus, a gap in financial literacy widens between the partners. A study published in the *Journal of Consumer Research* reveals that while the financial knowledge of the "household CFO" expands, the other partner's financial literacy not only remains stagnant, but even declines over time. This divergence in financial skills creates a few problems. Firstly, in the event of a divorce or widowhood, the "non-CFO" partner may struggle to make sound financial decisions due to their lack of expertise. This doesn't happen as much when the end of the relationship is predictable or when the non-CFO is proactive in financial decision-making. However, developing financial expertise is a lengthy process, which may lead to a prolonged period of financial vulnerability.[65]

Secondly, lack of financial expertise and reliance on your partner to make financial decisions exposes you to financial abuse. Financial abuse entails gaining financial power over the victim by exerting total control over the money they spend, ruining their credit score, not including them in investment decisions for their money, or forcing them to work in a family business without pay.[66] More than a quarter of people who reached the National Domestic Violence Hotline reported experiencing financial abuse.[a,67]

Finally, relying solely on one person for financial oversight exposes couples to the risk of non-intentional mismanagement. Managing a couple's finances can be complex and time-consuming, and leaving this task in the hands of one person increases the risk of errors or poor financial decision-making. This can result in missed bill payments, late fees, poor investment choices, or failure to adequately plan for the future.

---

[a] If you or someone you know thinks they might be a victim of abuse, you can reach out to the National Domestic Violence Hotline at 1-800-799-SAFE or 1-800-799-7233, or have a live chat at www.thehotline.org.

Within a corporate setting, various audits are meant to catch errors and prevent questionable decisions from ruining the company's finances. It shouldn't hurt to take a similar approach when dealing with financial planning within a family setting.

PART TWO. ECONOMIC LITERACY

CHAPTER FOUR

INTRODUCTION TO ECONOMICS

Economic literacy is defined as an understanding of basic economic concepts and the implications they have on daily life. The second part of this book seeks to emphasize awareness regarding the state of the world through an intuitive approach, which we believe is an effective method for thinking about making well-informed decisions. We begin by (very briefly) introducing important economic concepts that will provide a foundation for discussions in the following chapters.

4.1 What is Economics?

Economics is the study of how people allocate their limited resources to satisfy their needs. In general, economics can be divided into microeconomics and macroeconomics. **Microeconomics** studies the behavior of individual economic agents, such as consumers, firms, and households, and their interactions within specific markets. It focuses on examining how agents make decisions regarding the allocation of scarce resources, how markets function in terms of supply and demand, and how prices are determined for goods and services. On the other hand, **macroeconomics** focuses on the economy as a whole, studying aggregate variables and phenomena that impact the overall performance of an economy. It examines topics such as economic growth, inflation, unemployment, fiscal and monetary policies, and international trade.

Utility

One of the most important concepts in economics is that of **utility**, a measure of satisfaction or happiness that an individual derives from consuming a particular good or service. Utility is used to explain why individuals make certain choices. We choose to do things that generate larger utility.

Utility is a subjective concept, and there is no universal scale or unit of measurement for it. The level of satisfaction derived from a particular good or service can vary from person to person, depending on an individual's preferences. We also face various constraints, such as budget limitations and time limits. Given this framework, the goal is to maximize utility, subject to various constraints. If a constraint did not exist, we would consume as much as we wanted, and the notion of maximizing utility may be irrelevant.

We can also compare utilities across different periods. That is, would you rather receive $1,000 today or $1,100 a year from now? We often prefer to have things today rather than in the future (think: "time is money"). Such preferences make you happier today, often, at the cost of having lower savings in the future.

To paint a general picture of utility, suppose you have two investment options, which are two different savings accounts offered by two different banks. The first account will pay you 3% in interest and the second will pay you 4%. If the interest rate were the only thing affecting your choice, you would simply pick the account with the higher interest rate as it generates larger utility.

What happens if we consider investment options that differ in some other ways? Returning to the two-investment example, suppose one will pay you an expected 11% return and another will pay you 14%. However, the first option does not guarantee an 11% return—rather, the return may be anywhere between negative 40% and positive 40%, with 11% being the average. The second option, however, guarantees a 14% return. In this new scenario, maximizing utility may involve considerations of one's risk tolerance. Which option would you choose?

The numbers above aren't random but rather represent the S&P 500 index returns and a hypothetical interest rate on credit cards. For many, the decision between where to put the money is straightforward: pay off your credit card debt and avoid paying 14% interest. After all, why opt for "maybe 11" when you can get "certainly 14"? That being said, it's possible that those with a higher risk tolerance will choose to try their luck in the stock market (i.e., attempt a higher than 14% return in the market).

Demand and supply

Two fundamental concepts in economics are **demand** (quantity buyers are willing and able to buy) and **supply** (quantity sellers are willing and able to sell). According to what economists call "the law of demand," as prices decrease, the quantity demanded tends to increase, and vice versa. Similarly, according to the law of supply, as prices rise, producers become more willing to supply a greater amount of a product or service.

When demand and supply are balanced, the market reaches equilibrium, where the quantity demanded equals the quantity supplied. Changes in demand or supply, such as shifts in consumer incomes or preferences, or the imposition of taxes, affect this equilibrium point, causing a shift in the equilibrium price, the equilibrium quantity, or both.

Here is how changes in demand for or supply of goods and services in competitive markets (more about them in the next section) affect the equilibrium price:

- An increase in demand without a change in supply leads to a higher price;
- A decrease in demand without a change in supply leads to a lower price;
- An increase in supply without a change in demand leads to a lower price;
- A decrease in supply without a change in demand leads to a higher price.

Elasticity is a concept that measures the responsiveness of quantity demanded or supplied to changes in various factors, such as price, income, or the prices of related goods. The demand for goods is considered "elastic" if the quantity demanded changes substantially in response to a change in price. When the price of an elastic good increases, consumers tend to significantly reduce the amount of the good they buy. Goods with close substitutes or those that aren't necessities, like restaurant meals, tend to have elastic demand. Inelastic goods, on the other hand, are those for which the quantity demanded changes relatively little in response to a change in price. Essential goods (like insulin for patients with diabetes) or goods that form habits (like tobacco products) tend to have an inelastic price elasticity of demand. For example, it's estimated that a 10% increase in the cigarette price will result in only a 5% reduction in cigarettes consumed.[1]

Types of market structures

Market structures are concepts in economics that describe the organization and characteristics of different markets in which businesses operate. These structures influence how firms compete, set prices, and interact with consumers and each other. A **competitive market** is one where numerous buyers and sellers interact with each other selling and buying identical goods or services. No seller or no buyer is important or big enough to influence the market. Firms in competitive markets are price takers because they must accept the prevailing equilibrium price. There are no barriers to becoming a seller, like enormous costs to set up a business. Competitive markets are a theoretical construct that economists use, and thus, very few exist in the real world that perfectly meet all the assumptions of a competitive market.

The market for bread can be used as a close-enough example of a competitive market. The bread itself is a fairly uniform product—loaves don't vary much across sellers. The ingredients are simple and inexpensive—flour, water, salt, yeast—creating low barriers for new bakers to enter the market. There is no proprietary technology or high-cost equipment needed. At a typical farmers market, you may see booths for a few different home bakers, creating a very competitive environment. Prices are clearly marked on tags or listed on their Facebook business page. You can also buy bread at almost any grocery store and customers can easily compare prices across sellers to find the bread they want. No single baker has an advantage or price control. Both buyers and sellers are small relative to the total size of the market.

Although sellers have no say in determining the price, outside forces such as the government are capable of setting prices through policies. In the absence of externalities (more about them later), the overall effect of these policies is usually concluded to be negative for consumers and firms. Say the government introduces a policy that sets the maximum price of a loaf at $3. If the maximum price is set below the equilibrium price determined by supply and demand, it may lead to shortages. Some bread producers may find it unprofitable to produce bread at the capped price, resulting in a decrease in the amount of bread available in the market. The bread market would be missing out on items that cost more than $3 to produce. To compensate for lower profit margins, some bakers might cut costs by reducing the quality of ingredients or production processes. Some consumers are also out of luck because of the lower availability of bread. Consumers willing to pay more than $3 for a loaf may still find it difficult to purchase bread due to the limited supply.

It's important to distinguish unregulated markets from perfectly competitive markets. Deregulation, when implemented appropriately, can enhance market performance and stimulate economic activity. Removing unnecessary barriers to entry, streamlining bureaucratic processes, and reducing regulatory burdens can foster competition, encourage innovation, and create opportunities for businesses to thrive. While the public focus is often on the potential negative impact of regulations, well-designed regulations can protect consumers from market failures, ensure fair competition, and promote public safety and welfare. For example, regulations may be necessary to address harmful byproducts, prevent monopolistic behavior, or safeguard consumer rights.

Another market structure is a **monopoly**, a market with one seller. Due to the lack of competition, the monopolist can set a price higher than the price a competitive market would converge on. As the sole participant in the market, a monopolist has the market power to influence prices by controlling the entire supply of the product or service. However, a firm does not necessarily have to be the only company in an industry to possess monopoly power. Rather, it's determined by the firm's market share and the extent to which it can act independently of competitive pressures. Despite not being a monopoly, Microsoft faced antitrust scrutiny due to its dominant position in the market for personal computer operating systems during the 1990s. The company was sued under the Sherman Antitrust Act of 1890, which outlawed monopolistic business practices. In the early twentieth century, the Sherman Act was also used to break up American Tobacco and Standard Oil, both of which were deemed to be monopolistic enterprises that stifled competition and controlled significant portions of their respective industries.

Next, we have a market that is called to be **monopolistically competitive**, in which goods aren't fully identical. This differentiation comes from different quality or branding, which leads to high expenditure on advertising costs. Each firm has some degree of market power, allowing it to exercise control over pricing and product characteristics. However, this market power is limited by the presence of close substitutes from other firms. A market for physicians can be described as a monopolistically competitive market as, in the eyes of a patient, physicians are imperfect substitutes. Often, patients choose a specific physician and continue using their services over the years rather than searching for a new doctor for each annual check-up.[2]

Oligopolies are markets with more than one but less than many (less than monopolistic competition) firms. In this market, sellers engage in strategic behavior, such as deciding to undercut each other's prices. The number of firms in an oligopoly is small enough that the actions of one firm can significantly impact the profits of the other firms in the market. Firms in oligopolies make their pricing and output decisions based not only on consumer demand but also on the anticipated reactions of their rivals. Oligopolistic firms may engage in non-price competition, such as product differentiation, advertising, and other marketing strategies, to gain a competitive edge. They may also collude, either explicitly or tacitly, to maintain higher prices (although such collusion is generally illegal). The airline industry in the United States is a textbook example of oligopoly. In 2015, 80% of the U.S. market was controlled by four major airlines. The market for baby formulas is another example of oligopoly. In 2021, the shortage of baby formulas brought attention to the market structure of the industry, where four companies control 97% of the market.[3]

Lastly, there are also monopsonies and oligopsonies, markets with one and a few buyers, respectively. In a **monopsony**, there is a single buyer who exercises significant market power over the sellers. This buyer can dictate the terms and conditions of transactions, like prices and quantities. **Oligopsony** involves a few large buyers that collectively exert significant market power over sellers. These buyers may engage in strategic behavior, similar to oligopolistic sellers, by coordinating their purchasing decisions or negotiating favorable terms with suppliers.

A textbook example of monopsonies are company towns, where a single large employer dominates the local labor market and effectively acts as a monopsonistic buyer of labor.[a,4] Company towns emerged in the late nineteenth and early twentieth centuries, particularly in industries like mining and manufacturing. The employer would establish housing, schools, and other amenities, creating a self-contained community. With limited alternative employment opportunities in the surrounding areas, workers in company towns had little

---

[a] Some research suggests, however, that the monopsony power of company towns is overstated.

bargaining power when it came to wages, working conditions, and other aspects of their employment. This monopsony power allowed companies to pay relatively low wages and impose strict rules and regulations on their employees.[5]

Like monopolies, monopsonies don't have to be the only firms in the market. They only need to be the firm with large monopsony power. We must also be careful in defining the "market." For example, when considering teenage employment, we can focus specifically on companies that hire teenagers. In this case, supermarkets and fast-food chains that employ a large portion of the teenage workforce without much competition in the area can be considered monopsonies.

Monopsonies are particularly interesting to economists because they provide a useful theoretical framework for explaining why multiple increases in minimum wages across different states did not lead to large job losses.[6] The competitive model of labor markets suggests that an increase in the minimum wage above the market equilibrium wage would result in a surplus of labor supply, leading firms to cut jobs to reduce costs. This belief stems from the assumption of competitive labor markets, where employers are price takers and have no wage-setting power. This line of reasoning has been a common argument against raising minimum wages, as it's believed to price some workers out of the labor market and reduce overall employment levels. In a monopsonistic labor market, employers can pay wages below the competitive level, using their market power to suppress wages. Thus, in the case of monopsonies, increasing minimum wages (up to a certain level) may not lead to job cuts.

When discussing the effects of various policies, it's easy to incorrectly assume that every market is a competitive one. Individuals will recall demand and supply curve interactions that they learned in introductory economics courses and will judge a policy based on its effect on competitive markets. However, in reality, markets often exhibit characteristics of imperfect competition or even monopolistic or monopsonistic behavior.

4.2 Econometric Analysis

To non-economists, economic theories can often seem too abstract in their scope. Models of government, firm, or individual behavior get introduced one after another, and the examples used to back up concepts often appear arbitrarily constructed. Is there a way to apply real-life data to these economic models?

In short, the answer is yes!—a subfield of economics known as **econometrics** combines statistical methods and economic theory to analyze economic relationships. Econometrics is used to both evaluate the past and make predictions about the future. How does class size affect learning outcomes? What are the effects of minimum wage laws on low-wage jobs? How big of an effect does an oil spill have on trips to the beach? How much do local amenities like parks affect property prices? What is the dollar value of policies aimed at gun violence prevention? These are just some of the questions you could attempt to answer with real-world data using econometric tools.

Causal claims

Let's suppose you're given data on class size and the average SAT (Scholastic Aptitude Test; college entrance exam) scores of students in those classes. Upon plotting the data points on a graph, you notice a negative relationship between class size and SAT scores. How do you know that the relationship you observe is causal? How do you know that smaller class size was the reason for higher SAT scores? It's plausible that something else is influencing SAT scores, possibly by affecting class size.

The availability of resources, such as well-equipped classrooms, instructional materials, or teaching quality, may influence both class size and SAT scores. Better-funded schools may be able to hire more teachers, reduce class size, and improve access to helpful study materials for students. Furthermore, wealthier families are more likely to have resources and opportunities for tutoring services, which may also positively impact SAT scores.

"Spurious Correlations" is a fascinating website created by Tyler Vigen dedicated to exploring and highlighting unusual correlations between events or variables that aren't causally related. As the tagline at the top of the website mentions, it aims to demonstrate the importance of distinguishing between correlation and causation. Below is a recreation of a graph from this website showcasing the correlation between the number of babies born in the U.S. named Aubrey and the stock price of Exxon Mobil. The correlation coefficient for these two variables is 0.87 on a scale from -1 (perfect negative correlation) to 1 (perfect positive correlation), where 0 indicates no correlation.[7]

Figure 17. Exxon Mobil stock price vs the number of Aubreys born

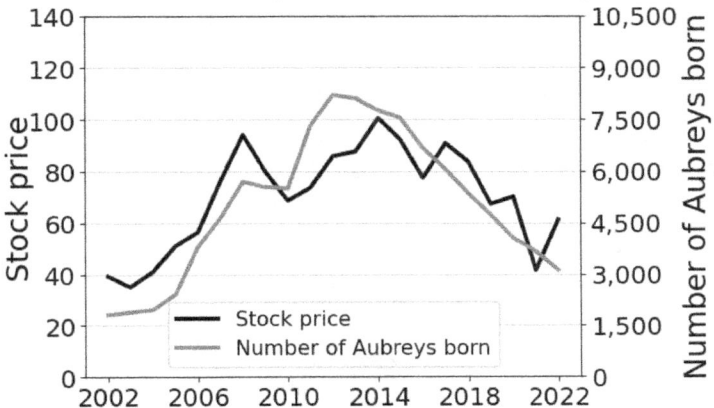

There are correlations (such as the Aubreys and Exxon Mobil example), where "common sense" informs us that the relationship is not causal. We think "A could not have plausibly caused B." The number of babies named Aubrey is not correlated with Exxon Mobil's stock price because these two variables are entirely unrelated and have no causal connection. There are also others, where people would disagree on whether the relationship is causal or not. How can we be certain of causality?

In economics, just like in the case of natural sciences, an ideal way to establish a causal link between two factors is to perform a controlled experiment. By manipulating one variable and holding all other factors constant, scientists can observe and measure the effect on their variable of interest. For example, changing the height from which an object falls while keeping other factors like the object's shape the same allows physicists to establish the relationship between the height of a fall and the time it takes for the object to hit the ground. Although rare, there are situations where economists too can conduct controlled experiments, usually in a lab or field experiment setting.[a]

For the most part, however, economists often grapple with a different reality. They deal with complex human behaviors where it may not be feasible or ethical to manipulate variables in a controlled setting. For instance, it would be unethical to bar a random group of high school graduates from attending college to estimate the economic returns of college education (by comparing those who went and those who were barred).[b] It would also be impractical to assign countries to different

---

[a] A common scenario is where participants answer survey-type questions on a computer screen, which has been designed by an experimental economist.

[b] Random assignment ensures that the treatment group and the control group are, on average, identical apart from the "treatment."

monetary or fiscal policies to study their effects on economic growth.

Instead, economists often leverage **natural experiments** where nature or external factors have led to a quasi-random assignment of a treatment. For example, economists can study the impact of random events like hurricanes on local economies by comparing areas that were hit by the hurricane to similar areas that were not.

Besides using random events like natural disasters, economists developed a multitude of methods for comparing changes in outcomes over time between a treatment group and a control group. To ensure the validity of their findings, economists carefully select control groups that closely resemble the treatment group in terms of relevant characteristics such as demographics, economic structure, or geographical location. Sometimes, economists choose a control group by matching individuals (or other "units" like counties or cities) on similar characteristics like income and education. Sometimes, economists can generate a fully new "synthetic" control group by combining multiple poorly matching control groups into one better-fitting one. This ensures that any observed differences in outcomes can be attributed to the treatment, rather than other confounding factors.

CHAPTER FIVE

INCOME

If you ask an economist what determines a person's wage, you're likely to hear a long list of things—including **human capital** (knowledge and skills received from training and education), **compensating differential** (differing pay based on job characteristics), effort someone puts into their work, union membership (workers in unions make more than their nonunionized counterparts, are more likely to receive paid leave and employer-provided health insurance, and be in employer-provided pension plans), and random events (like person's looks and whether technological progress makes certain jobs obsolete).[1,2]

Sometimes, even being "at the right place, at the right time" can be crucial. For example, consider the economic outcome possibilities for an individual who graduates from college in early 2009, at the height of the Great Recession, versus another who has just started college (and will graduate in 2013, when the unemployment rate was on the downward trend for the past three years).

Let's explore the various determinants of income distribution in the United States. On a practical level, this knowledge can help you make informed choices about pursuing higher education, investing in skills, or considering job opportunities in different locations. More generally, these concepts provide insight into why some jobs pay more than others and how various factors contribute to wage differences.

5.1 Income Distribution in the United States

How much do Americans make per year? In 2023, the real (inflation-adjusted) median salary in the U.S. was about 42,000. That number differed by location: in the South, it was slightly under $41,000, while in other regions, it was a little above the national median. The median income also differed by educational attainment and gender, factors we'll explore in the upcoming chapters.

The mean salary in the U.S. was much higher, $63,000. The average salary being higher than the median salary suggests that there are wealthy individuals who are "pulling" the average income up. Thus, relying on the mean statistic alone to measure an economy's "typical" income wouldn't be right.[a]

The graph below shows the history of real median personal income since 1980. Note that the median income would occasionally stall and even decrease for extended periods (like during the Great Recession). Nevertheless, overall, it increased by more than 40% in the past 40 years.

---

[a] If you want a refresher on these topics, we provide a short overview of means and medians in the Appendix.

Figure 18. Real (inflation-adjusted) median individual incomes

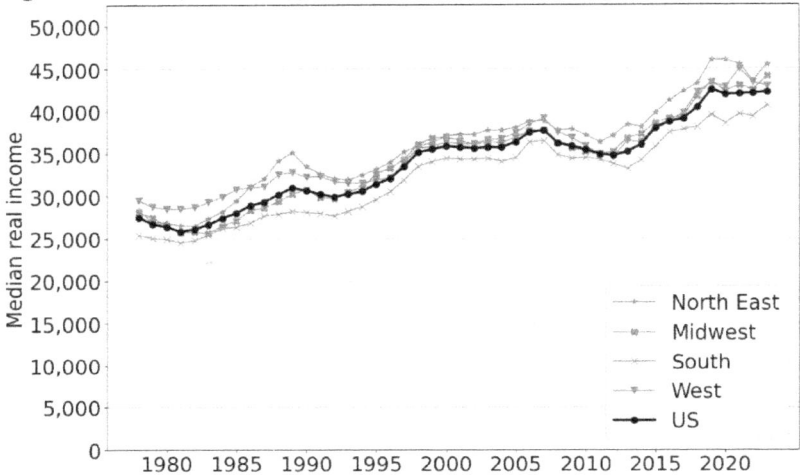

While encouraging, the positive trend in the graph does not tell us much about the distribution of income and how it changed. For example, prior to the 1970s, the pace of income growth was the same for the rich (for this context, defined as families with incomes in the top 20%) and the poor (families with incomes below the bottom 20%).[3] Since 1973, the richest families have seen their income grow by 80%, while the incomes of the poorest families grew by 20%.[4]

Some find the disparity in growth rates concerning, as they interpret this unequal growth as evidence that the income gains of the wealthy have come at the expense of the poor. Supporters of this view argue that the disparity in income growth rates suggests that the economic policies and market dynamics of recent decades have disproportionately favored the wealthy.

Social scientists attribute the growth in inequality to factors like the decline in jobs for less skilled workers, strong demand for college graduates (who usually come from more fortunate families), gains by the rich resulting from deregulation and speculation in the financial services industry, and the U.S. government doing less compared to governments of other wealthy countries to smooth the income distribution. [5] Economist Thomas Piketty also stresses the importance of financial markets in raising the wealth of high-income earners. In his book, *Capital in the Twenty-First Century*, he argues that it has been much easier for people who can invest their disposable income to accumulate wealth.[6,7]

Ultimately, the historical and economic causes of growing inequality deserve a more detailed discussion. Unfortunately, for the purposes of this book, such an analysis is well outside of our scope. However, to ensure we address the topic in some capacity, we'll still explore how inequality is defined, and we briefly cover the state of intergenerational mobility in the United States.

Defining inequality

There are different ways to define inequality. Generally, income inequality is defined as the uneven distribution of income among individuals. One measure of this distribution is the **Gini index**, a number between 0 (perfect equality) and 100 (a single person gets all the income). In 2019, the Gini index for the United States was 41.5, a statistic that is higher than those found in France (31.2), Canada (31.7), Germany (31.7), the United Kingdom (32.8), Iran (36.5), Russia (37.7) and China (38.2). Of the about 80 countries, for which the Gini index was calculated in 2019, the countries with the highest index values were Brazil (53.5), Colombia (51.3), and Mozambique (50.5).

Another approach we can use to quantify inequality is to look at the share of income earned by the highest earners. The figure below shows the share of income earned by the top 1% and bottom 50% of earners in the United States. The share of income earned by the highest earners was decreasing in the early twentieth century, but this trend reversed in the 1970s.

Figure 19. Share of income earned by groups of earners in the U.S.

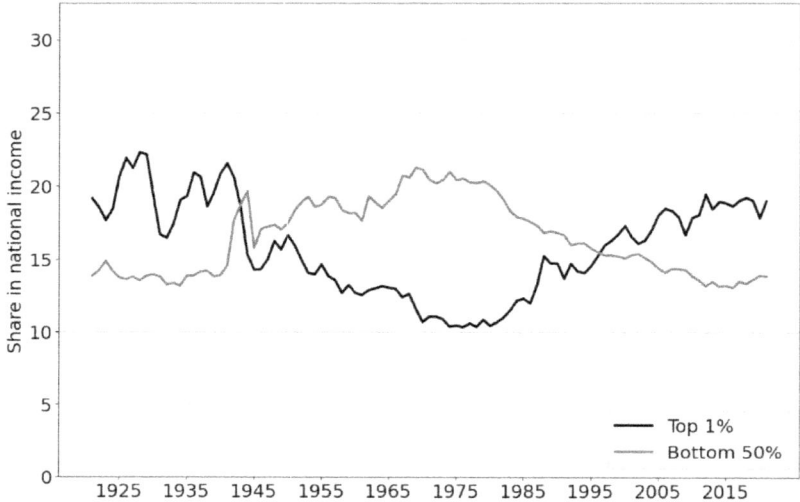

In the 1950s, economist Simon Kuznets observed that the share of income earned by the highest-earning 10% of the population in the U.S. was decreasing for the preceding 30 years. Kuznets suggested a theory that inequality increases in the early stages of development as some sectors of the economy grow faster than others and decreases at higher levels of development as more people can enjoy the benefits of a growing economy. While Kuznets has since admitted that this theory was mostly speculative, it became highly popular and the bell-curve relationship between income inequality and income per capita became known as the **Kuznets curve**. The theory suggests that inequality during development is inevitable. However, as you can observe from the graph, income inequality in the United States started growing again in the late 1970s.

Income inequality and high levels of wealth aren't exclusive of each other, as the United States maintains a relatively high level of inequality compared to other rich countries while having one of the highest median incomes. In fact, only Luxembourg, Norway, and Switzerland had median disposable household income higher than the U.S. in 2021. Incomes in France and Germany were only three-quarters of the income in the U.S., Russia's was only 40%, and income in China was only 14% of the income in the U.S.[8]

On the lower end of the income distribution are individuals the economists define as living "under the poverty threshold." The **poverty threshold** is defined by the government and depends on the size of the family. For example, in 2022, individuals living on their own would be considered as being in poverty if they earned less than $15,225 annually. For a family with two adults and two children under the age of 18, the threshold was about $30,000. These thresholds are determined based on the cost of a "minimum food diet" and gets adjusted for inflation every year.[9]

Intergenerational mobility

One major factor that will affect your income is the family you were born into. However, economic research has not always fully captured the impacts of family background on lifetime earnings. In 1986, economists Gary Becker (who, six years later, received a Nobel prize in economics) and Nigel Tomes analyzed intergenerational mobility in the U.S. and other wealthy countries. They found that "aside from families victimized by discrimination," incomes of children and grandchildren rapidly regress to the mean. That is, children born to both rich and poor parents often end up with medium-level incomes. They claim that most of the income "advantages and disadvantages of ancestors are wiped out in three generations."

A few other researchers in the 1980s also concluded that there is little correlation between a parent's and a child's income. They estimated that the intergenerational correlation in incomes was only 0.2 on a scale from 0 to 1 with higher numbers representing higher correlations.

The biggest issue with these studies was that the people whose incomes were used in these analyses were not representative of the entire US population. For example, one study focused on a sample of Wisconsin high school students and their incomes 7 to 10 years after graduation. This sample not only focused on a racially non-representative sample but also estimated people's incomes in their mid 20s, which may be an underestimation of their permanent incomes. Another study relied on the National Academy of Sciences-National Research Council (NAS-NRC) Twin Registry. The registry contained data on white male veteran twins born between 1917 and 1927. The data were then complemented with the data on the children of these twins. Again, the data were not representative of the entire US population.

More recent studies find a bigger effect of family background on incomes. One such work utilized the Panel Study of Income Dynamics (PSID), which, to date, is the longest-running longitudinal household survey in the world.[a] It estimated that the intergenerational correlation was 0.4, or twice the previously estimated amount. A 2005 study estimated the correlation to be 0.6 and suggested that "for a family living in poverty it might take five generations before their descendants (on average) would be close to the national average of income."

According to an analysis by the Brookings Institution, it's equally difficult for economically poor individuals to become

---

[a] "Longitudinal" or "panel" means that the same households are being surveyed throughout the years. This type of data helps control for unobserved variables, leading to more accurate and reliable analyses.

rich as it is for rich people to become poor. The table below shows the probabilities of children born into families in the top and bottom parts of income distribution ending up in different income groups as adults. About a third of people born into families in the bottom 20% of the distribution will remain in the bottom 20% by the time they reach 40. At the same time, a similar share of those born in the top 20% will remain in the top 20%.

Table 10. Probability of income groups given income group at birth

		Income group at age 40	
		Bottom 20%	Top 20%
Income group of the family at birth	Bottom 20%	36%	10%
	Top 20%	11%	30%

Overall, even though more recent studies show lower levels of intergenerational mobility than those found by early studies, people in the U.S. born into low-income families still have decent opportunities to improve their economic status. Note that most people (about two-thirds, in each case) will end up in an income group different from the one they were born into. Moreover, one in 10 individuals born into the lowest income group will end up in the highest income group by the time they turn 40.[10]

5.2 Effects of College Degrees

In the U.S., public education is provided for free through high school. Some states even mandate that all children attend school until they reach a certain age, usually 16 or 18. In doing so, the government is investing in the public, knowing that obtaining some level of schooling provides payoffs and benefits to its citizens and the country.

However, when it comes to higher education, the situation becomes more complex. College degrees have historically been associated with higher income levels and better job prospects. On the other hand, the cost of college has been rising dramatically in recent years. This increase in expenses has led to concerns about the financial feasibility of pursuing higher education.

What are the effects of college degrees on income? How expensive has college become in recent years? And, putting the answers to the previous two questions together, is college still worth it?

Before diving into the effects of postsecondary education, it's important to note that attending college is not a decision that will work for everyone, as evidenced by millions of full-time employed Americans without college degrees. However, in lieu of a college degree, many occupations that don't require them may have longer periods of on-the-job training or require various certifications.

For example, commercial pilots generally don't need to have a college degree, but the occupation requires extensive certification and hundreds to thousands of hours of on-the-job training. Similarly, joining the U.S. armed forces requires only a high school degree (or a GED), but the specialty you choose once in the armed forces (e.g., combat, construction, engineering, linguist) requires training. The table below lists some of the well-paying occupations that don't require a college degree, with a projected large growth of employment (according to the Bureau of Labor Statistics).

Table 11. Occupations that don't require a college degree

Occupation	On-the-job Training (to start)	Median Annual Wage	Employment Growth (2020–2030, %)
Wind turbine technician	Long term	$56,000	68
Tile and stone setters	Long term	$48,000	12
Farm service technician	Long term	$47,000	11
Commercial pilots	Moderate term	$99,000	11
Subway operators	Moderate term	$81,000	10
Private detectives	Moderate term	$59,000	13
Community health workers	Short term	$47,000	21

College degrees and wages

When conducting a job search, one of the first pieces of information that the job listing highlights is the qualifications required for that position. The listing may require that applicants hold a license or certification and have a certain number of years of experience, a specific college degree, or a minimum level of education. On the employer side, the weeding-out process allows the company to efficiently sort out qualified applicants from others, which may result in faster employer-employee matches. In today's digital age, job applications may even be automatically declined by software if the applicant fails to have the necessary background. Applicants may also be rejected for being "over-qualified" (for example, by holding a master's degree when applying for a position looking for undergraduate student interns).

The graphs below show the inflation-adjusted wage "premiums" for holders (ages 25 and higher) of high school, bachelor's, master's, and doctorate degrees, compared to high school dropouts. The first graph shows the premiums for men, and the second one shows the premiums for women. Overall, the wage premiums of each degree seem to have been constant over time. We can also conclude that premiums are different for men and women, a topic we explore in more detail in a later section.

Figure 20. Wage premiums for men, compared to high school dropouts

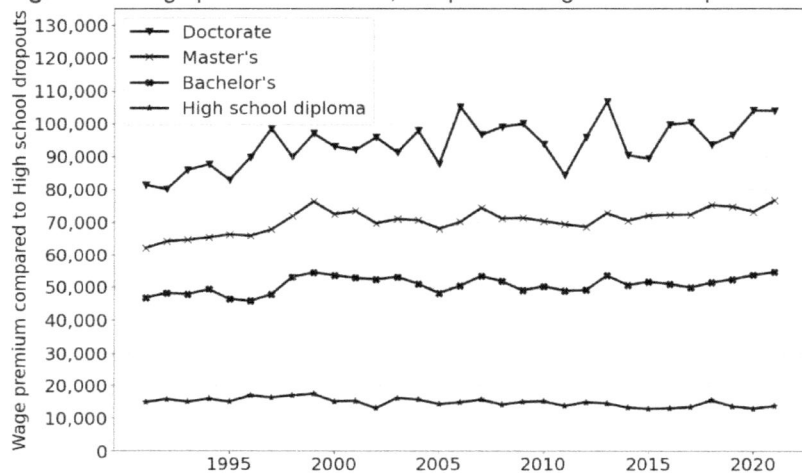

Figure 21. Wage premiums for women, compared to high school dropouts

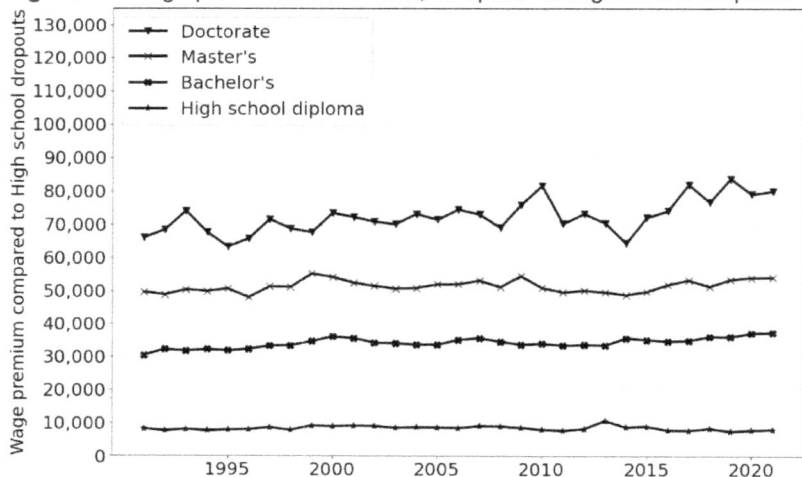

Economic theories: human capital and signaling

At first look, attending college seems to be beneficial. But why? Two prevalent views are the human capital theory and signaling theory. The human capital theory suggests that education and training, like tools and machinery (referred to as "capital" by economists), are crucial for producing goods and services in the modern economy. Attending college is valuable due to the essential knowledge and skills that students acquire during their time there, ultimately preparing them to become more productive employees upon graduation. Hence, people with college degrees are compensated more in the labor market for additional knowledge and skills.

According to signaling theory, the value of a college degree lies not in the specific training and skills acquired during the course of education but in the message the degree communicates to potential employers about the abilities of the degree holder. The theory says that if individuals have successfully completed all the tasks required of them during their college education, it signals to employers that such an individual is capable of completing future work tasks with equal success. In other words, the degree serves as a signal of the individual's competence and potential value as an employee.

It's fair to ask about the relationship between schooling and being a "good employee", specifically whether the relationship is causal. There is no way to measure one's innate ability, and thus, although schooling is not a perfect measure of whether an applicant would be highly productive, it does provide a sufficient signal of success to the employer.

To illustrate, suppose there are two types of workers in our economy: "low-productivity" and "high-productivity." Employers would like to pay each type of worker what they are "worth" in terms of the value they bring to the company (value of productivity). That is, companies would like to pay the low-productive individual a wage of $25,000 and the high-productive individual a wage of $30,000. However, the employer does not know each applicant's productivity level—all applicants may say that they are "highly productive," even though only 50% truly are.

Table 12. Productivity value example

Productivity	Population share	Value of Productivity
Low	50%	$25,000
High	50%	$30,000

If the company has no other information to gauge one's productivity, it will offer one wage to all workers regardless of true productivity. The wage offered is a simple average of what is expected in the market:

$$(\$25,000 \times 0.50) + (\$30,000 \times 0.50) = \$27,500$$

In this scenario, high-productivity workers are paid the same amount as the low-productivity workers. The low-productivity workers are receiving $2,500 extra (at a cost to the high-productive worker) due to the employer's inability to separate worker types.

Now, let's add schooling as a signaling tool that employers can utilize. Suppose that employers believe that applicants with an associate's degree are more likely to be highly productive than those without. Thus, an employee will be offered $30,000 if she has an associate's degree and $25,000 if she does not. In doing so, employers have created a scenario, where individuals who deem it "worth it" to provide the education signal will go on to college, and those who deem it "not worth it" won't pursue college and accept the lower $25,000 wage.

The signaling theory received much attention in the 1990s from numerous economists whose results could not agree on whether this effect actually exists. Early work in this area found that people who received degrees tended to have higher earnings than people who completed a similar number of college credits but did not get a degree. However, these studies did not account for the fact that individuals who don't complete their degrees may be different from those who do. For instance, those who have completed almost all the necessary credits for graduation but ended up not graduating may have encountered negative experiences, such as the loss of a parent, which hindered their ability to complete their degree. These experiences could potentially have a negative impact on their work productivity as well.[11]

Reality lies somewhere in between these two theories. Additionally, the value of a college degree can vary depending on the field of study and the specific job market. Some fields may place a greater emphasis on specific technical skills learned in college, while others may place a greater emphasis on simply the completion of a degree.

On a final note, we should be careful when interpreting data on college "premiums," as it may reflect a combination of factors rather than a direct effect of college education alone. The relationship between college education and higher earnings is often interpreted as a causal one: the "premiums" are the result of completing college. However, individuals who go to college may already possess qualities that predispose them to higher earnings, irrespective of their college education. For example, people who attend college may come from wealthier families or parents with college degrees and higher-income jobs, which can provide better resources and networks that can enhance earning potential.[a,12]

---

[a] Footnote: In fact, in 2006, more than two-thirds of students attending the most competitive colleges (those requiring high grades and SAT scores) came from families in the top 25% of the income distribution. Less than 5% were from families in the bottom 25% of the income distribution.

College as an investment: return

While higher education and learning are important, one should remember that a college degree is a means to an end goal of getting a well-paying job. Colleges are often presented as an opportunity for young adults to learn more about the fields they are interested in. This, unfortunately, often leads to cases where people choose to pursue majors that will make it very difficult to repay their student loans.

The amount of debt students at four-year colleges graduate with ranges between \$20,000 and \$30,000.[13] This may seem like a lot, but given that college graduates make about \$25,000 to \$40,000 more per year compared to individuals without college degrees, a student loan may be a worthwhile investment.[14,15]

Given a wide range of academic programs with varying levels of rigor and training, how should you choose the one that will be the most beneficial to you? After all, don't they all lead to a "college degree?"

Firstly, the quality of the college one attends matters. Employers seeking high-performing employees often have a list of "target schools" from which they prefer to recruit. These schools are typically defined by their selectivity, which is often based on the ACT and SAT scores of first-year students.[16]

Secondly, the field of study one chooses can be just as important as the college one attends. Engineering degrees, for instance, tend to offer higher returns than degrees in the humanities. Additionally, degrees that require less time to complete, such as associate degrees, generally offer lower returns than bachelor's degrees.

The table below shows the majors paying the most upon graduation for college graduates aged 22 to 27 according to the 2022 data. The three best-compensated majors are Computer

Engineering, Chemical Engineering, and Computer Science.[a,17] Note that the tables presented in this section show wages for people with bachelor's degrees only. That is, higher wages in the mid-career column aren't a result of a premium from graduate school completion. Many of us think that STEM (science, technology, engineering, and mathematics) majors typically earn higher salaries, but that is not always the case. Early career median wage for students majoring in Communications, a major that often gets a bad reputation for the perceived easiness of the program, was $47,000, almost $3,000 higher than for those majoring in Biology and $6,000 higher than for those majoring in Biochemistry. And, while Biochemistry majors' salaries outpace those of Communications majors by the time individuals turn 35-45 years old, Biology majors will still earn $2,000 less than Communications majors in the middle of their careers.

Table 13. Majors paying the most upon graduation[18]

Major	Median Wage Early Career	Median Wage Mid-Career
Computer Engineering	$80,000	$125,000
Chemical Engineering	$79,000	$133,000
Computer Science	$78,000	$110,000
Aerospace Engineering	$74,000	$120,000
Electrical Engineering	$72,000	$112,000
Industrial Engineering	$71,000	$100,000
Mechanical Engineering	$70,000	$111,000
Misc. Engineering	$68,000	$100,000
General Engineering	$68,000	$100,000
Finance	$66,000	$104,000
Mathematics	$65,000	$92,000
Economics	$65,000	$100,000
Civil Engineering	$65,000	$100,000

[a] Fun piece of trivia: among the 10 highest paid majors only Computer Science and Finance do not contain the word "engineering" in them.

Business Analytics	$65,000	$100,000
Pharmacy	$64,000	$85,000

In general, majors that pay the most upon graduation are also the majors that pay the most in the later stages of your career.

Table 14. Majors paying the most for those aged 35-45

Major	Median Wage Early Career	Median Wage Mid-Career
Chemical Engineering	$79,000	$133,000
Computer Science	$78,000	$110,000
Aerospace Engineering	$74,000	$120,000
Electrical Engineering	$72,000	$112,000
Mechanical Engineering	$70,000	$111,000
Computer Science	$78,000	$110,000
Finance	$66,000	$104,000
Misc. Engineering	$68,000	$100,000
Industrial Engineering	$71,000	$100,000
General Engineering	$68,000	$100,000
Economics	$65,000	$100,000
Construction Services	$64,000	$100,000
Civil Engineering	$65,000	$100,000
Business Analytics	$65,000	$100,000
Physics	$62,000	$95,000

Majors that pay the least upon graduation are Liberal Arts, Performing Arts, and Theology and Religion. Note that the early career wages for these majors are less than the median salary in the country. Later in their careers, however, holders of these degrees do start earning significantly more.

Table 15. Majors paying the least upon graduation

Major	Median Wage Early Career	Median Wage Mid-Career
Liberal Arts	$38,000	$65,000
Performing Arts	$38,000	$64,000
Theology and Religion	$38,000	$56,000
Leisure and Hospitality	$38,000	$56,000
Anthropology	$40,000	$65,000

Early Childhood Education	$40,000	$48,000
Elementary Education	$40,000	$52,000
Family and Consumer Sciences	$40,000	$59,000
Fine Arts	$40,000	$68,000
General Social Sciences	$40,000	$70,000
History	$40,000	$70,000
Misc. Biological Sciences	$40,000	$68,000
Nutrition Sciences	$40,000	$65,000
Psychology	$40,000	$65,000
Social Services	$40,000	$56,000

Table 16. Majors paying the least for those aged 35-45

Major	Median Wage Early Career	Median Wage Mid-Career
Early Childhood Education	$40,000	$48,000
Elementary Education	$40,000	$52,000
General Education	$41,000	$52,000
Secondary Education	$41,000	$55,000
Misc. Education	$43,000	$56,000
Social Services	$40,000	$56,000
Theology and Religion	$38,000	$56,000
Special Education	$43,000	$57,000
Family and Consumer Sciences	$40,000	$59,000
Performing Arts	$38,000	$64,000
Anthropology	$40,000	$65,000
Health Services	$45,000	$65,000
Liberal Arts	$38,000	$65,000
Nutrition Sciences	$40,000	$65,000
Psychology	$40,000	$65,000

In light of such big income differences (over a lifetime, highest-earning majors earn $3 million more than the lowest-earning majors), you may be wondering: why would anyone choose to major in something that does not pay well?

Some of the low-paying majors serve as a step toward high-paying graduate degrees. For example, while it's possible to enter medical school having majored in something seemingly unrelated like Computer Science, majoring in subjects like

Biology can help ensure you have the necessary prerequisites for medical school.

Another answer lies in the personal satisfaction that individuals can derive from their chosen fields. Many people find joy and fulfillment in studying subjects they are passionate about, whether it's the arts, humanities, or social sciences. The utility gained from their work can often outweigh the sacrifice in potential earnings.

We should warn prospective students considering the low-paying majors that the utility they get from pursuing these degrees will be different from satisfaction with the degree when they enter the job market. Online employment marketplace ZipRecruiter surveyed its users and found that jobseekers' satisfaction with their majors was tied to their job prospects and their earnings. According to the survey, the most regretted majors are Journalism, Sociology, Liberal Arts and General Studies, Communications, and Education. The most regret-free majors are Computer and Information Sciences, Criminology, Engineering, Nursing, and Health.[19]

Finally, it's possible that students choosing low-paying majors aren't aware that their fields of study don't pay well. The table below shows the results of two surveys asking college students about their salary expectations.[20,21] Interestingly, while the 2019 estimates seem reasonable, the 2022 survey results suggest that students across all majors overestimate how much they will make upon graduation. The 2022 survey was done in March of 2022, when the 12-month inflation exceeded 8%, a value not seen since the 1980s. It's possible that with inflation being constantly in the news, students were worried about rising prices and, hence, were expecting higher salaries.

Table 17. Salary expectations among college students of different majors

Major	Average expected salary, one year after college, Nominal Dollars		Actual Median Wage, Early Career, Nominal Dollars
	2019	2022	2022
Phys. or Life Sci.	$64,428	$110,360	$52,000
Nursing	$62,417	$104,270	$55,000
Business	$61,085	$101,120	$50,000
Computer Sci.	$59,303	$95,690	$73,000
Pol. Sci. / Econ.	$58,601	$108,160	$50,000 / $60,000
Finance / Account.	$56,638	$111,240	$60,000 / $54,000
Psychology	$53,673	$104,120	$37,400
Commun. / Journal.	$51,730	$107,040	$47,000 / $45,000
Education	$46,616	$99,090	$40,200

College as an investment: cost

Although returns to college education are large, the cost of college education is also significant. In fact, between 2000 and 2022, the cost of college tuition, fees, and textbooks increased by more than 160%. For comparison, prices of food and beverages in the same period increased by "only" 80%. At the same time, the cost of cellphone services, computer software, and TVs decreased by more than 40%.[22]

But why is college so expensive?

The first major reason is limited competition. For a significant portion of the student population, colleges that are available to them are geographically constrained, limiting competition and enabling local institutions to maintain higher tuition rates. Tuition and fees for full-time undergraduate students at public four-year universities are nearly three times higher for out-of-state students than they are for in-state students.[a,23] In addition to out-of-state fees, moving away from your family to another state or even another city is both financially and emotionally costly.

---

[a] Students at private universities pay three and a half times more than the in-state students at public universities.

In the same sense, universities are often only competing with institutions that are similar in rankings and perceived prestige. Thus, universities can charge tuition rates closely aligned with their few competitors in the same institutional category.

At the international level, American universities generally have very limited competition from foreign universities. Yes, there are world-renowned universities in countries like Canada, China, Singapore, and the UK. Nevertheless, nearly half of the 50 highest-ranked universities in the world in 2024 are located in the United States. No other country has more than seven universities in the top 50.[24] U.S. universities attract more than 260,000 new students from around the world every year. In total, there were 1,057,188 international students in the U.S. in the academic year 2022-2023.[25] That is more than the number of people living in states like Alaska, Delaware, North Dakota, South Dakota, Vermont, and Wyoming![26]

The second reason can be explained by the **Bennet Hypothesis**. In 1987, Secretary of Education William J. Bennett wrote an article for the New York Times titled "Our Greedy Colleges." He criticized colleges for raising tuition at rates far exceeding inflation (6-8% tuition hikes versus 1.8% inflation in 1986). While presidents of universities partially attributed their university's tuition hikes to changes in government support for student aid, Bennet refuted that argument by showing that the federal student aid funding increased 57% from 1980 to 1987 (far outpacing 26% inflation over that period). In fact, colleges were raising prices while also seeing huge cash infusions from state governments, corporations, foundations, and alumni donations during this time. Bennett argued that increases in federal student aid allowed colleges to raise tuition without improving affordability, as the aid simply enabled higher prices rather than making education more affordable for students by covering more of the cost burden.[27] The premise is straightforward: if you were already willing and able to pay $10,000 out of your own funds for college, receiving an additional $2,500 in financial aid means the school can now charge you $10,000 + $2,500. Over the next 30 years, more than two dozen academic articles will be published analyzing increases in federal student aid and colleges' tuition increases. The majority of these articles found that Bennett's hypothesis was indeed true: subsidies for college education increased the price of higher education.[28]

The third reason for the high cost of college is the lack of transparency on the benefits and costs of a college education. The main sources of revenue for public universities are government grants, contracts, and appropriations. At the same time, 16% of their revenues come from tuition and fees.[29] For private nonprofit universities, the share of tuition and fees stands at 19%. For private for-profit universities, it stands at staggering 93%. But what do universities spend that money on? What are students paying for?

Some of this spending raises questions about whether universities spend money wisely. For example, the University of Kentucky has, on average, spent more than $800,000 per day for more than a decade on campus upgrades. The University of Oklahoma spent $14.3 million to buy and renovate a monastery in Italy for its new study-abroad program. [30] Campuses throughout the U.S. also increased inflation-adjusted spending on athletic coaches by 50% between 2010 and 2022. For some colleges, this is a justified increase in expenses. About 10% of Division I athletic programs generate enough revenue to pay for themselves. The rest, however, rely heavily on subsidies from student fees and other sources to cover the costs of their athletic programs.[31]

Unfortunately, colleges don't have strict uniform requirements for reporting how they spend their money. According to data from the National Center for Education Statistics, in the academic year 2020-21, 34% of expenses of public four-year institutions were spent on instruction. About 28% of expenses were spread across "academic support" (activities that support instruction, research, and public service), "student services" (support of students' physical and emotional well-being; the category can include intercollegiate athletics except when operated as self-supporting auxiliary enterprises), and "institutional support" (day-to-day operational expenses of the institution).[32] The remaining funds were spent on "research and public service" (22%) and "other core expenses" (15%). All of these numbers and categories seem reasonable on the surface. But because there are no uniform reporting requirements, any "unreasonable" expense could be hiding somewhere in the details.

The fourth reason is the limited incentives for colleges to consider their students' future earnings potential. Their revenue streams are primarily based on tuition payments made upfront before students even enter the job market. Without a direct stake in graduate earnings, universities face less pressure to prioritize career preparation, salary prospects, and overall return on investment for students. This is not always a bad thing. If colleges start prioritizing admitting students who are more likely to earn higher incomes after graduating, they may become more inclined to admit students already coming from wealthy backgrounds. Colleges may pass over talented students from underprivileged backgrounds who could flourish in college but don't (yet) have the same earnings potential profiles.

Income share agreements (ISAs) were initially viewed as a promising alternative to traditional student loans for funding higher education. The key idea behind ISAs was that students would receive upfront funding for their education costs in exchange for agreeing to pay a percentage of their future income over a set period after graduating. Unfortunately, ISAs have not had major success. Many of the pioneering institutions and programs offering ISAs have now suspended their initiatives.[33]

Finally, for many students, the increased tuition and fees charged by colleges are still justifiable given the substantial "college premium" in earnings. However, with rising costs, the decision on whether college is worth it is becoming more difficult every year.

College as an investment: paying for college

A major challenge in assessing the true cost of college is the difference between the advertised "sticker" price and the actual net cost after factoring in various types of financial aid. Many students receive aid in the form of grants, scholarships, work-study programs, and student loans, which can significantly reduce the out-of-pocket cost of attendance. During the 2019-2020 academic year, more than 70% of undergraduate students received some form of financial aid averaging $14,100.[a,34]

What are some of the ways to pay for college outside of out-of-pocket expenses and scholarships? A large one is **student loans**. The common types of these loans are:

- **Direct Subsidized Loans** are available to undergraduate students who can demonstrate significant financial need. The defining feature of these loans is that the government covers the interest charges while the student is enrolled or during the grace period after the student leaves school.

---

[a] This number includes all forms of financial aid including loans to students and Direct PLUS Loans to parents but does not include federal tax credits for education or emergency aid related to the COVID-19 pandemic.

- **Direct Unsubsidized Loans**, on the other hand, don't require students to show the same level of financial need for eligibility. However, interest accrues even while the student is still attending school. These loans are available to both undergraduate and graduate students.
- For parents of undergraduate students or graduate and professional students themselves, the **Direct PLUS Loan** program offers another borrowing option. These loans require a basic credit check but have higher loan limits than direct subsidized/unsubsidized loans. If you're not able to pass a credit check, you can add a cosigner who will be liable if you fail to make payments.
- Finally, the **Direct Consolidation Loan** allows students to combine multiple existing federal student loans into a new single loan, sometimes with an extended repayment period. This option can help borrowers simplify managing their monthly payments to a single loan servicer.[35]

Like with other types of loans, it's important to consider paying off student loans early. While we often think of student loans as a problem of young people, this is not always the case. In fact, in 2023, there were 3.5 million Americans aged 60 and above who collectively held more than $125 billion in student loans. Although some of the balance was for their children, most was for their own education. Being behind on student loan payments in retirement can lead to a reduction in Social Security payments. In fact, in 2015, the government withheld $171 million in Social Security payments from older Americans who were not paying their student loans.

For those who may be planning for college in the future, a 529 plan is a tax-advantaged investment account designed to help families save for education expenses. The key benefits include:

- *Tax-deferred growth*: Earnings in the account grow tax-deferred. That is, you don't pay taxes until you withdraw the money.
- *Tax-free withdrawals for qualified expenses*: Withdrawals used for qualified education expenses are exempt from federal income tax. This includes costs like tuition, fees, books, room and board.
- *Limited impact on financial aid*: 529 assets are considered parental assets in the **Student Aid Index** (SAI) formula used to calculate a student's financial need. The SAI formula weighs student and parent assets differently, and a child's assets can have a greater effect on federal financial aid eligibility.[36]

Finally, in lieu of or to offset student loans, many students work part-time jobs. In fact, about a quarter of full-time undergraduate students report working 20 or more hours per week.[37] Many older readers may remember working part-time to put themselves through college. Unfortunately, today, minimum wage jobs alone may not generate sufficient funds to fully cover the costs of higher education. The federal minimum wage in 1970 was $1.60 per hour. If that number had kept up with inflation, the federal minimum wage would have been a little above $13 in 2023. The actual federal minimum wage in 2023 was $7.25 per hour, about 55% of the inflation-adjusted 1970 value.

5.3 Gender Pay Gap and Income Discrimination

In the previous section, we learned about the impact of college degrees on income. People with more training (or more years of education), on average, make more than people without.

Besides education, other factors employers consider when deciding how much to pay their employees include various job characteristics. For example, employers can offer higher wages to compensate for the undesirable characteristics of a job, such as an overnight shift or working in unsanitary places. On the other hand, they may offer lower salaries for jobs that aren't very stressful or allow you to work from home.

As you probably understood from the title of this section, we'll be examining the effects of these job characteristics in one very specific context. The gender pay gap remains a hotly debated topic. In popular media, there seem to be two camps with opposite views on the nature of the gender pay gap. One side argues that a substantial gender pay gap persists, attributing this disparity primarily to discrimination and societal biases that undervalue women's work. On the other hand, critics argue that the gender pay gap is largely a myth, saying that when differences in factors like job characteristics, work hours, and individual choices are accounted for, the gap disappears.[38,39,40,41] The reality is more nuanced.

The gender pay gap

January of 1985 brought a monumental moment in history being the first month during which more than 50% of women in the United States held employment. Apart from a decrease in employment during the COVID-19 pandemic, that statistic—referred to as **employment-population ratio**—has never fallen below 50% for women since 1985.

Figure 22. The employment-population ratio for men and women

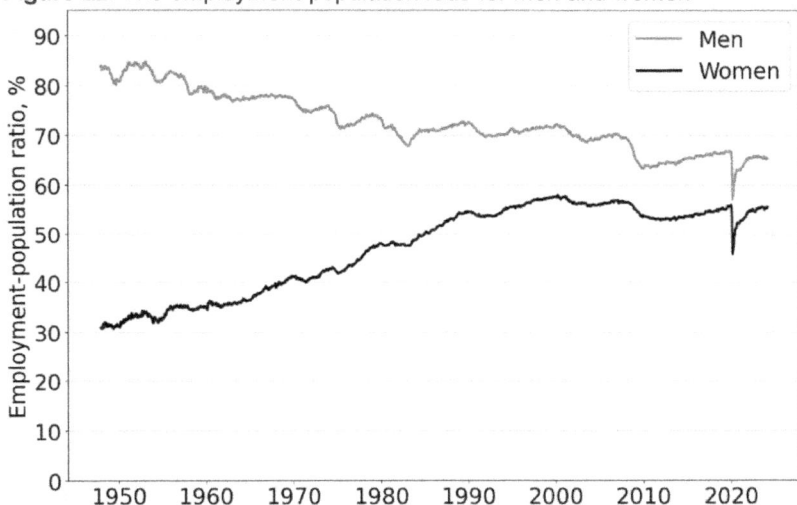

At the same time, we have seen women's wages rise as percent of men's wages from 65% in 1982 to 82% in 2022. For workers aged 25-34, that percentage increased from 74% in 1982 to 92% in 2022.[42] What prevents this gap from vanishing completely? How much of it is caused by discrimination against women in the workforce? If we take into account differences between men and women (for example, in terms of the types of jobs the two groups tend to work), will the size of the gap decrease significantly?

In the U.S., the gender of a child is not expected to be correlated with parents' income (as opposed to countries and cultures that favor boys over girls). Based on medical factors like the types of chromosomes and reproductive anatomy, most people are assigned either male or female at birth. We often assume that the probability of a child being a boy or a girl is 50%, although there are slightly fewer girls born in the United States than there are boys.[43] The unusually high proportion of boys compared to girls in countries like Armenia, Azerbaijan, China, and India is often taken as evidence for selective abortion of girls. Despite the slightly higher number of boys born, no strong evidence exists for selective abortions being prevalent in the U.S. Whether heterosexual couples earn a low, middle or high income, they remain just as likely to give birth to a baby boy or girl.[a,44,45] Thus, we do not expect income differences among men and women. Then, what factors are responsible for the difference in wages?

Compensating wage differentials

As people seek different types of jobs, **compensating wage differentials** arise to compensate workers for the differences in non-wage characteristics of jobs. For example, people working jobs that are dangerous may require a premium (higher salary) to compensate for taking upon the risk of injury. On the other hand, individuals working from home don't have to spend time and money on commuting and, hence, may be willing to accept lower compensation. Salaries can also vary due to a myriad of other job characteristics: the job is physically demanding, takes place in an undesirable geography or weather, requires a college degree, is "fun and interesting" (subjective to the employee), provides excellent benefits, is secure from layoffs, and much more.

To illustrate the concept of compensating wage differentials, let's consider one of the most dangerous (in terms of fatal on-the-job incidents) industries: logging. Loggers deal with heavy equipment to obtain raw building materials in harsh and

---

[a] Adoptive parents, however, tend to prefer girls. Given that adoptive parents tend to have higher incomes and education levels, we may expect a disproportionate number of girls in richer families if the share of adopted children were significant. However, only about 50,000 children get adopted every year, much less than the 3.6 million children born.

physically demanding environments, which led to 100.7 fatal accidents per 100,000 workers in 2022.[a] By comparison, the fatality rate across all jobs averages approximately 3.7 per 100,000 workers.[46]

Figure 23. Workplace fatal injuries

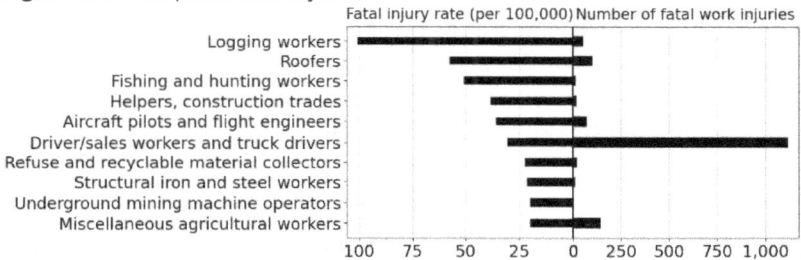

Fatal injury rate (per 100,000) Number of fatal work injuries

Logging workers
Roofers
Fishing and hunting workers
Helpers, construction trades
Aircraft pilots and flight engineers
Driver/sales workers and truck drivers
Refuse and recyclable material collectors
Structural iron and steel workers
Underground mining machine operators
Miscellaneous agricultural workers

100   75   50   25   0   250   500   750   1,000

Suppose there are two logging companies, the "Beaver" company and the "Woodpecker" company. Each company employs 10,000 workers but differs in terms of the level of risk. Due to better training practices, the Beaver company has one fewer fatal accidents each year. However, nothing is free—the tradeoff of one fewer fatal accident is the extra money spent on training, which ultimately means lower pay for workers at the Beaver company.

Table 18. Fatal accidents and pay at two logging companies

Company	Fatal accidents	Annual pay
Beaver	8	$40,000
Woodpecker	9	$41,250

Specifically, workers at the Beaver company receive $104.17 less on their monthly paycheck, or a total of $1,250 on a yearly basis. An alternative interpretation is that workers employed by

[a] The U.S. Bureau of Labor Statistics bases fatality rate per 100,000 workers. Thus, the industry with the highest total number of fatalities may not necessarily be the same industry with the highest fatality rate.

Woodpecker are accepting the higher risk (of fatality) in exchange for the extra pay of $1,250.

How do the compensating wage differentials explain the gender pay gap? Consider the risk of injury as an example. Jobs that are perceived as more dangerous or have less desirable working conditions often pay more to attract workers willing to endure these conditions. Historically, men were more likely to work in these higher-risk jobs, which can contribute to higher average wages for men compared to women. Interestingly, a 2003 study found that men received an earnings premium for accepting a higher risk of workplace fatal accidents, but women did not.[a] At the same time, both genders received an earnings premium for accepting a higher risk of workplace nonfatal injury at non-physically demanding jobs, but women's premium was over three times larger than men's.[47]

Table 19. Earnings premium

Premium	Men	Women
Fatal Injury Risk (vs. no fatal injury risk)	0.53% to 0.89%	Statistically not significant
In Monetary Terms	$166 to $277	N/A[b]
Non-Fatal Injury Risk (vs. no fatal injury risk)	0.93% to 1.38%	2.87% to 4.49%
In Monetary Terms	$290 to $429	$714 to $1,119

At first glance, it seems that men are provided extra pay for the additional risk of a fatal injury, and women are not. However, careful examination of the distribution of job types (i.e., what industries men and women typically work in) shows that the findings are driven by the disparity in job choices. That is, women were more likely to work in non-hazardous jobs.

---

[a] Across all industries.
[b] Estimates ranged from negative to positive

174

Therefore, the data could not capture a higher earnings premium for accepting a higher risk of workplace fatal accidents for women.

Table 20. Distribution of women by select major industries[48]

Industry	Women, %
Agriculture, Forestry, Fishing, and Hunting	29.3
Construction	10.8
Education and Health Services	74.4
Manufacturing	29.5
Mining	15.3
Transportation and Utilities	24.3

Discrimination in the labor market

What if differences in wages persist even if all differences in the non-wage characteristics are accounted for? In such cases, the observed wage differences may be due to **discrimination**.

The economics of discrimination was motivated by economist Gary Becker (whom we mentioned in the chapter on intergenerational mobility) through his doctoral dissertation in 1957, which discussed taste discrimination. "Taste" is inferred through three avenues: employer, employee, and customer, which help explain differences in labor market outcomes like wages and employment.

An employer is said to be discriminatory if the hiring company pays two workers differently due to the "perceived cost" of hiring an individual as opposed to the actual cost. If two individuals have the same set of skills and level of education, it would be reasonable to think any actual hiring costs (like onboarding and training) would be the same for both applicants.

Employee discrimination refers to prejudiced employees who may not want to work with certain groups of individuals. The discriminating employee perceives their wage to be lower than what it should be when working with certain individuals and, thus, may demand higher pay to remain at the same place of employment. However, this type of discrimination is rarely a factor in determining wage differences, as prejudiced employees rarely have any power to demand higher wages from employers, especially if the demand is based on discrimination. Lastly, customer discrimination refers to the notion that consumers can perceive the cost (of a good or a service) to be higher when interacting with certain types of workers. For example, individuals may feel more comfortable receiving an annual physical exam from a doctor who is of the same gender and thus may place a higher cost on receiving a physical exam from a person of a different gender.

Following Becker, a leading alternative theory of discrimination in economics was introduced in 1972 by Edmund Phelps (who won the Nobel Prize in economics in 2006). The main intuition behind Phelps's theory of **statistical discrimination** is quite simple—that discrimination in the labor market may be based on known statistics, such as the average performance of certain groups. For example, a company looking to hire a younger employee may choose to offer a higher wage to the male applicant over the female applicant if the company's historical data suggest that female employees on average tend to leave the company at higher rates as workers approach 30 years of age (perhaps, due to motherhood).

Let's consider the scenario where the company decides to utilize statistical discrimination to set wages for new employees. In this case, women seem to be negatively discriminated against, as the company places a "higher cost" on retaining female employees, driven by the company's own historical data. On the other hand, men aren't associated with this higher cost and thus receive a wage that is not discounted.

Breaking down this further, women who end up staying with the company well past their thirties—some even staying longer than their male counterparts—are the ones that are most negatively impacted by the statistical discrimination. These workers did not incur higher costs for the employer but were treated as if they would, based on the company's historical data. On the other hand, it could be argued that women who left the company as they approached 30 years of age were paid "fairly" based on the company's own data.

Similarly, men who stayed past their thirties were paid "fairly," while men who left as they approached 30 years of age were over-paid and benefited from the statistical discrimination imposed on women. Depending on the scenario, statistical discrimination based on gender can be reversed (i.e., women receive more pay on average), be driven by race, or any other characteristic the employer deems appropriate to utilize to discriminate based on statistical means.

A well-known study in the economics of discrimination is a 1973 article by Ronald Oaxaca, in which the author decomposed various defining characteristics of a wage, including education, industry, occupation, health problems, marital status, and location, using U.S. Census data from the 1960s. What is referred to today as the "Oaxaca-Blinder Decomposition" method (Alan Blinder's work used a similar method and was published in the same year as Oaxaca's paper), Oaxaca concluded that while wage gaps exist between men and women, much of the difference was due to compensating wage differentials. In other words, there seemed to be "men's jobs" and "women's jobs" and "men's jobs" paid more.[49,50]

The table below showcases the power of Oaxaca's decomposition, where most of the gender pay gap can be explained by the difference in the number of years of education. Note that this is a hypothetical example, meant to introduce the mechanism behind the gap we see in the real world. However, we'll consider real-world numbers in a later section.

Table 21. Wage and the number of years of schooling

	Man #1	Man #2	Woman #1	Woman #2
Schooling	12	20	12	16
Wage	$25/hr	$33/hr	$24/hr	$27.60/hr

Suppose there are four workers (two men and two women) at some firm. Each person has a certain number of years of schooling and a certain hourly wage. A simple comparison of the average wages between the genders gives $29 per hour for men and $25.80 per hour for women.

Although intuitive, these numbers fail to fully represent any wage gaps brought on by discrimination. Why? We aren't accounting for other characteristics that may affect wages. So, let's introduce one such determinant—the number of years of schooling. We see that men, on average, have 16 years of schooling while women have 14. Thus, part of the wage gap we see—the $3.20 per hour difference—can be attributed to the schooling gap. Specifically, how much? To calculate that, we'll need to use the Oaxaca-Blinder Decomposition. The result of the decomposition is provided in the table below. You can verify the numbers by multiplying the extra wage received for a year of education by the number of years of schooling. Then, add the wage received for 0 years of education. For example, for "Man #1," that would be $13 + $1 * 12 = $25.

Table 22. Implied values

Category	Men	Women
Wage received with no education	$13.00/hr	$13.20/hr
Extra wage for an extra year of education	$1.00/hr	$0.90/hr

Note that, in this example, if women had the same average level of education as men, their wages would be slightly higher. Specifically, part of the $3.20 per hour difference attributable to the schooling gap is $1 * (16 - 14) = 2, representing more than half of the wage gap. The remaining $1.20 per hour represents wage differentials stemming from other aspects. The implied values given in the table showcase where the discrimination is coming from – the fact that women are receiving $0.90 per extra year of education compared to men's $1.00. Interestingly, women are paid slightly more without any education compared to men, meaning that the discrimination (holding education constant) is on the men.

Reality is more complicated as we need to consider all sorts of variables that may have an impact on earnings, and not just education alone. In a later section, we'll look into all of these factors together.

Psychological and societal factors

Another explanation for the gender pay gap is the one proposed by economists Muriel Niederle and Lise Vesterlund. In their 2007 study, they suggested that men tend to choose to go into competitive environments more often than women, which could lead to men having higher-paying jobs.

It's virtually impossible to test this theory in the real world because of how difficult it would be to get relevant data. Collecting data on the employment decisions of hundreds of thousands or millions of people and figuring out which cases of employment were due to a competitive work environment is not feasible. To circumvent the problem of the lack of "real-world" data, economists often resort to lab experiments, which usually involve the recruitment of students on university campuses.

In one such experiment, Niederle and Vesterlund asked groups of female and male participants to add up sets of five two-digit numbers for five minutes. Students were paid for correct answers according to one of two systems: piece rate (each person received 50 cents for a correct answer) and tournament (a person with the largest number of correct answers in the group received $2). Both men and women performed similarly under either system, which rules out any gender-related differences in math abilities in the subjects. After becoming familiar with both systems, students were asked to play again and choose which system they wanted to play in. While 73% of men chose the tournament system, only 35% of women chose the same system. Thus, the authors suggested that men and women have different preferences for competition.

Suppose the gap between men's and women's competitiveness holds up outside of the lab setting of this experiment. What could explain this pattern? Social scientists, perhaps, can answer it by referring to some established cultural norms and various social factors. Niederle and Vesterlund claim that findings in their experiments are consistent with observations made by economists Linda Babcock and Sara Laschever, who, in their book *Women Don't Ask: Negotiation and the Gender Divide* consider the possibility that the gender pay gap can be partially explained due to women disliking negotiations. Niederle and Vesterlund suggest that aversion to negotiations can be seen as a tendency to avoid competition and, hence, is consistent with their results.[51] There are, of course, numerous other factors that help explain why women may be less willing than men to negotiate for higher wages. We recommend reading the aforementioned book for a more in-depth discussion. Interestingly, a 2023 study revealed that while women were less likely to negotiate wages before the twenty-first century, women today are more likely than men to initiate salary negotiations.[52]

Our upbringing may also partly explain the difference in competition. Economists Jonas Tungodden and Alexander Willén implemented an experiment similar to the one used by Niederle and Vesterlund and focused on nearly 1,500 subjects in Norway (a country that is often praised for its success in combating the gender gap in education and income). They slightly modified the experiments by making parents of middle school students decide whether their children should play according to competitive or noncompetitive schemes. Tungodden and Willén found that parents were much more likely to choose competitive settings for sons.[53]

Bringing it all together

So, what happens to the gender pay gap after we take all of these factors into account?

The table below shows results from a 2020 study from the Center for Economic Studies (part of the U.S. Census Bureau) on the quantifiable factors explaining the gender pay gap. It used data from the Current Population Survey and American Community Survey, matching it with data from the Social Security Administration and the Internal Revenue Service. The study estimated the wage gap to be about 21%. However, only about 30% of the gap could be explained by the factors the analysis considered. That is, when we consider these factors, the gap remains but reduces to about 14%.[54]

The biggest contributors to the (explained portion of the) gap are the types of jobs that women work. The study shows that women are less represented in competitive and hazardous occupations, which widens the wage gap. This confirms the role of compensating wage differentials in determining the wage gap. On the other hand, factors like location, work history, and age have only a small contribution to the gender pay gap.[a,55]

Note that education also has a large coefficient, although it's a negative one. This is the result of women surpassing men in

---

[a] Work history used to be a more important factor in explaining the gender pay gap as men had more experience compared to women in the past. However, between 1981 and 2011, the gap in the number of years of experience between men and women decreased from 7 to about 1.4 years.

educational attainment. Thus, if women had the same level of educational attainment as men, the wage gap would have been bigger.

Table 23. Share of the pay gap explained

Factor	Percent of the gap	As addends to the 21% gap
Industry	23.37	4.91
Competition	14.87	3.12
Proportion female	9.65	2.03
Race/ethnicity	2.87	0.60
Working 41-49 hours	2.73	0.57
Occupational hazards	2.15	0.45
Region	0.87	0.18
Work history	0.49	0.10
Metropolitan status	0.04	0.01
Time pressure	-0.38	-0.08
Age	-0.45	-0.09
Working 50+ hours	-0.56	-0.12
Autonomy	-0.91	-0.19
Usual weekly hours	-0.98	-0.21
Communication and teamwork	-5.09	-1.07
Education	-16.64	4.91
Unexplained	*67.97*	*14.27*

The gender pay gap has been found in other rich countries as well. For example, a 2022 study found wage gaps across various industries between men and women by using data from New Zealand. The authors note that although gender differences in pay can be partially explained by occupation choices, industries, and companies, a gap of approximately 15% persists between genders.[a] Of the 15%, the authors argue that 10% can be explained by less successful bargaining by women and differences in productivity (both through statistical

---

[a] Overall gender wage gap was between 20% and 28% before considering occupation choices, industries, and companies.

discrimination), leaving a 5% wage gap that can be attributed to taste discrimination (or other unexplained reasons).[56] Research by economist Claudia Goldin (who won the Nobel Prize in economics in 2023) explains that one of the major factors affecting the gender pay gap is motherhood. Part of the reason is that women who are mothers or who are taking care of others are less likely to have jobs that require long hours. And these are the jobs that pay the most.[a] Conversely, women who aren't raising children or taking care of the elderly earn salaries similar to the ones earned by men, although researchers can still find "a residual gap." Goldin explains that, today, there is still discrimination contributing to the pay gap, but it's unclear how much of it is there exactly. In the past, we could find employers openly admitting to paying women less, but today, it is harder to find "smoking gun" admissions like this because no employer would risk a lawsuit.[b,57,58,59]

5.4 Migration

Where you reside affects your income, which ultimately can also be a determinant of your standard of living. Cities like Honolulu, New York City, and San Francisco are well known for their high cost of living, which means that the income that individuals take home in those cities is likely to be nominally larger (that is, their paychecks are higher) but may not necessarily equate to higher standards of living. For example, a $50,000 salary in Cincinnati, Ohio, would require approximately $71,000 in San Francisco, $72,000 in New York

---

[a] There is, however, evidence from laboratory and field experiments suggesting that mothers are perceived as less competent and less committed to work. "Evaluators" in the lab experiments would recommend lower starting salaries for mothers compared to other women.

[b] Famously, in a 1983 article in New York Times (as well as in his 2007 book, *The Age of Turbulence*) Alan Greenspan admitted that he hired female vice presidents because he could pay women less for the same quality of work men did.

City, and $73,000 in Honolulu to maintain a similar standard of living.

Why do some people leave their hometowns, even if it means paying more for rent or food? Why do others decide to stay where they are, even if they could earn more somewhere else? How does migration transform local labor markets?

Attachment to home?

The decision to move is not an easy one, as it can be costly in both monetary (hiring a moving company, taking time off from work) and non-monetary (time and effort spent on packing and unpacking, and the emotional cost of leaving "home") terms. Thus, to incentivize an individual to move, the reward must be great. For example, such a reward could be starting your undergraduate career at your dream college or receiving a high-paying job offer. In fact, the cost is so significant that less than 3% of individuals in the U.S. moved between states in 2019. What would incentivize you to leave your home?

In 2021, the average yearly salary of a construction worker in Puerto Rico was approximately $17,800. Since there are no legal barriers for a U.S. person to migrate from Puerto Rico to a U.S. state, the theory would suggest that if the average salary were large "enough" compared to the $17,800 in Puerto Rico, people would be incentivized to move. Although wages vary among states, the average yearly pay of a construction worker across the U.S. was approximately $37,800. That is $20,000 more than the average pay offered in Puerto Rico.

Yet, employers often face difficulty finding employees for such positions, and many job listings and opportunities go unfulfilled. In our case, even if it may be more costly to move across waters from Puerto Rico to the mainland, the potential lifetime earnings far outweigh any one-time costs. You may counter and point out that the living costs are more expensive in the U.S. than in Puerto Rico. While true, the difference in living cost is said to vary between 15-25%, which is much less than the annual difference in pay (112%).

Thus, if people choose not to migrate after having considered the difference in living cost, and the higher pay, we can hypothesize that the "non-monetary" costs are exorbitantly high. Suppose this construction worker ends up being employed for 20 additional years, meaning that (without any raises), working in the U.S. would net $400,000 in additional pay compared to working in Puerto Rico. From here, let's take away a living cost difference of 20%, which leaves $320,000 in additional pay. We can also take out $20,000 in monetary moving costs (i.e., moving company, finding a new place to stay), which implies that the non-monetary cost of moving is $300,000![a] Since the non-monetary costs of moving can be large, employees will have to be incentivized enough to move, which means the pay has to be large enough to outweigh the value people place on their hometowns, their cultures, and their friends and families.

What other forces shape migration decisions?

Internal migration

In 2020, 58% of Americans lived in the state where they were born, down from a peak of 70% in 1940. The remaining 42% was divided between those who were born outside the U.S. (14%) and those who were born in the U.S. but did not reside in their state of birth (28%). The state of Nevada has the least number of Nevada-born residents, with 78% of the population having immigrated from outside the U.S. or moved to the state from another state. An opposing statistic can be seen in the state

---

[a] Over 20 years.

of Louisiana, where approximately 78% of the population are Louisiana-born residents.[60]

The map below shows **net domestic migration** (NDM) across the U.S. from 2021 to 2022. The NDM statistic is the number of individuals entering minus the number of individuals who leave. Thus, a positive value indicates population growth, while a negative one implies a decrease in the population. Between 2021 and 2022, many Americans left large metropolitan areas on the West Coast and Northeast for places such as Arizona, Texas, Georgia, North Carolina, and Florida.

Figure 24. Net Migration in Thousands (2021–2022)

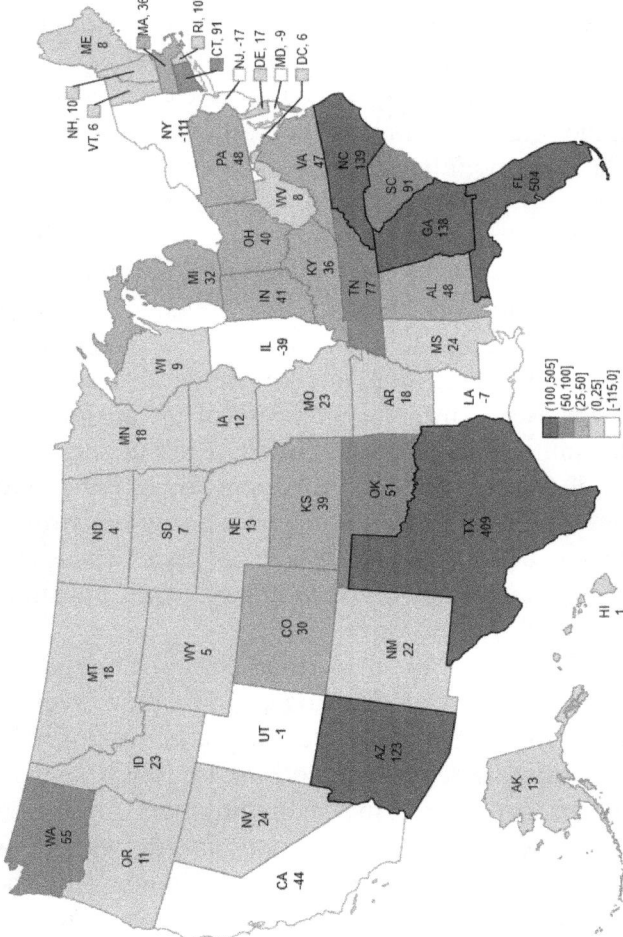

Part of this large move can be attributed to the ongoing migration trends, where Americans were already moving away from large cities and counties, especially those with a population size greater than one million. At the same time, smaller communities (with a population size of less than 30,000

individuals) also had negative net domestic migration rates, with many individuals moving to more populated areas (with population sizes between 30,000 and 999,999).

In addition to existing trends, the COVID-19 pandemic affected the migration choices for many, as some wanted to get out of heavily populated areas as a direct response to the pandemic. For other people, the pandemic may have accelerated the move (i.e., people who were already thinking about moving prior to the pandemic). Furthermore, as the option for remote work became more prevalent, employees had more freedom to migrate across states.

Besides unexpected events like pandemics, two common reasons Americans migrate within the U.S. are to seek better job opportunities and to attend college, both undergraduate and graduate degrees. Another big reason for moving within the U.S. (including within the same state) is the desire for newer, or larger house or apartment. According to a Census survey, in 2022, nearly half of survey respondents cited housing-related reasons for their relocation.[61]

From the first look, the theoretical effect of migration on the economic outcomes of the local population seems to be straightforward. One might expect that an influx of individuals from out of state increases competition for jobs, thereby driving down wages and increasing unemployment among "native" (commonly used term used by economists to describe workers who were already present in the area) workers. This should be especially true for domestic migrants because they have the same educational background, have similar skills, and speak the same language as the "locals."

The data evidence, however, suggests that the impact of internal migration is more interesting. A 2010 study looked at the effect of extensive internal migration during the 1930s. This period was ideal for such a study because low immigration from abroad (partly caused by the Great Depression) meant that any effect would be coming from internal migration. The study found no effect of in-migration on the hourly earnings of existing residents. However, in-migration did encourage some locals to move away and did reduce the number of weeks worked during the year by locals. Specifically, for every 100 immigrants, 19 locals left the area, 21 "were prevented from finding a relief job" (jobs offered by the Works Progress Administration, which was part of the New Deal), and 19 locals converted from full-time to part-time work.[a,62,63]

It's difficult to say if domestic migration has similar effects today. A significant number of international migration rates makes it difficult to single out the effects of internal migrants on local economies. Furthermore, the rate of internal migration has been steadily declining in the U.S. since the 1980s.[b,64,65]

International migration (immigration)

Despite its prevalence, migration between states is rarely a topic of news coverage, although it was an important issue a century ago. In the 1930s, California became concerned by the influx of millions of people migrating from Arkansas, Oklahoma, and Texas, suffering from the devastation caused by the Dust Bowl. As a result, the California Indigent Act of 1933 made it illegal to bring poor people into the state and was used to turn back poor migrants at the state's major entry points. In 1941, however, the Supreme Court ruled the Act to be an "unconstitutional barrier to interstate commerce."[66,67,68] Today,

---

[a] A decline in employment, rather than in wages, aligns with the concept of "sticky wages" in economics. When companies encounter weak demand, they can sell goods at discounted prices to ensure they are generating some revenue. In contrast, when employees face low demand for their labor, they usually don't negotiate for lower wages; instead, they are often laid off.

[b] Americans are still more mobile than citizens of most European countries.

migration between states is seen as normal and often necessary for individuals seeking better opportunities and quality of life.

Migration of foreign-born individuals into the U.S. (**immigration**), however, is one of the most controversial political issues on people's minds. In February 2024, according to a Gallup survey, immigration became the "most important problem" in the U.S., placing higher than even inflation, a pressing economic issue of the early 2020s.[69]

Immigrants tend to possess distinct characteristics that differentiate them from both their origin population and the receiving population. These often include a higher tolerance for risk, a strong entrepreneurial spirit, specialized education, or a powerful motivation to improve their economic circumstances. The "incentive" to immigrate must be sufficiently large, as immigrants face additional costs of moving including immigration fees, long-distance moving costs, and learning a new language.

Which subset of workers finds it worthwhile to move—the "most" or "least" skilled?

Not only is this question difficult to answer practically (it's hard to find relevant data), but even theory is complicated. Suppose that earnings in both countries (the sending country and the U.S.) only depend on the person's skills and abilities. That is, a more skilled worker will receive higher pay in both countries. Since countries value professions (and compensate them) differently, the self-selection of immigrants may be "positive" or "negative," depending on the labor market conditions. We say that immigrants are positively selected if they are highly skilled, and because their country does not compensate them as well as the U.S. does, they choose to immigrate to the U.S. On the other hand, immigrants are said to be negatively selected if individuals aren't highly skilled and the U.S. provides higher pay than what is offered back at their home country. At the onset, it may seem that the positively selected immigrants may be more beneficial to the U.S. than the negatively selected immigrants. Some may think that a doctor or a physicist may be "better" for our economy than the day laborer or the meat plant worker. However, oversimplifying the immigration process to prioritize either positively selected or negatively selected individuals may have unintended consequences. For example, hiring too many professors from outside the U.S. may create reliance on non-American researchers and teachers, which may ultimately discourage U.S. natives from pursuing becoming professors. At the same time, college students (of which the majority are U.S. citizens or permanent residents) may prefer to be taught or mentored by professors from the U.S., someone with whom they share a common background (for example, if sharing the same background helps professors be better at explaining topics).

Research on the effects of immigration on native workers (U.S. citizens and permanent residents) shows that immigrants tend to find roles that are typically not sought by the native population and generally have little to no impact on the labor market outcomes of native workers. [70, 71, 72] Although not common, in industries where the working population lacks high-school education, native workers may face higher competition with immigrants. The competition is on the wage front rather than employment itself. That is, while native workers without high-school diplomas may face higher competition due to a larger population of non-educated immigrants, often this is shown in lower wages rather than loss of employment. [73] Furthermore, immigrants spend money on things like groceries, home supplies, haircuts, and other services. This spending creates jobs, often for people without high-school or college degrees. The resulting increased demand for labor helps to counteract the potential downward pressure on wages caused by the increased labor supply.[74]

A lot of the foreigners living in the U.S. are staying here on non-immigrant working visas. One such visa is the H-1B visa, which allows U.S. employers to temporarily employ highly skilled foreign workers in specialty occupations. These occupations generally require a bachelor's degree or higher in a specific field, such as technology, engineering, or medicine. The H-1B visa must be sponsored by a U.S. employer; it does not guarantee permanent residence and requires renewal after three years. The process is not guaranteed, as receiving the visa depends on a lottery. The program is designed to protect U.S. natives, as it requires the employer to apply for a certification of Labor Condition Application from the Department of Labor (an additional cost), as well as to make sure that the job posting is clearly available and accessible to qualified U.S. natives. If the employer is unable to find a qualified U.S. individual for the position after a certain amount of time, then a qualified immigrant would be able to accept that position. There are also annual caps (65,000 as of 2024) set for the program. Despite these requirements, many job listings will only be fulfilled by an immigrant, as no qualified U.S. person has applied.

Because H-1B visas are assigned to firms using lotteries, there is an interesting opportunity to study the effects of these visas on firms' hiring decisions. A 2022 study found that winning an additional H-1B visa "crowds out" about one and a half workers (that the firm would have otherwise hired). The study suggests a couple of possible explanations, including that H-1B workers work harder than other workers (perhaps due to fewer opportunities compared to workers who don't need visas or because they are simply more hard-working) or that H-1B workers have unique skills that let firms reduce hiring of other employees.

It's important not to interpret these results as an irrefutable sign that H-1B workers are displacing American workers. This study, while interesting, follows multiple other studies published in the decade prior that did not find evidence of H-1B workers taking jobs from Americans. Thus, at this time, the evidence regarding the effect of H-1B workers on native workers remains mixed.[75]

As a final thought, it's important to recognize one major difficulty in studying the effect of immigrants on native workers. Two individuals can "look" similar and have similar skills but have different immigration statuses. The term immigrant does not only include nor is dominated by recently arrived individuals. Millions of individuals who have lived in the U.S. for many years are considered immigrants by the U.S. government. Even permanent residents (green card holders). Similarly, millions more are naturalized U.S. citizens and aren't considered immigrants. Even if their outwardly appearance or language skills seem to be no different than those of immigrants from similar backgrounds. In such situations, it becomes challenging to isolate the impact of immigration status itself on labor market outcomes, as any observed differences may be confounded by unobserved (in the data) factors like language skills, social connections, cultural knowledge, and many more.

5.5 Other Things that Can Affect Your Salary

So far, we have covered some of the fundamental factors that affect your salary. There are, however, plenty of other factors that can affect the size of your paycheck. Social interactions and physical appearance are some of the interesting ones.

Social interactions with your manager are an important determinant of promotions and, hence, your income. For example, a study done in collaboration with a large commercial bank in Southeast Asia found that smokers who transition from working for non-smoking to a smoking manager are promoted more quickly. Smoke breaks are an excellent ground for an informal interaction with your supervisor.[76]

Another factor that affects your income is your looks. In the 1970s, Canadian and US researchers conducted several surveys to understand people's employment conditions. Along with asking participants about their earnings, the interviewers also evaluated their physical appearance. Fast forward two decades later, economists Daniel Hamermesh and Jeff Biddle used the data from these surveys to examine the correlation between physical attractiveness and higher earnings. Their analysis revealed that good-looking individuals earned approximately 5% more than their average-looking peers, while "plain" (terminology used by the authors) individuals received a 5% penalty compared to those with average looks.

The authors also discovered that attractive people were more likely to work as salespeople or servers, jobs where good looks can be advantageous. However, it remains unclear whether individuals chose these professions themselves or whether these industries exhibit some degree of discrimination based on looks. There may even be a degree of reverse causality, where individuals with higher pay have the means to take better care of themselves, leading to higher beauty ratings.

About 20 years after Hamermesh and Biddle's seminal article was published, another group of economists, tried to quantity how beauty contributes to your income. Specifically, they considered the effect of looks on income through the salary negotiation step. Due to the lack of available negotiation data from actual companies, they experimented with college students. The participants were divided into "workers" and "employers," and each worker was matched with five employers. All employers received a worker's resume. While some employers were not aware of how workers looked, others saw a passport-like photograph of a worker. Additionally, some employers performed either a blind or a face-to-face interview with the workers. The employers were then asked to estimate the worker's ability to solve maze puzzles, while the workers were given 15 minutes to solve as many puzzles as possible. Prior to the start of the experiment, workers were also asked to estimate how well they think they will perform and their guesses were later used as proxies for their confidence. The study found that physical attractiveness was positively correlated with confidence but had no effect on actual maze-solving performance. Furthermore, the authors discovered that for a given level of confidence, employers tended to overestimate the abilities of more attractive workers.[77]

Career advancement and income aren't determined solely by skills, education, or job performance. Biases stemming from the extent of social interactions between managers and their employees, as well as biases based on physical attractiveness, play an important role too. Ideally, awareness of these factors should help address them and foster a more meritocratic work environment. As we tell our students, on a practical level, this means that it doesn't hurt to look your best if you're aiming for a promotion. And, of course, it doesn't hurt to be polite to your manager.

CHAPTER SIX

HOUSING

For a while, home ownership has been an important part of the American dream. One survey found that when asked about what they associated with the American dream, three-quarters of the Americans cited home ownership, 62% mentioned a successful career, and 42% mentioned having children. Nevertheless, a recurring theme in the media about house prices is how unaffordable housing has become in recent years. This is often discussed in the context of the despair of younger generations, for whom buying a house became much more difficult compared to older groups like the baby boomers (people born between 1946 and 1964). Indeed, the same survey found that the most cited reasons for not owning a house (respondents could choose multiple options) were "Not enough income" (46%), "Prices are too high" (42%), and "Can't afford downpayment" (40%).[1]

6.1 Upward Trends

Looking at data confirms the perception shared by so many people today: real (adjusted for inflation) house prices have been steadily growing for the past 50 years. The median sale price for a single-family house in the 1980s was around $200,000 (measured in 2023 dollars) across the country. By 2020, the median price skyrocketed to nearly $400,000 in the Midwest and the South and nearly 600,000 in the West and the Northeast.

Figure 25. Real (inflation-adjusted) median sales price by region

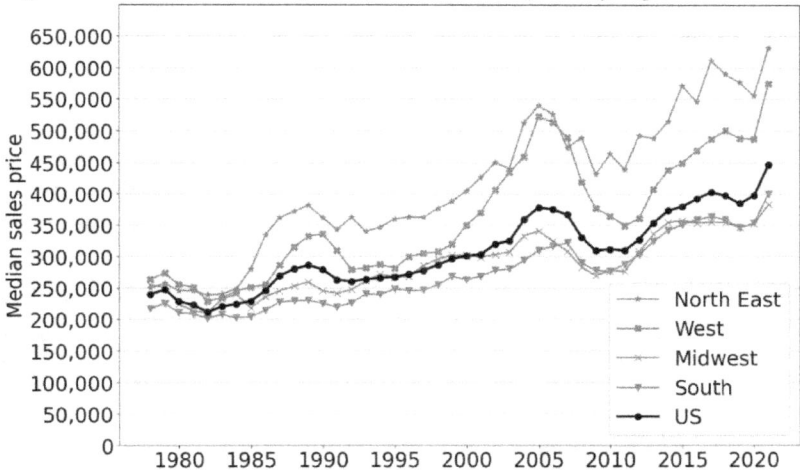

However, there is another upward trend that we should consider. In the 1980s, a median house sold in the United States had slightly more than 1,500 square feet of area. Four decades later, this number increased by nearly 1,000 square feet, a 67% increase. Yes, the American dream is becoming more expensive, but it's also becoming bigger.

Figure 26. Median square footage by region

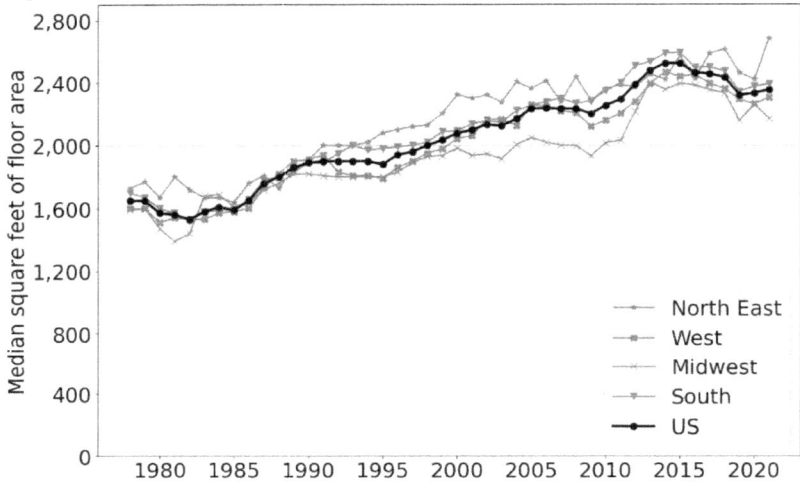

It's hard to say definitively why the houses got larger. Growth in real incomes could be one reason: wealthier Americans are able to afford larger houses.[a] Various land use regulations (like minimum requirements for lots and building sizes) are sometimes named as another reason. For example, in the city of Boston, between 1980 and 2002, an increase in lot size requirements by one acre was associated with a 40% decrease in the number of building permits, decreasing the housing supply and, hence, increasing the prices.[2] In cities like San Francisco and San Jose (both in California), zoning regulations were estimated to have increased house prices by about 50%.[3]

Given the median prices and median square footage, we may be inclined to divide one by the other to get the median price

---

[a] Remember from our discussion in the earlier chapter that even the poorest Americans today are wealthier than the poorest Americans 40 years ago. Even when adjusting for inflation.

per square foot. There is, however, a mathematical problem: a ratio of medians is not equal to the median of ratios.

Luckily for us, the Census Bureau also provides the data on median price per square foot, although it goes back only to 1992. We cannot be sure how the prices have changed compared to the 1970s. But we still have three decades of data available to us. From the graph, we notice that the price per square foot has been relatively stable for decades. There is, however, undoubtedly, an upward trend in the recent years.

Figure 27. Real median price per square foot by region

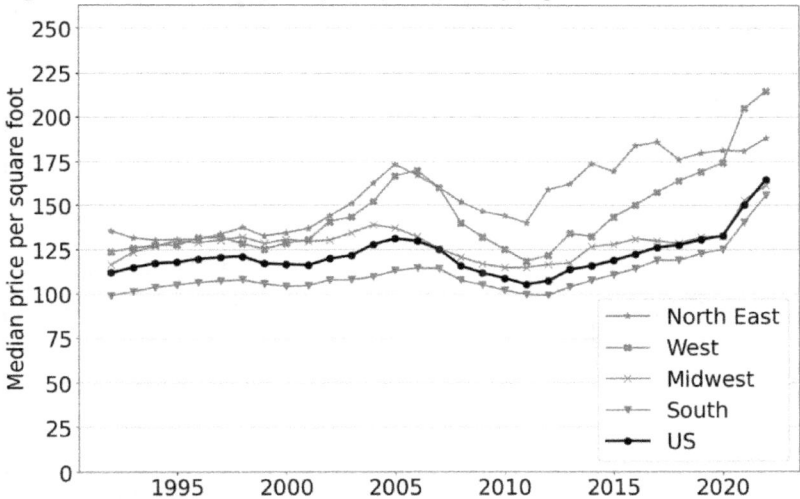

6.2 Prices Relative to Income

In 2000, economist Robbert Shiller, who in 2013 (jointly with two other economists) won the Nobel Memorial Prize in Economic Sciences, published his book *Irrational Exuberance*, in which he argued that the stock market was overvalued at the time. As we know now, the book was published at the peak of the dot-com bubble. The bubble burst the same year, and markets fell by almost 45% over the next two years. In the second edition of the book, published in 2005, Shiller argued that the housing market was overheated, with house prices at the time far exceeding median incomes and construction prices.[4,5] The second edition was published at the height of the housing bubble that ultimately led to the Great Recession a couple of years later.

What does the comparison of incomes and prices tell us about how affordable the houses are today? Let's look at how many yearly incomes it takes to buy a house. The graph below shows the ratio of median inflation-adjusted sale prices to median inflation-adjusted incomes across the country.

Figure 28. Real median sales price divided by real median income

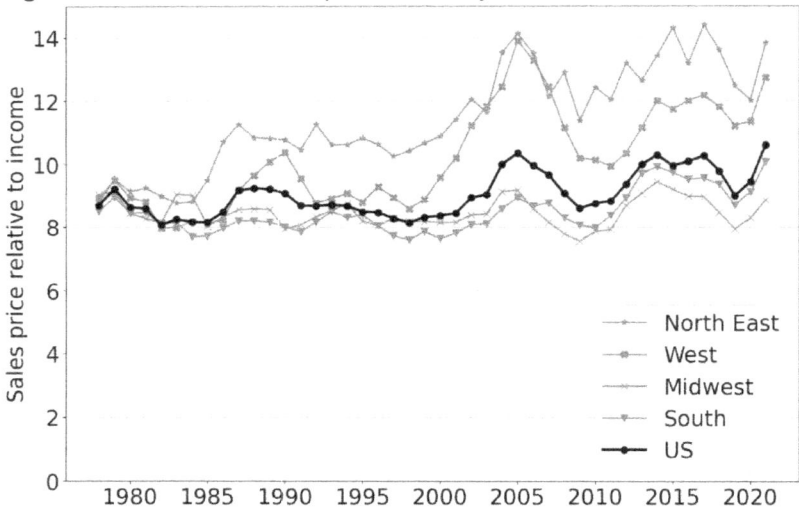

We can see that the market was overheated right before the subprime mortgage crisis of 2007-2010. In the Northeast and West regions, houses were being sold for as much as 14 times the median annual income. This ratio has again reached the

country-wide pre-Great Recession values by 2015. After a short drop during the COVID pandemic, the prices shot back up and, today, slightly exceed the pre-Great Recession values.

Does this imply the presence of another housing bubble on the verge of bursting? It's challenging to assert such a scenario based solely on this simple graph. It's important for the reader to exercise caution when encountering economic "experts" who make such predictions, even if their forecasts seem grounded in data. Professional economists are decent at forecasting recessions for the upcoming quarter, but their accuracy diminishes when projecting further into the future. [6] Furthermore, note that experts who make incorrect forecasts face no consequences. The motivation to predict an impending recession may outweigh the motivation to suggest a limited possibility of one. The former type of forecast generates interviews and recognition, while the latter may appear unexciting.

We can combine the previous two graphs and divide the price per square foot by the median income in each region. Doing so reveals the affordability by square foot, which looks to have been the same in the 1990s as it is today. Specifically, a square foot of a house used to cost slightly under 0.4% of the median salary in the 1990s. Three decades later, it still does not exceed 0.4%.

Figure 29. Real median price per sq ft as percent of real median income

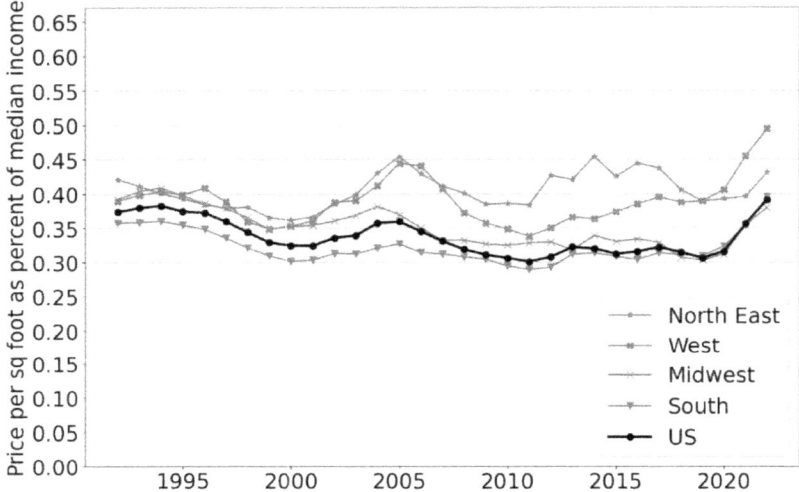

6.3 Affordability of Mortgage Payments

Of the 81 million owner-occupied housing units ("a house, an apartment, a mobile home, a group of rooms, or a single room that is occupied as separate living quarters"), 60% had a **mortgage** in 2022. [7] Several factors influence mortgage payments. One of the most significant factors is the interest rate, which determines the cost of borrowing money. As we learned earlier in the book, even a small difference in interest rates can significantly impact the total payments. The length of the loan term also plays a crucial role; while longer terms typically result in lower monthly payments, they ultimately lead to paying more in total due to accumulated interest.

Other factors affecting mortgage payments include the principal, property taxes, and insurance costs, which are often bundled into the monthly payment. The **principal** is the remaining loan amount after the downpayment is subtracted from the total purchase price. The **downpayment** is the initial amount a buyer pays upfront when purchasing a home. A larger downpayment reduces the principal, leading to smaller monthly mortgage payments and potentially lower interest costs over the life of the loan.

What should your downpayment be? A typical suggestion is around 20%. Over the last three decades, the average downpayment has ranged from 2% before the Great Recession to 25% in the early 2000s. [8] This means that the principal portion people were required to cover fell between 75% and 98%. Striving for a larger downpayment can help reduce your principal amount. Yet, it's vital to factor in potential unforeseen events, such as job loss, that could impact your ability to manage monthly payments. Collaborating with your loan officer to devise a comprehensive financial strategy tailored to your circumstances is crucial. Together, you can outline a plan that balances a substantial downpayment with maintaining a comfortable financial safety net for any unexpected challenges that may arise in the future.

Mortgages differ in how they charge interest. **Fixed-Rate Mortgages** offer borrowers a stable interest rate throughout the loan term, ensuring consistent monthly payments. In contrast, **Graduated Payment Mortgages** are structured to have increasing payments over time, which can be advantageous for young individuals anticipating income growth. On the other hand, **Adjustable-Rate Mortgages** (ARMs) start with lower initial rates that can fluctuate, leading to varying monthly payments. Notably, during the Great Recession, many individuals who held ARMs faced financial strain and foreclosure, as rising interest rates made their mortgage payments unmanageable.[9,10]

Are mortgage payments more or less affordable today? While houses are more expensive today than they were four decades ago (as we learned earlier, mainly because they are larger today), interest rates are much lower. How do these two factors compare in their effect on the mortgage payments?

There are various mortgage calculators available online, but you should be cautious about the assumptions each one makes. Generally, you will see the following fixed-rate mortgage payment formula:

$$Monthly\ Payment = Principal\ \frac{r(1+r)^n}{(1+r)^n - 1},$$

where $Principal$ is the amount borrowed, r is the interest rate, and n is the number of payments.

The graph below shows the estimated monthly mortgage payments as a percent of individual and household incomes. Even though house prices have been consistently rising, the estimated monthly mortgage payments have been decreasing over the past four decades. A big reason for this is that the 30-year fixed-rate mortgage interest rate average has decreased from 18% in 1980 to less than 3% in 2019. However, there is also a significant uptick in the share of mortgage payments as a percent of income in the early 2020s.

Figure 30. Estimated monthly mortgage payment as a percent of income

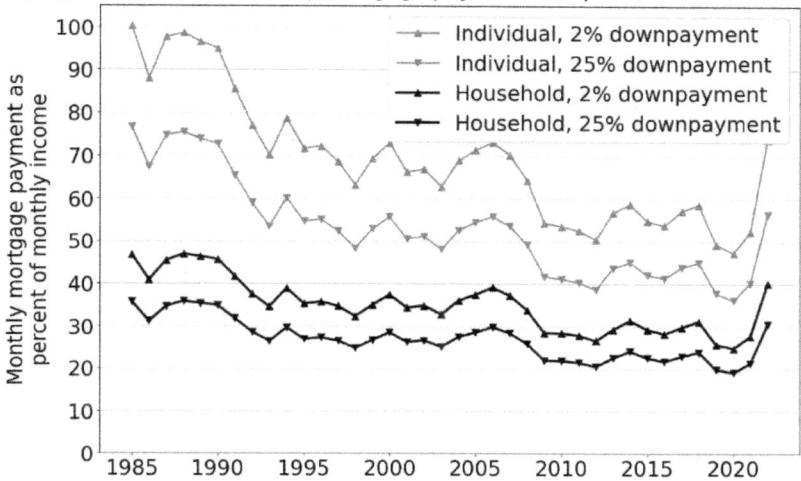

While these are just estimates, the Census data for recent years does confirm that they are somewhat reflective of actual costs. Specifically, for 70% of the housing units with a mortgage in 2022, monthly owner costs (mortgage, real estate taxes, property insurance, and utilities) were below 30% of the household income.[11]

6.4 Diverging from the Median: Minimum Wage

So far, our discussion of housing affordability has focused on median incomes. We should, however, also consider the housing affordability by the lowest earners. A piece of evidence suggested for the existence of the affordability crisis is that it's much more difficult today for minimum wage earners to afford a house. It's not uncommon for young people to express their frustration toward some representatives of the Baby Boomer generation who claim to have managed to put themselves through college, purchase homes, and support their families while earning minimum wages.

That frustration is not completely ungrounded. It's true that the minimum wage has not kept up with inflation. The federal minimum wage in 1978 was $2.90 per hour and the median price of a house in 1978 (unadjusted for inflation) was $55,700. That translates to 19,200 hours of work at the minimum wage required to buy a house. In 2023, the federal minimum wage was $7.25 and the median price of a house was $420,000, which translated to about 58,000 hours required to buy a house, triple the number of hours required in 1978. Thus, even taking into account the fact that houses today are larger than they were 40 years ago (remember, the houses sold today are 67% larger than the houses sold in 1978), the houses today are less affordable for minimum-wage workers.

Some may argue that the significance of minimum wage has changed. That, while it was an essential policy in the past to ensure a basic standard of living for workers, today it's mostly relevant for entry-level positions only. The graph below shows the share of minimum wage workers in the United States, which partially confirms that argument. The percentage of workers who earn minimum wage has decreased significantly over time. Over the past four decades, the share of workers earning minimum wage (out of all wage and salary workers) decreased from nearly 9% to less than 1%. A major reason for the decrease is that the federal minimum wage has not kept up with inflation. In addition, this statistic misses workers who earn only slightly more than minimum wage. According to a 2014 report, almost 30% of workers are paid wages that are below or equal to 150% of the minimum wage in their state.

Figure 31. Share of minimum wage workers

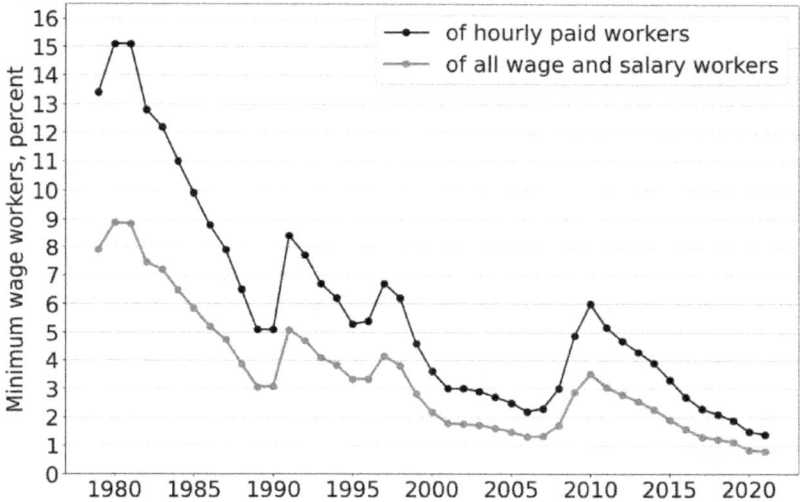

Thus, for around a third of American workers employed in near-minimum-wage positions, the affordability of a median-priced house has decreased significantly over the years. The number of hours required to purchase a home has nearly tripled since 1978, surpassing the growth in price per square foot.

6.5 Institutional Investors

One frequently expressed concern is that large corporations ("institutional investors") are purchasing homes and displacing ordinary individuals from the housing market. We know that institutional investors are playing a bigger role today than they used to. According to the National Association of Realtors (NAR), the share of institutional buyers in residential home purchases was 13.2% in 2021, up from 6% in the early 2000s.[12]

We would expect institutional investors to exert significant influence on the housing market due to their substantial market power. Unfortunately, there is little research or open data available that could help us assess the exact effects of institutional investors on house prices. We do know that making money in this market can be difficult. In 2021, Zillow cut its homebuying business laying off 25% of its workforce.[13] The following year, Redfin cut 13% of its workforce. A third of the laid-off employees worked at RedfinNow, the house-flipping arm of the company.[14] But we don't know much outside of that.

An interesting data point on the effects of market power on housing comes from the rental market. From the inflation chapter, we know that in the past three decades, rents have grown by 200%. Some of it is "natural" as landlords increase rent to cover their growing costs or face higher demand from renters. Not always, however, can the increases in rent be attributed to "honest" market forces.

Today, many landlords are using software that analyzes rental data and often recommends raising rents to maximize profits. These algorithms consider various details about the apartments to estimate how much landlords can charge. If only a handful of landlords used such algorithms to simply suggest prices, it would not necessarily have a negative effect on the housing market. In that case, the competition in the market should keep rents in check, as tenants would move from high-charging landlords to those with more reasonable prices.

However, the problem arises when a significant number of landlords start using these algorithmic pricing tools. When these algorithms become the primary price-setters in the market, they lead to concerning outcomes. In 2022, ProPublica published a report about the work of YieldStar, a software developed by the Texas-based company RealPage, which often recommended that landlords set higher rents. The ProPublica investigation found that in one Seattle neighborhood, 70% of apartments were managed by 10 property managers, all of whom used RealPage's software. Troublingly, the report revealed that RealPage's software advised landlords to accept lower occupancy rates (resulting from the higher rents) because the higher rents would compensate for the reduced occupancy. While apartment managers could reject the software's recommendations, nine out of 10 accepted them.[15]

Shortly after the ProPublica article was published, renters filed a lawsuit alleging that RealPage and the nation's biggest property managers had formed a cartel to inflate rent prices.[16] A year later, the U.S. Department of Justice backed the tenants suing RealPage, further increasing the legal pressure on the company.[17]

Several pieces of legislation have been proposed to make it more difficult for institutional investors to purchase houses. One recent proposal is the "End Hedge Fund Control of American Homes Act", introduced in 2023. This bill would impose a $20,000 federal tax penalty on each single-family home owned beyond 100 properties. Investors would be allowed to sell excess properties over several years, provided they sell at least 10% of their properties annually.[18] The "Stop Wall Street Landlords Act" of 2022 proposed, among other measures, to prevent institutional investors from claiming certain tax breaks, such as the mortgage interest deduction.[19] However, none of these acts became law as of 2024.

CHAPTER SEVEN

HEALTHCARE

Alec Smith was in search of an insurance plan as his birthday approached. He was about to reach the age of 26, which meant he could no longer remain on his mother's insurance. Having been diagnosed with diabetes a year earlier, Alec had to consider the cost of insulin when deciding on a suitable plan. Without insurance, the price of his insulin amounted to a staggering $1,300 per month. In his quest for alternatives, Alec came across an insurance plan, but it had a steep annual deductible of $7,600. This meant that in addition to the $450 monthly premium, Alec had to pay $7,600 out of pocket before his insurance coverage would begin. Faced with this overwhelming financial burden, he made the difficult decision to forgo insurance altogether, deeming it a more manageable option. His family thinks that because of the high cost, Alec decided to ration insulin. Less than a month after his 26th birthday, he passed away due to diabetic ketoacidosis, a severe complication of diabetes often caused by missing insulin doses.[1]

How could such an event happen in an advanced economy? A major reason for the exorbitant insulin prices can be attributed to the fact that three companies (U.S.-based Eli Lilly, Danish Novo Nordisk, and French Sanofi) control about 90% of the U.S. insulin market.[2] With little to no competition and lax regulatory oversight, prices are set at the mercy of these companies. Cases like Alec's and countless others have stirred up lawsuits. Eli Lilly is trying to settle the matter by proposing to pay $13 million in a settlement for a 2023 case. They also agreed to cap the out-of-pocket price of insulin to $35 per month for the next four years.[3] Their plans after four years remain unclear.

Let's look at the important aspects of the healthcare system in the United States, learn how healthcare insurance works, and try to answer why healthcare is so expensive in the U.S. The complexity of the U.S. healthcare system often leads to confusion and anxiety. This chapter aims to demystify healthcare-related concepts, providing a clearer picture of how the system functions. By breaking down these complex issues, we hope to equip readers with the knowledge to make informed decisions about their healthcare, understand their insurance options, and be able to critically assess proposed healthcare policies.

7.1 History of Health Insurance in the U.S.

A century and a half ago, hospitals were very different from what they are today. They were often places that provided care for the poor. Surgeries and most childbirths were often performed at home. [4] As medical technology advanced, healthcare costs began to rise. Hospitals also started positioning themselves as places for surgeries and childbirth. Though this seemed like a perfect scenario for introducing and growing the health insurance industry, hospitals were hesitant to fully adopt them.

In 1929, Baylor University Hospital started offering health insurance to teachers in Dallas. The insurance plan provided coverage for 21 days of hospital care, with teachers paying an annual fee of $6 (equivalent to around $110 in 2024). This approach helped mitigate negative selection (only individuals who are likely to get sick purchasing health insurance, a concept we'll discuss later) by attracting a pool of healthier individuals. These plans also promoted individual responsibilities, as patients could not admit themselves to the hospital.

The popularity of employer-sponsored health plans continued to grow and was further boosted in the 1940s following World War II. With unemployment at a record low of 1.2%, the government instituted wage controls to prevent employers from attracting scarce workers with higher salaries, which could have disrupted wartime production. To work around these limitations, companies began offering fringe benefits like health insurance. This trend was reinforced in 1943 when a tax ruling allowed employers to reduce their taxable income by deducting contributions to employee health plans.[5]

In the second half of the twentieth century, many policymakers started realizing that an employer-based market could not deliver healthcare to socially and economically vulnerable groups like the elderly, the poor, and disabled people. For the private insurance markets, this illness-prone population was a "bad risk." In 1965, President Lyndon Johnson signed the Social Security Amendments establishing Medicare and Medicaid. These programs provided health insurance for people 65 years old or older and people with low income, respectively.

In 1985, the Consolidated Omnibus Budget Reconciliation Act (COBRA) was passed, marking a development in health insurance continuation provisions for employees. COBRA mandates that group health plans provide a temporary continuation of health coverage at group rates for former employees in the event of job loss. Because the insurance rates are employer-negotiated, these rates are typically lower than those available on the open market.[6]

The Affordable Care Act was signed into law in 2010 with the goal of expanding access to healthcare, improving the quality of care, and reducing health care costs. The ACA provided health insurance subsidies, expanded Medicaid access to low income families, and mandated that insurance companies cover pre-existing conditions. The ACA is also the reason that young people like Alec Smith could remain on their parents' health insurance until the age of 26.

Finally, the ACA mandated the operation of state-based health insurance exchanges (also known as marketplaces), one-stop (online) shops where people can compare the benefits and prices of different plans and choose the option that best suits their needs. Health insurance plans in the marketplace are divided into different tiers: from the cheapest Bronze plan (where the insurance company covers approximately 60% of the costs) to the most expensive Platinum plan (where the insurance company covers approximately 90% of the costs). In 2023, the average monthly premium (amount you pay each month to maintain your health insurance coverage) for the Bronze plans across the country was $342, while the cheapest Platinum plans cost more than $700 per month. People under the age of 30 also have access to the Catastrophic plan, which is even cheaper and has lower coverage than the Bronze plan.

7.2 The U.S. Healthcare System

The United States healthcare system relies on a mix of private and public insurers and providers. The U.S. does not have universal health insurance coverage, with about 8% of the population (28 million people) being uninsured. Of those with health insurance in 2021, approximately half had employer-provided insurance, 19% had Medicaid (covers low-income families, the blind, and individuals with disabilities), 18% had Medicare (covers people over the age of 65 and some individuals under age 65 with long-term disabilities; only 15% of Medicare beneficiaries are under 65), 10% purchased insurance on their own, and approximately 5% had insurance received from military service or through a family member who served. [7] Some children are also covered by the Children's Health Insurance Program if they come from families that earn too much to make them eligible for Medicaid but not enough to afford private insurance.

Health insurance operates similarly to other types of insurance like car insurance. Individuals (and families) pay regular payments (premiums) to an insurance company, which then assumes the responsibility of covering a portion or the entirety of their healthcare costs. Unlike car insurance, health insurance comes with some unfamiliar terms, and understanding them is important for making informed decisions about your healthcare.

- *Deductible*: This is the amount of money you have to pay before your insurance starts covering costs. For example, if you have a $2,000 deductible and receive medical care that costs $10,000, you would need to pay the first $2,000 out of your pocket, and then your insurance would cover part of or the full amount of the remaining $8,000. In 2022, the average annual deductible for employer-based health insurance was around $2,000. [8] The average deductible for

Bronze plans in the marketplace can go as high as $7,000, while the average deductible for Platinum plans is under $100.[9]

- *Copayment*: A copay is a fixed amount you pay for a specific healthcare service. For instance, you may have a $25 copay for doctor visits. This means that each time you visit the doctor, you would pay $25. The average copayment for an office visit to a physician is under $30. The average copayment for a hospital admission is about $320 per day. Generally, copayments don't count toward deductibles.

- *Coinsurance*: Coinsurance is the percentage of costs you're responsible for after meeting your deductible. For example, if your coinsurance is 20% and you've already paid your deductible, you would pay 20% of the cost for a covered service, while your insurance would cover the remaining 80%. The average coinsurance for an office visit to a physician and a hospital stay is around 20%.

- *Out-of-pocket maximum:* This is the maximum amount you will have to pay in a given year for covered services. Once you reach this limit, your insurance will typically cover all remaining eligible expenses for the rest of the year. The average out-of-pocket maximum for single enrollees is about $4,600.

- *Network*: Insurance plans often have a network of preferred doctors, hospitals, and other healthcare providers. Staying within the network usually results in lower out-of-pocket costs. Going outside the network may result in higher expenses or limited coverage.

Let's break down how much you would pay for a healthcare service that costs $6,000, given an annual deductible of $2,000, a coinsurance of 20%, and a maximum out-of-pocket limit of $5,000. Additionally, let's assume that there's a $30 copay for the service, which does not count toward your deductible.

Table 24. Insurance payments

Stage	You pay	Insurance pays	Amount remaining
Initial amount			$6,030
Copay	$30		$6,000
Deductible	$2,000		$4,000
Coinsurance	20% of $4,000 = $800	$3,200	$0

First, you're responsible for paying the $2,000 deductible. After meeting the deductible, your insurance begins to share the cost and covers 80% of the remaining $4,000, which totals $3,200. You're then left to pay the remaining 20% or $800. Your total payment for this service would be the sum of your deductible, coinsurance, and copay, which is $2,000 (deductible) + $800 (coinsurance) + $30 (copay) = $2,830. Thus, thanks to your insurance, you're paying less than half the billed amount. If your salary is around the national median (approximately $42,000 per year), this represents 7% of your annual income.

7.3 Healthcare Costs in the U.S.

In 2021, spending on healthcare in the U.S. amounted to $4.3 trillion or 18.3% of GDP.[10] In 1960, that number was only 5%. The current number is higher when compared to other peer nations too. For example, France, Germany, Japan, and Canada spend only around 11% of their GDP on healthcare. In 2019, 86% of the U.S. adult civilian population (those who were 16 years and older, not serving in the Armed Forces, and not residing in penal or mental institutions or senior care homes; approximately 260 million individuals) incurred some level of personal healthcare expenses. [11] The total of these expenses was a staggering $2.4 trillion when adjusted to 2023 dollars.

The importance of having insurance cannot be overstated. Without it, individuals risk facing the full burden of these potentially exorbitant costs on their own. In the table below, we can see a negative relationship between the size of the average bill and the percent paid out-of-pocket. As the size of the bill increases, the percentage paid out-of-pocket tends to decrease. This is often due to the out-of-pocket maximums. These limits ensure that individuals won't be burdened with excessively high out-of-pocket expenses, even if the bill size is substantial. For the majority of people, health expenditures are very modest. A smaller percentage of people bore a disproportionately larger share of the healthcare expenses. Roughly 5% of the population had healthcare costs exceeding $31,000, with the average bill for this group reaching $72,000. This small group was responsible for more than $1.1 trillion in healthcare costs, which is nearly half of all expenses. Although a bill totaling almost twice the national median income may sound ridiculous, only 7.3% of this amount was paid out of pocket, and the majority of these costs were covered by private insurance, Medicare, and Medicaid.

Table 25. Average medical bill vs out-of-pocket expenses

	Average bill, 2023 dollars	Percent paid out-of-pocket
Overall	7,400	13.3
Bottom 50%	440	26.7
Top 50%	14,400	12.8
Top 5%	72,400	7.3

Note that the numbers above omit people like Alec who could not spend any money on doctor visits or medication. We are missing many people who "choose" not to get medical help when they need it. In a 2018 survey, almost a third of Americans admitted that in the previous year, they either didn't fill a prescribed medication or took less than the prescribed dose.[12] The same survey revealed that 44% didn't visit a doctor when they fell ill due to high healthcare costs. While a third of Americans are afraid of contracting a severe illness, a larger portion (40%) fear the medical bills that such an illness would likely bring. That is, many Americans are more worried about the steep cost of treatment than the illness itself.

7.4 Why is Healthcare So Expensive?

There is no shortage of solutions proposed to curb healthcare costs. Unfortunately, discussing the advantages and disadvantages of each of the numerous proposals would likely take a book of its own. To limit our scope, we'll only focus on the economics behind growing healthcare costs. We believe this should help the reader understand the merits and shortcomings of any solutions proposed by lawmakers.

Market structure

The healthcare industry operates differently from the perfectly competitive market of local bakers that we described earlier in the book. The healthcare industry has a high **market concentration**, which measures the extent to which a market is dominated by a few large firms. The Herfindahl-Hirschman index (HHI) is a commonly used tool to assess market concentration. For an industry represented by N firms, it's calculated by adding squares of shares of each of the N firms:

$$HHI = (share_{Firm\,1})^2 + (share_{Firm\,2})^2 + \cdots + (share_{Firm\,N})^2$$

For example, if an industry consists of three firms with shares of 50%, 30%, and 20%, the HHI is 3,800.

$$HHI = 50^2 + 30^2 + 20^2 = 3,800$$

If two of the largest firms by market share merge (the largest firm, thus, having 80% market share), the HHI index increases to 6,800.

$$HHI = (50 + 30)^2 + 20^2 = 6,800$$

Thus, if there is only one firm, the HHI of the industry is 10,000.

$$HHI = 100^2 = 10,000$$

On the other hand, if there are a lot of small firms, the HHI index gets relatively close to 0. For example, if there are 1000 firms, each with 0.1% of the market share, the HHI index is 10.[a]

$$HHI = 0.1^2 + \cdots + 0.1^2 = 0.01 + \cdots + 0.01 = 10$$

The U.S. Department of Justice uses the HHI to evaluate market concentration. HHIs between 1,500 and 2,500 points indicate moderate concentration. Values exceeding 2,500 points suggest high concentration. Estimated HHIs for primary care physicians range between 2,000 and 2,500. The HHI for insurers is slightly below 3,000. Hospitals exhibit significant market concentration, with HHIs exceeding 5,500 in some estimates.[13]

High market concentration lets hospitals dictate their prices. Medicare reimbursement rates for services are standardized and set by federal regulation. In contrast, private insurers negotiate individualized rates with each hospital based on local market dynamics. This frequently results in payments to hospitals that are approximately double the Medicare rates for equivalent services. Studies show that, on average, private insurers pay 199% (twice the amount) of Medicare rates for hospital services and 143% of Medicare rates for physician services.[14]

Lack of price transparency

Price transparency is critical in perfectly competitive markets. When shopping for a loaf of bread at the farmer's market, you can compare prices across different sellers. When prices are clearly visible, buyers and sellers can make informed decisions. With transparent pricing, buyers can compare offerings to find the best deal. If a seller sets prices too high, buyers will purchase from a competitor. This pushes sellers to set the same,

---

[a] Sometimes, economist only focus on the largest N companies, when calculating such indexes. In such cases, the value of N could be anything from four all the way to (and even more than) 50.

or similar price. Likewise, sellers can easily monitor the going price of their product. If profits are strong, new sellers will enter to compete, increasing supply and lowering prices.

Unfortunately, consumers are often uninformed about the costs of medical treatments in advance, leaving them with little or no ability to compare prices. Just as high charges for medical bills can be shocking, it's also unfortunate when the fear of high bills, caused by lack of price transparency, prevents someone from seeking medical help.

Steps toward better price transparency are already being undertaken. Since 2021, every hospital in the United States is required to provide clear prices on their services online. Hospitals can be charged a monetary penalty, which can be pretty hefty depending on the hospital's capacity and the number of days that the hospital was found to be non-compliant after the initial warning. For example, in 2023, the Centers for Medicare and Medicaid Services imposed a penalty of $979,000 on the UF Health North medical center in Florida.[15] Starting in 2022, similar rules went into effect for health insurance companies. These companies also have to publish the prices they are paying for hospital care, outpatient centers, and physician services. And, just like hospitals, they can be fined for non-compliance.

Effective January 1, 2022, the No Surprises Act provides protection against surprise billing. **Surprise billing** is an unexpected bill for services from a healthcare provider or facility that was out-of-network, which you did not realize you were going to pay until you got the bill. Your health insurance may not cover the full cost of out-of-network care, leaving you to pay the remainder. In 2017, roughly one-fifth of emergency room visits and one-sixth of in-network hospital stays had at least one out-of-network charge. If you have group or individual health insurance, the Act protects you by prohibiting:

- Surprise bills for emergency services from out-of-network providers without prior approval
- Out-of-network cost-sharing, like coinsurance or copayments, for emergency and some non-emergency services
- Out-of-network charges for supplemental care like radiology or anesthesiology provided by out-of-network providers at an in-network facility

Ground ambulances aren't covered under the No Surprises Act, though air ambulances are. As a result, even insured patients can face exorbitant charges for ambulance rides due to surprise billing. This is a major concern given the prevalence of ambulance use in emergencies when patients have little control over the provider. In 2018 alone, ground ambulances transported three million privately insured individuals. Over half of emergency transports and 40% of non-emergency transports resulted in out-of-network charges. Approximately 10% of emergency room visits for the privately insured involve an ambulance ride.[16]

Administrative fees

In the United States, healthcare administration accounts for the largest portion of medical spending. Roughly one-third of healthcare dollars are spent on administrative costs, much higher than what countries like Canada spend. Part of the reason is that in the U.S., hospitals have to juggle requirements and claims forms used by multiple insurers. Engaging with multiple insurance providers who have different fee structures, deductibles, prior-approval criteria, formularies, and referral networks, along with patients frequently switching between insurers, contributes to increased overhead costs for physicians in the United States. Consequently, physicians must charge higher fees. In contrast, Canadian physicians submit bills to a single insurer, all hospitals and physicians are considered "in-network," and copayments and deductibles are strictly regulated. The key to reducing administrative expenses is not necessarily switching to a Canada-style single-insurer system. In countries like Germany and Switzerland, which have multiple payers and private providers, administrative costs are less than half of what they are in the United States. What the U.S. system lacks is the standardization of medical records. Despite the prevalence of electronic medical records in most hospitals, sending medical records electronically from one hospital to another remains a significant challenge due to the absence of federal requirements for interoperability. Some healthcare providers are even said to intentionally avoid electronic interchange to prevent patients from switching doctors.[17,18]

Baumol effect and doctor fees

Economists also attribute the rising costs in the healthcare industry to the Baumol effect (or Baumol's cost disease). The **Baumol effect** refers to the phenomenon of costs increasing in industries where labor productivity has not improved as rapidly as in other sectors. In their 1965 paper, economists William Baumol and William Bowen highlighted the performing arts industry as an example where technological advancements have had a limited impact on labor productivity. The output produced by a violinist, for instance, remains relatively fixed over time. Regardless of technological advancements, a composition written for a quartet of violins will always require four violinists. To attract talented artists and remain competitive, the performing arts industry must offer wages comparable to those in other sectors. However, since the output per worker has remained stable, the overall costs in the performing arts industry have continued to rise. In other words, the cost per violinist increased over the past 200 years, yet the requirement of having four violinists in a quartet remains unchanged. In fact, economists do find some evidence that the Baumol effect is responsible for part of the increase in healthcare costs in the U.S.[19,20,21]

The dark side of generous insurance

The fundamental purpose of insurance, as a business, is to reduce financial uncertainty by spreading risk across a group of people. The more people sign up, the better. Then, when only a few people get sick, health insurance companies can pay for their treatment and still have enough money to operate. Two significant problems the hospitals of the early twentieth century perceived about health insurance were adverse selection and moral hazard.

Adverse selection refers to situations where buyers and sellers have asymmetric (unequal) information. Consider the case of comprehensive car insurance. People who are more likely to make claims or have a higher risk of accidents are the ones who choose to purchase the insurance. This can happen when people have prior knowledge about their higher risk, such as a history of accidents or living in an area with high rates of car theft or vandalism. In the context of health insurance, adverse selection occurs when individuals with existing health issues are the only ones who purchase insurance and subsequently utilize its benefits.

Moral hazard is the risk that an individual will engage in risky behavior because they are protected from the consequences of their actions. For example, if you only have liability car insurance (which only pays for the other driver's expenses in the event of a car accident), you may be more careful about where you park your car because you would not want damage done to your car while you're away. On the other hand, if you have comprehensive insurance, you may become less careful about where you park your car and expose it to a higher risk, because you know that your insurance will cover the cost of repairs. In the context of health insurance, moral hazard refers to the consumption of more medical services as a result of purchasing the insurance.

Health insurance is good because it makes medical procedures more affordable. But lower prices also encourage bigger consumption. In the 1970s and 1980s, economists at the RAND Corporation think tank ran a large study trying to figure out how lower healthcare costs might affect utilization and health outcomes. Participants were divided into four groups: one received free care, the second paid 25% of costs, the third paid 50%, and the fourth paid 95%. As expected, patients who paid more for care used fewer services than those receiving free care.[22]

Hospitals also have incentives to provide unnecessary services due to the predominant fee-for-service payment model, and patients may accept them due to their limited professional knowledge and the relatively low cost of services when covered by insurance. Hospitals are paid based on quantity rather than quality of care. In 2021, over 40% of healthcare payments were fee-for-service with no link to value.[23] Consequently, we find ourselves in a situation where doctors have financial motivation to provide more services. One study estimates that the expansion of health insurance between 1950 and 1990 contributed to around half of the increase in per capita healthcare spending during that period.[24]

Increasing incomes and longer lives

Part of the increase in expenditures on healthcare is natural and is an indicator of a flourishing economy. The richer people become, the more they can afford to spend on healthcare. With access to better healthcare, people live longer. Between 1970 and 2018, the real incomes of high-income households increased by nearly 70%, while the real incomes of low-income households increased by still impressive 45%.[25] At the same time, life expectancy at birth in the United States has increased slightly, from under 74 years to nearly 76 years. In 2019, it actually reached 79 years but later decreased during the COVID-19 pandemic.[26]

With increased longevity comes a higher likelihood of encountering health issues and the need for ongoing medical care. Individuals may require sustained treatments and management of chronic conditions over an extended period. Of the people who spent more than $31,000 on healthcare in 2019, the largest share (nearly 41%) were people over the age of 65. Thus, as people receive better healthcare and live longer, they naturally tend to spend more on healthcare throughout their extended lifetimes.

We can see a correlation between healthcare spending and life expectancy when comparing data across countries.[27] The graph below illustrates a generally positive relationship between spending on healthcare and life expectancy. Labeled are the 10 countries with the highest healthcare spending as a percentage of GDP. The United States is among this group, spending a similar proportion of GDP on healthcare as Afghanistan, Armenia, Lesotho, and a few small island nations in the Pacific. The size of the circles represents each country's GDP per capita, with larger circles indicating higher GDP per capita. Switzerland and Germany are two other high-income countries that rank among the top healthcare spenders. However, both have notably higher life expectancies than the United States. In fact, the U.S. is the only country with high GDP per capita that falls below the 80-year mark for life expectancy.

Figure 32. Life expectancy and health expenditures around the world

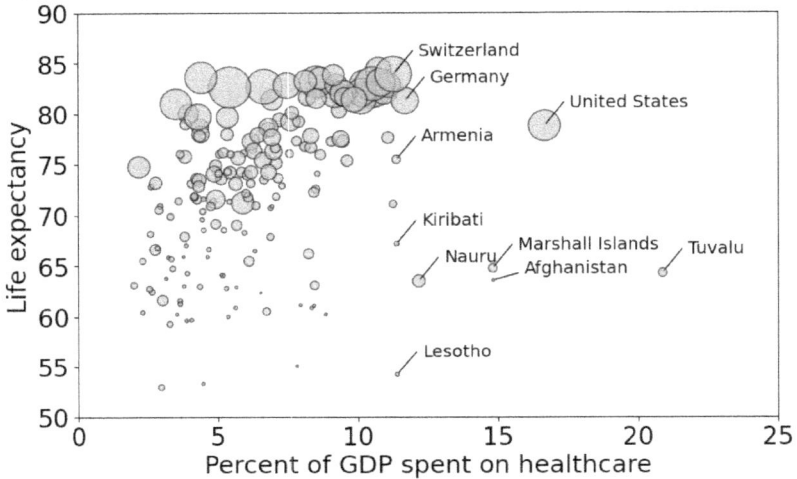

The plot below shows the evolution of healthcare spending and life expectancy over the past four decades in some of the rich countries. The left ends of the arrows represent the data for 1980, while the right ends (arrow tips) represent the data for 2019. All of these countries, including the global trend, witnessed a positive correlation between increased life expectancy and higher healthcare spending. Greater spending resulted in longer lives, and longer lives, in turn, led to higher healthcare expenditures.

Figure 33. Changes in life expectancy and health expenditures, 1980–2019

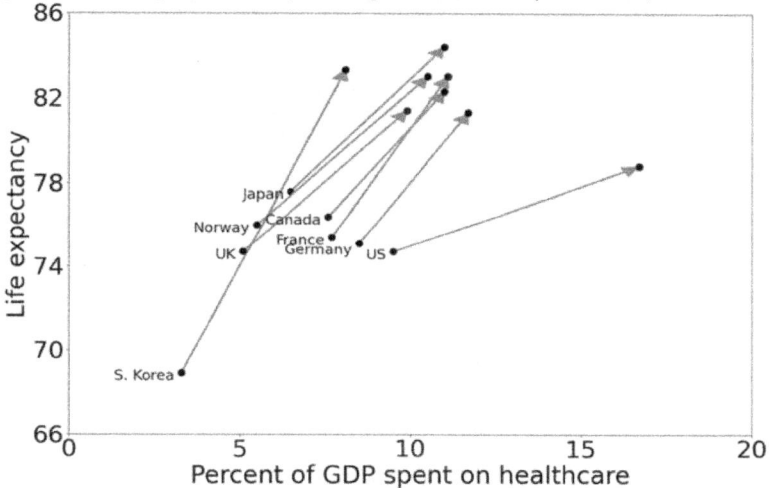

South Korea appears as an outlier on this graph. The country experienced tremendous economic growth in the second half of the twentieth century. We observe that life expectancy in South Korea soared from 69 to 83 years. However, this came at the cost of doubling healthcare expenditures from 5.5% to 10.5%. Many other affluent countries also witnessed an increase in life expectancy, surpassing 80 years, when their healthcare spending reached double digits.

The United States also appears as an outlier on this graph, but not in a positive manner. In 1985, the U.S. was already spending more on healthcare compared to other affluent countries, although its life expectancy was not too unfavorable. Over the next 35 years, healthcare spending in the U.S. increased to more than 15%. However, life expectancy did not surpass 80 years, as it did in other countries. Consequently, for every 1% increase in healthcare spending, the U.S. only gained 7 months in life expectancy. In comparison, the UK, which had a very similar life expectancy in the 1980s, gained more than twice as much in life expectancy.

Table 26. Years gained for a percent of healthcare spending (1985—2019)

Country	Years gained
S. Korea	3.00
France	2.24
New Zealand	1.98
Germany	1.94
Australia	1.80
Sweden	1.78
Switzerland	1.75
Canada	1.74
Netherlands	1.58
Japan	1.51
Norway	1.40
UK	1.40
US	0.57

7.5 Concerns Related to Universal Healthcare

Despite what some may believe, in countries with so called "socialized" medicine, not all healthcare costs are picked up by the government. That being said, governments in such countries do play a more significant role in the health industry. For example, in France, a country where 99% of residents have baseline coverage, government insurance covers 80% of hospitalization costs, 70% of doctor consultation fees, and 55% of transportation fees. That is, a doctor consultation, which costs 25 euros (less than 27 USD as of 2024), would result in an out-of-pocket expense of 8 euros for the patient after factoring in the 70% coverage.[28]

However, in addition to the baseline coverage, 96% of the French population also has voluntary health insurance, commonly referred to as "mutuelle." [29, 30] This additional insurance typically costs between 30 to 100 euros per month ($400 to $1,300 per year) and is used to cover the remaining costs not covered by the government insurance.

A common concern about the U.S. adopting a healthcare system similar to the ones in other rich countries is that the quality of care could diminish under a "universal healthcare system." The argument is that the competitive nature of private healthcare is a driver for innovation and quality improvements. Thus, the U.S. remains the only rich country that doesn't have universal health coverage.[31] However, many countries that are considered as having universal healthcare have consistently high standards of care as well. But how does their quality of care compare against healthcare in the United States?

One particular concern about universal healthcare is the long wait times that supposedly persist in countries with universal healthcare. Data show that the wait times for Americans for some services are indeed better than in some of the other rich countries. For example, in 2016, the share of people waiting one month or more for a specialist appointment in the United States was 27%. This number was smaller for the Netherlands (25%), Germany (25%), and Switzerland (23%). But it was way larger for Canada and Norway (each standing at 61%), Sweden (52%), New Zealand (48%), United Kingdom (41%), Australia (39%), and France (36%).[32]

In 2017, the Canadian Institute for Health Information produced a report comparing healthcare quality across 11 wealthy countries. Data on various measures of wait time are shown in the table below. For the first two categories, the U.S. is located in the middle of the distribution. On the bright side, for the remaining two categories, the numbers for the U.S. are lower than the median across countries. The following are the measures presented in each column:

(a) Percent of survey respondents who said it was very/somewhat easy to get medical care in the evenings, on weekends, or on holidays without going to the hospital emergency department.

(b) Percent of emergency department patients who reported waiting four or more hours.

(c) Percent of patients who waited four weeks or longer to see a specialist after they were advised or decided to see one in the last two years.

(d) Patients who waited four months or longer for elective surgery in the last two years.[33]

Table 27. Healthcare quality indicators across rich countries

Country	(a)	(b)	(c)	(d)
United States	42	11	24	3
Australia	29	10	35	8
Canda	34	29	56	18
France	35	1	36	2
Germany	36	3	25	0
Netherlands	72	4	23	4
New Zealand	53	10	44	15
Norway	49	13	52	15
Sweden	24	20	42	12
Switzerland	41	7	22	6
United Kingdom	43	8	37	12
Median	*41*	*10*	*36*	*8*

Despite seemingly encouraging results, the U.S. healthcare system still fares worse than the systems of other rich countries. In a 2021 analysis of the same 11 countries, prepared by the Commonwealth Fund, the U.S. scored the lowest in

- *Access to care*: Affordability and how quickly patients can obtain information, make appointments, and obtain urgent care after hours.

- *Administrative efficiency*: Time and effort spent dealing with paperwork.

- *Equity*: Performance for higher- and lower-income individuals.

- *Care outcomes*: 10 measures of health besides life expectancy at birth.

To be fair, the U.S. did place second in the category of "care process," which included the subdomains of preventive care (mammography screening, vaccination rates, rates of avoidable hospital admissions for prevalent chronic conditions), safe care (rates of medical and laboratory mistakes), and engagement and patient preferences (13 measures around the delivery of care and clinician-patient communication).[34]

In conclusion, while the current U.S. healthcare system performs well in certain areas, such as specialist or elective surgery wait times and care process, it is generally either on par with or lags behind the healthcare systems of other wealthy nations in key measures like access to medical care after hours, emergency department wait times, affordability, amount of paperwork, access for low-income individuals, and overall health outcomes.

CHAPTER EIGHT

TAXES AND PUBLIC DEBT

On September 29, 2010, a fire engulfed the home of Paulette and Gene Cranick in rural Tennessee. The blaze was started by the couple's grandson in a backyard burn barrel but slowly spread from there to a nearby shed and then to the house. The Cranicks called 911 for help, but the fire department refused to assist in putting out the flames. Obion County, in which the house was located, did not provide county-wide firefighting services. Instead, rural residents had to rely on the fire department in the nearby city of South Fulton, but only if they paid an annual fee of $75. As it happened, the Cranicks had forgotten to pay the fee for that year. Although the firefighters arrived to contain the fire before it reached the property of a neighbor who had paid the fee, they allowed the flames to consume the Cranicks' house. In the fire, the family lost their house, as well as three dogs and a cat.

The story garnered significant media attention. Some, including the Cranicks' neighbors who offered the firefighters thousands of dollars to extinguish the blaze, expressed outrage. Others viewed this as a case of market forces at play: the Cranicks simply did not receive a service for which they had not paid. The immense media coverage, however, compelled the local government to alter the policy. Beginning in March 2012, residents who had not paid the $75 fee but called upon the fire department would be charged $3,500 per call.[1,2,3,4]

Despite what three-quarters of Americans believe, firefighter services aren't always free to you.[5] For example, if you get into an accident on the road and a firetruck gets called, you may be charged a "crash tax." While medical insurance covers your health expenses and car insurance pays for your car damage, you would have to pay the crash tax yourself. These fees are a way for local governments to raise money for their services without raising taxes. The practice of charging crash taxes became more prevalent in the early 2010s when cash-strapped local governments struggled to support their operations through taxes in the wake of the Great Recession.

Why do we pay taxes, and where do our tax dollars go?

8.1 The Need for Taxes

Article 1 of the U.S. Constitution grants the government power to collect taxes "to pay the Debts and provide for the common Defense and general Welfare of the United States." Thus, the intended reason for tax collection is to fund operations that are beneficial to the people of the United States. Some examples of these operations include education, scientific research, infrastructure, and military defense.

Why can't private markets provide these services? There are certain areas where they may not be able to fully address societal needs and achieve "socially optimal" outcomes. Some goods and services have characteristics that make it difficult for private markets to supply efficiently. Public goods, such as national defense, clean air, and law enforcement, are **non-excludable** and **non-rivalrous**. This means that it's difficult to exclude others from benefiting or using the good, and one person's consumption does not reduce the availability to others. Think of a civil defense (tornado) siren. Once a siren is activated, it's difficult to exclude individuals within its range from hearing the warning. At the same time, the use of a siren by one person (hearing the warning sound) does not reduce its availability or effectiveness for others in the community. Private markets tend to underprovide public goods because individuals have an incentive to "free-ride," enjoying the benefits without contributing their fair share. How can a private firm provide a siren warning just to people who paid for it? If you can hear the siren without paying for it, why would anyone pay for it? This concept extends to many other public goods and services. National security benefits all citizens, regardless of whether they contributed to its funding. It's impractical to protect only those who paid for the police protection service while ignoring crimes against non-payers in the same neighborhood. Efforts to reduce air pollution benefit everyone in an area, not just those who pay for pollution control measures.

Another reason for governments to impose taxes is to address externalities. **Negative externalities** occur when the actions of someone, like a business or individual, have uncompensated harmful impacts on other people or the environment. The rationale behind imposing taxes on things that generate negative externalities is to make them more expensive. Taxing harmful activities (or products) can reduce their consumption (or production) and mitigate the negative societal impacts. When people drive their cars, they usually only think about the immediate costs they encounter, such as the price of gasoline. They fill up their tanks regularly, and that's the expense they are directly aware of. They may not consider the negative consequences on the environment and public health because they don't directly pay for these costs. The social cost of air pollution caused by cars is higher than the private cost borne by individual drivers. Society as a whole has to deal with the adverse effects of pollution, such as increased healthcare expenses due to respiratory illnesses, damage to ecosystems, and the need for environmental remediation.

The negative effects of externalities don't have to be as material as health impacts. Visual or aesthetic impacts, like the haze ruining scenic views at the Grand Canyon, are negative externalities too. In September 1991, President George H.W. Bush introduced regulations aimed at reducing air pollution in the Grand Canyon. A coal-fired plant located near the canyon was required to install pollution-reducing equipment to eliminate the haze that was obstructing the views from within the canyon.

The government can allocate the funds it has raised toward activities that generate **positive externalities** (beneficial spillover effects). These activities include areas such as education, research, and public transportation. Similar to negative externalities, when the unintended consequences of an activity extend to third parties who aren't directly involved in the market transaction, the market may not adequately factor in these positive external effects. For example, individuals with higher levels of education often secure higher-paying jobs, which not only benefit them personally but also have positive spillover effects on the economy as a whole. These effects can include increased tax revenues, reduced dependence on social welfare programs, and a more skilled and productive workforce that drives innovation and economic growth. However, private markets may not fully account for these positive externalities, as the benefits extend beyond the immediate transaction and aren't captured in the price of education.

Sin taxes are taxes that target goods and behaviors considered undesirable or harmful. These include taxes on products like alcohol, tobacco, gambling, and sugary drinks. The rationale behind sin taxes is twofold—to discourage overconsumption of these potentially addictive or unhealthy products (by making them more expensive), and to raise revenue that can be used to fund public health initiatives, education, or other programs that address the societal costs associated with their use.

8.2 How Much We Pay

Businesses and individuals making money in the United States have to pay part of the money they make to the government in the form of an income tax. The federal personal income tax was established in 1913 with the adoption of the Sixteenth Amendment, which gave Congress the power to tax income. Since then, income tax has become a major source of revenue for the federal government. Income taxes are also collected by state governments. As of 2024, only nine states (Alaska, Florida, Nevada, New Hampshire, South Dakota, Tennessee, Texas, Washington, and Wyoming) don't have individual income tax.

The United States utilizes a progressive tax system, which means that the income tax rate increases as a person's income rises.[a] Imagine Alice, who made $60,000 in taxable income in a given year. To simplify the explanation, we'll come up with tax rates that are easy to work with. Say the taxes are 10% on income from $0 to $50,000 and 20% on income above $50,000. That is, for the first $50,000 of Alice's income, the tax rate is

---

[a] Individuals pay income taxes based on their gross income (total amount of money they made from wages, rents, interest payments, and other sources) minus various adjustments to income and deductions.

10%. Therefore, the tax Alice owed on this portion is $5,000. For the remaining $10,000 of income, the tax rate is 20%. That is an additional $2,000 in taxes. So, in total, Alice owed $7,000 in taxes.

A rather common misconception is that the progressive tax system means that earning more money can result in paying higher taxes and bringing home less income overall. The higher tax rate only applies to the income within that specific tax bracket. In our example, Alice does not have to pay 20% on the entire $60,000. The 20% rate only applies to the portion above $50,000.

For a better understanding of how much people are paying in taxes, we often calculate the **effective tax rate**, which is the share of your income that you pay in taxes. In the example above, the effective tax rate is 11.67%.

$$\frac{7,000}{60,000} * 100\% = 11.67\%$$

In 2020, the effective federal tax rate in the U.S. was 0.2% for people whose **Adjusted Gross Income** (AGI) was $15,000 or less, 4.3% for people with AGI between $30,000 and $50,000, and 26% for people with AGI above $5 million. At the same time, more than five million people did not owe any taxes because their AGI was zero. AGI is the total income from wages, rents, and other sources minus adjustments (more about them in a moment) like retirement plan contributions.[6]

A tax deduction lets you reduce your taxable income. Recall Alice, who made $60,000. With the tax rates we described earlier, we know that Alice is supposed to pay $7,000 in taxes. Suppose Alice qualifies for a $5,000 deduction. Then, Alice's taxable income would be reduced to $55,000. Using the same 10% and 20% progressive tax rate, Alice would now owe $6,000 in taxes instead of $7,000.

The U.S. government allows taxpayers to choose between a standard deduction and itemized deductions. The **standard deduction** is a fixed amount (in 2023, $13,850 for single filers), while itemizing involves listing specific expenses to reduce taxable income. Common **itemized deductions** include mortgage interest, charitable contributions, student loan interest, gambling losses, and many other categories.[7,8,9]

Another common misconception is that receiving a higher income automatically leads to owing taxes come tax season. Whether you owe taxes or receive a refund primarily depends on how much you have already paid in taxes throughout the year through payroll deductions. If your employer has withheld an appropriate amount from your paychecks based on your income level and filing status, you may not owe additional taxes when you file your return.

8.3 Where Do Our Tax Payments Go?

In 2023, the U.S. government spent $6.1 trillion. That is about $1.4 trillion more than it collected in revenue. Thus, the government had to borrow money to cover this deficit, increasing the national debt.

Who does the government borrow this money from?

Technically speaking, not all of the "public debt" is held by individuals, as the debt may be owned by foreign investors, mutual funds, banks, state and local governments, insurance companies, and the government. Approximately 20% of the total amount is held by intragovernmental holdings, which represent the amounts the U.S. Treasury owes to other federal agencies, such as the Social Security Trust Fund and the Military Retirement Fund. These two funds provide benefits to their respective beneficiaries, and if their year-to-year expenses are less than how much money they take in (i.e., money received from taxes), leftover money can be used to buy Treasury bills, notes, and bonds (from the U.S. Treasury). Of the remaining 80%, approximately 25% is owned by foreign investors, with the three largest foreign owners of U.S. debt being Japan, followed by China and Britain. In practice, this means that the U.S. government owes seven to eight trillion dollars to foreign governments and individuals, plus any interest stated on the loan.

What exactly does the government spend this money on?

The largest category is health insurance at 24% of the budget ($1.5 trillion). This covers Medicare, Medicaid, Children's Health Insurance, and Affordable Care Act subsidies. Medicare alone is $828 billion and supports 66 million elderly and disabled people. Medicaid and CHIP provide coverage to 94 million low-income Americans. The ACA subsidies make marketplace health insurance affordable for 14.3 million people.

The next category is Social Security at 21% of the budget ($1.4 trillion). Social Security provides monthly retirement benefits averaging $1,836 to nearly 50 million retired workers.[10] It also provides benefits to six million spouses and children of deceased and nine million disabled workers. We have covered Social Security in the "Financial Literacy" part of this book, and we can only reiterate the importance of this program in protecting the economically vulnerable segments of the population.

Defense accounts for 13% ($806 billion), mostly going to military operations, personnel, weapons, and research. Our military expenditure surpasses the combined defense budgets of China, Russia, India, Saudi Arabia, the United Kingdom, Germany, France, South Korea, and Japan, combined. However, when considering these expenses as a percentage of GDP, the U.S. expenditure represents less than 5% of its GDP.

This puts the U.S. on par with countries such as China, Russia, India, and the United Kingdom in terms of relative spending.

The graph below shows the 10 countries that spend the most on defense (in terms of absolute size) and what percent of GDP these expenditures correspond to. In 2023, the United States' allocation of GDP toward defense expenditure ranked twentieth globally.[11]

Figure 34. Defense spending across select big spenders

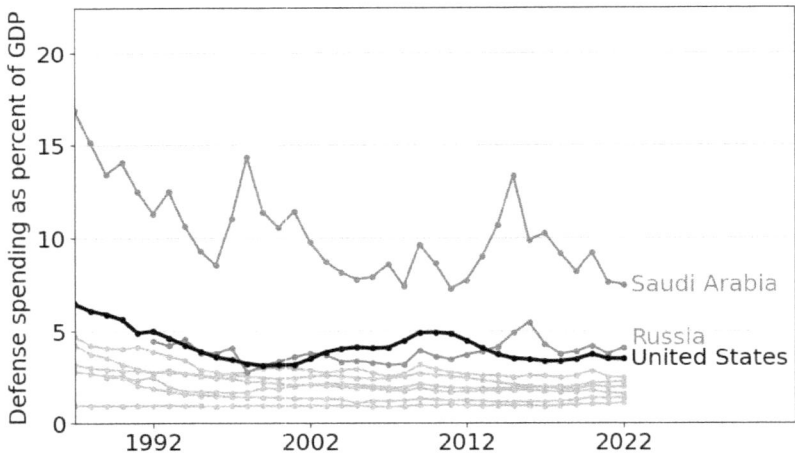

The fourth largest category is interest payments on the money the federal government borrowed to cover previous deficits. In 2023, these interest payments amounted to $663 billion, 10% of the budget. According to the Congressional Budget Office, these payments will increase to $1.4 trillion in 2033.[12] We'll talk a little more about this debt in the next section. We would only reiterate here that this is an important part of expenditure that will likely become larger in the future. In fact, in 2024, the federal government spent more on interest than on defense.[13]

Economic security programs account for 8% of the budget ($522 billion). These include tax credits for working families, unemployment benefits, food stamps, housing assistance, and other aid programs that keep millions out of poverty. These programs, combined with Social Security, keep 40 million people a year above the poverty line. It's estimated that, overall, these expenses cut poverty by half nationwide.[14]

Another 8% of the budget goes for the benefits for veterans and federal retirees. Most of these benefits are disability payments and medical care for the 18.5 million veterans. Of the benefits for veterans, about 90% are either disability payments or medical care. Spending on veteran support has increased from about $50 billion to nearly $300 billion dollars in the past two decades as more veterans returned from service in Afghanistan and Iraq.[15]

Approximately 8% is spent on education, science, law enforcement, and basic infrastructure such as roads, bridges, and airports. These are likely the categories that come to mind first when people think about government spending.

The last and smallest category of spending is foreign aid. This is an especially controversial part of the budget, which often comes up in political debates ("Why send money to other countries when we need it here?"). While many Americans believe that the U.S. spends a huge part of its federal budget (25%, according to one poll) on foreign aid, about only 1% of it goes to international programs like humanitarian aid.[16,17] The U.S. government spends approximately the same amount of money per American on development aid as what Americans spend per person on Halloween decorations.[18]

The U.S. is not the only country that provides aid to other countries. The United Nations has a target for spending on foreign aid, which is 0.7% of **Gross National Income** (GNI, value of output produced by U.S. residents, regardless of where they are located). However, between 1960 and 2023, only 15 countries have met that threshold.[19] The table below shows how much countries spent on foreign aid in 2023, both in dollars and as a percentage of GNI. Note that the U.S. is not even in the top 20. While the U.S. spent less than other countries as a percentage of GNI, thanks to the country's large GNI, it still spent more than Germany and the United Kingdom combined.[20]

Table 28. Largest spenders on foreign aid as percent of GNI, 2023

Country	Percent of GNI	In billions of U.S. dollars
Norway	1.09	5.55
Luxembourg	0.99	0.58
Sweden	0.91	5.61
Germany	0.79	36.68
Denmark	0.74	3.08
Ireland	0.67	2.82
Netherlands	0.66	7.36
Switzerland	0.60	5.16
United Kingdom	0.58	19.11
Finland	0.52	1.57
(15 more countries)		
United States	0.24	66.04

8.4 Debt Ceiling

On June 28, 1914, a 20-year-old Gavrilo Princip shot Archduke Franz Ferdinand, heir to the Austro-Hungarian throne. A young revolutionary believed that the assassination of a member of the imperial family would lead to the liberation of the Balkans from the Austro-Hungarian rule. Instead, it triggered a chain of events that ultimately led to the beginning of World War I.

In August of 1914, hesitant to join the war, the United States proclaimed neutrality. While many Americans sympathized with Britain and France in their war against Germany, nearly 10% of Americans identified as ethnic Germans, most of whom supported the country's policy of neutrality.

Public opinion, however, started changing when, in 1915, the German Empire sank the Lusitania, a British cruise liner traveling from New York to England, leading to the deaths of 1,195 people, including 123 Americans. [21] Because of the international outcry caused by the sinking of Lusitania, Germany paused indiscriminate attacks on ships in the Atlantic. However, the success of their army emboldened the German government. In early 1917, Russia essentially dropped out of the war against Germany because of the turmoil caused by the March Revolution (known as the "February Revolution" in Russian history, as the Russian Empire was still using the Julian calendar at the time). The revolution was preceded by a series of losses by Russia, which were noted by Germany who shifted their attention to the West. Germany resumed indiscriminate attacks of ships in the Atlantic leading to more losses of American lives. [22] Finally, in March of 1917, a telegram from the German Empire offering U.S. territory to Mexico in return for alliance hit the U.S. newspapers. [23] The telegram generated enough outrage, and in April 1917, the United States joined the war.

About two weeks after the declaration of war Congress passed the Liberty Loan Act authorizing the Treasury Secretary to issue Liberty Bonds worth $2 billion to fund the war efforts. Before 1917, each loan issued by the Treasury had to be approved by Congress. Through the Second Liberty Bond Act, however, Congress allowed the Treasury to borrow money for "other public purposes authorized by law," provided that bond sales don't exceed a given limit. The Act limited the quantity of long-term securities that could be issued as well as the quantity of outstanding short-term debt. Over the next two decades, Congress occasionally changed the limits on different types of securities until 1939, when it settled on a single aggregate limit of $45 billion (about one trillion in 2023 dollars), allowing more freedom for the Treasury to design and manage the debt. This point is commonly referred to as the start of the federal debt ceiling as we know it today.

In 2021, the debt limit was raised by $2.5 trillion to a total of $31.4 trillion, which was reached in early 2023. In June of 2023, President Joe Biden signed into law the Fiscal Responsibility Act of 2023, suspending the debt limit until January 1, 2025. In 2024, the national debt reached a staggering $35 trillion. As the debt grows, interest payments consume a larger portion of the federal budget. This means that interest costs reduce the funds available for other government expenditures, potentially decreasing spending on programs that benefit citizens. The increasing interest burden can lead to difficult choices, such as raising taxes, cutting services, or incurring even more debt. Over time, this cycle can limit the government's ability to respond to economic crises or invest in long-term projects that could benefit the public.

State of the debt

The **debt ceiling** is a limit set by Congress on the total amount of money the federal government can borrow to meet its financial obligations. As we already mentioned in an earlier chapter, when the government does not make enough money to cover its expenses (runs a deficit), it has to borrow money by selling Treasury Securities to federal government agencies, state and local governments, businesses, and ordinary people, as well as governments, businesses, and individuals from other countries.

The purpose of the debt ceiling is to control government spending and borrowing. Some argue that it encourages Congress to review the nation's debt levels regularly and maintain fiscal responsibility. Yet, the national debt has continued to grow since 1981, except for a short period between

1998 and 2001. As the federal government consistently faces deficits, the national debt continues to increase. In addition to paying borrowed money (principal), the U.S. government must also pay interest on the national debt. This interest expense escalates annual expenditures, thus contributing to increased spending (and consequently, deficits) as the debt continues to grow.[24] Thus, various presidents and policymakers are dealing with the debt left to them by previous generations. In the past six decades, Congress raised or temporarily extended the debt ceiling on 78 occasions.[25]

The **debt-to-GDP ratio** puts a country's debt in perspective by comparing it to the size of its economy. We present this graph below.

Figure 35. Debt as a percent of GDP

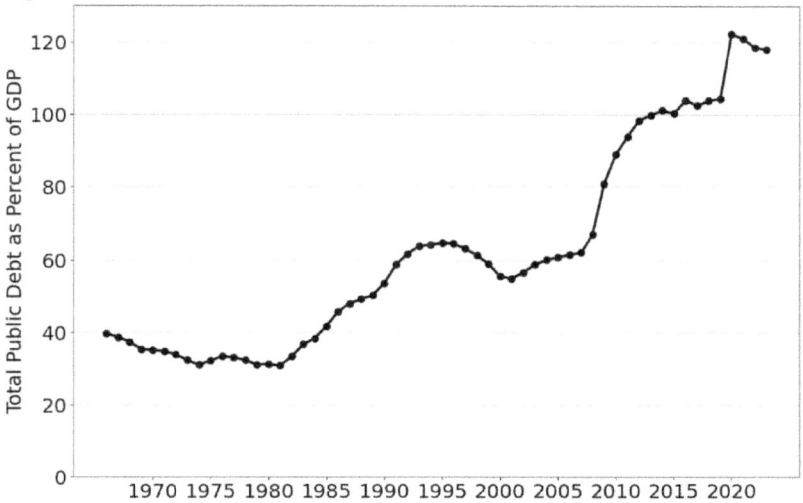

In the second half of the twentieth century, the debt-to-GDP ratio has been slowly decreasing from the high of more than 100% it reached during World War II. In his 1981 Inaugural

Address, Ronald Reagan raised concerns over excessive public spending and a deficit that had been growing for decades.[26] In his first year in office, Reagan worked on the passage of $39 billion dollars in budget cuts. However, these cuts were accompanied by reductions in both personal and business taxes, making it difficult for the government to reduce the deficit.[27,28] Additionally, defense spending as percent of GDP increased to 7%, the highest value the U.S. had since then.[29] Consequently, the debt-to-GDP ratio started growing again in the 1980s.

Tax increases enacted during the George H.W. Bush and Bill Clinton administrations in the 1990s, economic growth of the dot-com boom, as well as the decrease in defense spending resulting from the fall of the Soviet Union resulted in the first budget surplus the U.S. has experienced in decades. As a result, in 2001, the Congressional Budget Office projected that three-quarters of the public debt would be repaid in the following decade.[30]

However, this optimistic forecast was derailed by a series of unforeseen events and policy decisions. After the September 11 terrorist attacks in 2001, the government ramped up spending on defense. The economic slowdown during this period led to a decline in tax revenue. Compounding this issue, President George W. Bush implemented a series of tax cuts, which further reduced government income.[31] Finally, Bush's second term ended in one of the worst recessions in recent history, prompting the newly elected President Barack Obama to significantly increase government spending in an attempt to stabilize the economy.

The most recent and dramatic increase in government spending occurred in response to the COVID-19 pandemic. In 2020 and 2021, the U.S. government implemented unprecedented measures to address the public health crisis and its economic fallout. These measures pushed the national debt to new heights, with the debt-to-GDP ratio exceeding 100% for the first time since World War II.

The growing debt figure remains daunting for many, and discussions regarding a balanced budget or reducing the debt is an ongoing hotly debated topic. Economists also don't have a "yes or no" answer to whether we should take on more debt, although most agree that some debt can be necessary.

It's difficult to argue against the U.S. government taking on debt during the American Revolutionary War, which amounted to approximately $75 million by 1791. The U.S. would also look much different today if the Louisiana Purchase (for $15 million! in 1901) had not taken place. And everyone would not bat an eye to debt acquired ($211 billion) while fighting the Axis powers during World War II.

Government debt, much like personal debt, can serve as a crucial financial tool when used responsibly. Just as individuals might take on debt to purchase a home or invest in their education, governments can leverage debt to fund essential programs and initiatives that promote societal well-being and economic growth. Besides, if the interest rate on the loan is not too high, the benefits of taking on debt will often outweigh its costs.

Government debt can also be particularly useful in crisis response or during recessions. During a recession, private sector spending typically decreases as businesses and consumers become more cautious. This reduction in spending can further deepen the economic slowdown. In such situations, government borrowing and spending can help fill the gap left by the private sector. Thus, the government can stimulate economic activity, create jobs, and prevent a more severe economic contraction. Not all economists agree that the government should spend more money during recessions, especially if it means taking on more debt. However, the U.S.

government has been consistent in increasing spending during economic downturns.

But how much debt is too much? Some suggest that serious problems will occur if the debt-to-GDP ratio reaches 200%, and even project that this ratio will be achieved in the next 20 years.[32] Based on historical data across various countries, a 2010 study proposed a threshold of 77%, stating that values in excess of that threshold will slow down a country's growth.[33] Another study published the same year named a threshold of 90%.[34] As of 2024, the debt-to-GDP ratio stands at 120%.

Who pays for the debt?

You can donate your own money to help reduce the public debt. In fact, in 2022, the government received one million dollars in the special debt fund, which can only be used for the repayment of the national debt.[35] It's a negligible amount compared to the overall debt. But the existence of such a fund and the fact that people donate to it is an interesting indication of the deep-seated concern many Americans feel toward addressing the national debt. How do we pay the rest of the debt?

Let's consider the intragovernmental debt, specifically the amounts held by the Social Security Trust Fund. If the trust fund wanted to redeem its holdings, the Treasury would have to provide money, which it may or may not have on hand. If the Treasury does not, it may have to take on further debt or make the money up elsewhere, such as through increased tax rates—which requires Congress's action.

Congress can allow the U.S. government to "make" more Treasury bills available and sell them to investors to take on more debt. Doing so creates more U.S. currency in the long run, which can decrease the value of the dollar. Alternatively, Congress can increase tax rates—for corporations, individuals, or both—to increase the revenue needed to fund the government. Doing so may have negative impacts on spending for companies and individuals. In short, the U.S. economy "pays" for the debt.

Why doesn't the U.S. government just print money to pay for its debt? Assuming that the political environment exists where Congress would approve such a plan, a major issue would be the collapse of the U.S. dollar. That is, to pay more than $30 trillion overnight would require the U.S. to inject the same amount of cash into the market, an amount greater than our yearly GDP value. The value of your money would decline sharply overnight. The economic downfall would also be felt across the world, as holders of U.S. debt would see the value of their U.S. dollar fall drastically. Furthermore, increased uncertainty about the credibility of the U.S. government may cause heightened risk aversion, resulting in less country-to-country investing and trade, along with a loss of confidence. In this case, the whole world would "pay."

You will often hear the debt ceiling being discussed on the news. The core issue is straightforward: if the debt ceiling is not raised in a timely manner, it could lead to dire consequences for the American economy and people's livelihoods. Failure to increase the debt ceiling risks the federal government defaulting on its financial obligations, which could trigger an economic crisis, soaring unemployment rates, plummeting retirement accounts, and an overall decline in the standard of living for millions of Americans. And, given the role of the United States in the world markets, a default on U.S. debt obligations could potentially have cascading effects that destabilize the global financial system. The U.S. dollar is the world's leading reserve currency, and U.S. Treasury securities are considered among the safest investments due to the full faith and credit of the

American government. A default would shatter this foundational assumption and severely erode confidence in U.S. economic leadership. Global markets could plunge, and the repercussions would likely be felt through disrupted trade, investment flows, and economic growth worldwide. These are just some of the gloomy predictions that economic experts have warned about.

While these predictions sound dire, so far, Congress has always stepped up when called upon to raise the limit.[36] Also, the Treasury can take some "extraordinary measures" like suspending new investments, redeeming existing investments early, and temporarily reducing the debt using some accounting techniques.[37]

Growing public debt is an issue that we need to address. Unfortunately, it gets politicized and overshadowed by short-term electoral considerations, making meaningful long-term fiscal reform extremely challenging. We hope that readers have gained a deeper understanding of public debt and its implications. We encourage you to stay informed and participate actively in conversations about fiscal policy, ensuring that our collective future is shaped by sound economic decisions.

CONCLUDING REMARKS

While some earlier studies suggested that financial literacy education has no effect on people's actual behavior, there is a growing body of research suggesting otherwise. These newer studies show that financial literacy education in high schools leads to a myriad of life improvements like reduced default rates, increased credit scores, reduced non-student debt, shifts toward lower interest methods for student loans, and reduced payday loan borrowing.[1]

The importance of financial literacy and economic education has been recognized for over a century in the United States, though efforts towards enacting it have significantly varied over time. In the early 1900s, initiatives began to emerge with the founding of organizations such as Junior Achievement during World War I and the Council for Economic Education in 1949. Junior Achievement, established in 1919, aimed to prepare young people for the workforce by teaching them through hands-on extracurricular programs and encouraging them to create their own functioning companies.[2] The Council for Economic Education, on the other hand, focused on improving the economic and financial education of K-12 students by providing educators with the necessary resources and training. These early programs aimed to teach basic personal finance skills and economic concepts, laying the groundwork for a more financially literate society.

In the second half of the twentieth century, a policy shift took place when states started mandating the inclusion of personal finance, economics, and consumer education topics in K-12 curriculums. This marked an increased focus by policymakers on developing financial literacy among young Americans.[3]

Fast forwarding to 2011, the Consumer Financial Protection Bureau (CFPB) was founded with the goal of ensuring that "markets for consumer financial products are fair, transparent, and competitive." To achieve its goal, the CFPB develops programs for varying population segments. It publishes materials on managing money, dealing with student loans, and building credit for students and young consumers. It also partners with military and veteran services organizations to spread awareness and resolve various issues faced by service members and veterans, from housing rights to costly auto loans. To address elder financial exploitation, the Bureau publishes various resources for caregivers and service providers. And for people with limited English proficiency, the Bureau makes its financial literacy materials available in languages like Arabic, Chinese, Haitian Créole, Korean, Russian, Spanish, Tagalog, and Vietnamese.[4]

Over recent years, the push for financial education has intensified further. As of 2024, 35 U.S. states require high school students to complete a personal finance course, and 28 states require students to take an economics course prior to graduation. These courses typically cover a wide range of topics, from understanding financial markets and institutions to practical skills like budgeting, building credit, and planning for retirement. Despite many improvements, studies show there is still significant room for progress when it comes to financial literacy levels across the United States.[5,6]

One such study reveals a startling statistic that only 57% of American adults can be considered financially literate. That 57% figure comes from a study that tested knowledge of just four basic financial concepts: risk diversification (is it safer to put your money into multiple investments or one investment?), inflation (if the prices of goods you buy and your income both double, will you be able to purchase more than you can today?), understanding interest (which is larger, $105 or $100 plus 3% interest?), and interest compounding. While these are indeed basic concepts, they serve as crucial building blocks for overall financial literacy.

In the preceding chapters, we've touched upon each of these four core concepts in detail and gone beyond these basics. While we couldn't have possibly covered every single detail and nuance about the financial and economic world around us, we have tried to lay a strong foundation by explaining the essential concepts and principles.

We hope that this book was not only informative but also provided practical knowledge that readers can apply in their everyday lives.

We would greatly appreciate your feedback—whether you liked the book or not—by leaving a review on your preferred platform, or by sharing your thoughts with us at contact@FinEconLit.com.

ACKNOWLEDGMENTS

This book wouldn't have been possible without the generous contributions from many remarkable individuals. Mukhtar Sadykov was our first test reader, and his thoughtful comments helped us add important topics that had initially been overlooked. We would like to acknowledge our early readers—Anton Ogay and Temirlan Atambayev—for their constructive suggestions that guided our revisions. We are thankful to Nikki Thai for the support in reading multiple versions of this book and providing feedback that greatly enriched its final form. We are also deeply grateful to Walter Thurman, whose guidance helped us narrow our discussion to the most essential topics in finance and economics.

Many of the ideas presented in this book grew out of our teaching notes, which were refined through ongoing feedback from our students at North Carolina State University.

We appreciate Farrukh Khan for designing the book cover.

Finally, we are grateful to our diligent editors, Amy Lisane, Amanda Callisaya, and N.L. Carter, whose careful work helped shape the final version of this book.

APPENDIX

Mean versus median

We prefer to report median numbers rather than mean numbers because median numbers tend to be a better indicator of middle values. To see why, suppose that you were tasked with estimating the "typical" salary in the United States. How would you go about it? Some may take that prompt and think about finding the average pay for a worker in the United States—in other words, finding the mean. Others may opt for other methods, such as utilizing median values or finding the most common salary (mode).

Suppose we have the salaries of 10 people: $50,000, $52,000, $54,000, $55,000, $56,000, $58,000, $60,000, $62,000, $64,000, and $1,000,000. To find the mean income, we would add up all reported earnings and divide the sum by the total number of data points. Thus, the mean is $151,100.

The median can be found by identifying the middle value in an ordered data set when arranged from smallest to largest. We first need to arrange the salaries in ascending order (which was already done for us when the numbers were provided). Since there are 10 values, the median is the point between the fifth and the sixth values, which is $57,000. Note that the first nine salaries are relatively similar, while the tenth salary is an outlier at $1,000,000. When asked about a number that represents the "typical" salary of this population, you would likely specify a number around 55,000, rather than the value of more than $150,000. The outlier has a substantial impact on the average, but not on the median. As such, the median provides a better estimate of the "typical" worker's earnings and is thus the preferred statistic when making numerical comparisons.

College as investment: mathematical appendix

In this section, we'll examine a framework for deciding whether college is worth it for a hypothetical high school graduate. This section is slightly more mathematically rigorous than most other parts of the book. That's why we included it in the Appendix rather than in the main part of the book. It's important to note that the following estimations, while rough, are still useful for gaining a clearer picture of the potential outcomes. For those who are grappling with the decision of whether to enroll in college, this example can serve as a valuable starting point.

Although we've documented a general positive correlation between college degrees and higher earnings, we must be careful in asserting the need for a degree. Returns from college are very different for different people. To see why, let's look at a basic economic model which compares one's lifetime earnings with and without a degree.

Consider an 18-year-old high school graduate who is making plans for her future. She could decide to forgo a college education and enter the labor force to earn a wage of w_{HS} (where subscript "HS" stands for high school) or spend four years obtaining a college degree and earn a wage of w_{COL} (where subscript "COL" stands for college) after graduation.[a] How do we compare the value of going to college to the value of going straight into the job market? How do we compare all the wages she will make throughout the years? Ideally, we would want to have one number representing each of the decisions. We'll make a present value comparison of her future potential earnings with and without a college degree, considering all costs associated with attending college. If she decides to pursue a college degree following high school graduation, the present value of her earnings is

$$PV_{COL} = -H - \frac{H}{1+r} - \frac{H}{(1+r)^2} - \frac{H}{(1+r)^3} + \frac{w_{COL}}{(1+r)^4} + \cdots + \frac{w_{COL}}{(1+r)^{46}}$$

Here, the number 46 comes from the assumption that she will work up to age 64. H represents the yearly cost of attending college, such as tuition, fees, and books.[b] Similarly, if she decides to forgo college, the present value of her earnings is

$$PV_{HS} = w_{HS} + \frac{w_{HS}}{1+r} + \frac{w_{HS}}{(1+r)^2} + \cdots + \frac{w_{HS}}{(1+r)^{46}}$$

Intuitively, this individual should attend college if her present-value earnings are higher under PV_{COL} compared to PV_{HS}. That is, if her expected wage can make up for the lost income and the cost of college, she should pursue higher education. Numerically, she should attend if

$$PV_{COL} > PV_{HS}$$

We can write the above as

$$-H - \frac{H}{1+r} - \frac{H}{(1+r)^2} - \frac{H}{(1+r)^3} + \frac{w_{COL}}{(1+r)^4} + \cdots + \frac{w_{COL}}{(1+r)^{46}}$$
$$> w_{HS} + \frac{w_{HS}}{1+r} + \frac{w_{HS}}{(1+r)^2} + \cdots + \frac{w_{HS}}{(1+r)^{46}}$$

---

[a] This is a big assumption of this model, as real data shows that less than 50% of undergraduate students at four-year institutions graduate within 4 years. Furthermore, as of 2016 data, less than 62% of students graduated within six years.
[b] Notice that both future costs and future wages are discounted by rate r. Recall that due to inflation, a dollar is worth less tomorrow than it is today!

Let's apply what we've learned to real data. During the 2021-2022 academic year, the average cost of attendance at a four-year public university was $15,600 for students who lived off campus with family.[a] This number is net of any financial aid received, meaning the figure is how much the average family spent after receiving any financial assistance and grants.

Next, we need to apply an appropriate value of r to discount future measures of money. Although inflation rates may vary widely within a short period of time, historical rates have been under 4%. Putting it all together, we find that an individual should pursue college if:

$$-15,600 - \frac{15,600}{1.04} - \frac{15,600}{(1.04)^2} - \frac{15,600}{(1.04)^3} + \frac{w_{COL}}{(1.04)^4} + \cdots + \frac{w_{COL}}{(1+r)^{46}}$$
$$> w_{HS} + \frac{w_{HS}}{1.04} + \frac{w_{HS}}{(1.04)^2} + \cdots + \frac{w_{HS}}{(1.04)^{46}}$$

Rearranging and simplifying the above gives us:

$$-58,891.42 + \frac{w_{COL}}{(1.04)^4} + \cdots + \frac{w_{COL}}{(1.04)^{46}} > w_{HS} + \frac{w_{HS}}{1.04} + \frac{w_{HS}}{(1.04)^2} + \cdots + \frac{w_{HS}}{(1.04)^{46}}$$

With a little more work, we get the final result:

$$w_{COL} > 1.21 \times w_{HS} + 3,282.69$$

In words, this individual should attend college if the wage offered to her after graduating from college is at least 21% greater than the wage that would be offered to her with a high school degree, plus $3,282.69.

Note that we made some big assumptions while building this model. We assumed a non-changing yearly cost of $15,600, an individual living with family (versus on-campus), attending a public school with four years to completion, a discount rate of 4%, and retiring at the age of 65. The results can change somewhat significantly if we change these assumptions. For example, increasing the discount rate from 4% to 5% will

---

[a] Private four-year university: $43,900. Two-year public university: $9,800. Two-year private university: $21,400.

increase the required return from 21% to 24% to make college "worth it." Reducing the number of years worked will have a similar effect, as you'll need to "pay for college" in a smaller number of years.

INDEX

NOTES

PART ONE. FINANCIAL LITERACY

CHAPTER ONE. INFLATION

[1] U.S. Bureau of Labor Statistics, Consumer Price Index for All Urban Consumer, retrieved from FRED, Federal Reserve Bank of St. Louis. https://fred.stlouisfed.org/categories/9.

[2] Stoner, Lillian Bartlett. 2016. "A Mediterranean Game of Thrones: The Tumultuous Legacy of Alexander the Great - the Metropolitan Museum of Art."

[3] Temin, Peter. 2022. "Price behavior in ancient Babylon." Explorations in Economic History 39, no. 1: 46-60.

[4] Barzun, Jacques, Herlihy, David, Treasure, Geoffrey Russell Richards, Champion, et al. 2025. "History of Europe | Summary, Wars, Map, Ideas, & Colonialism." Encyclopedia Britannica. https://www.britannica.com/topic/history-of-Europe/Prices-and-inflation.

[5] World Economic Forum. 2022. "What is hyperinflation and should we be worried?" http://weforum.org/stories/2022/06/hyperinflation-inflation-interest-rate/.

[6] The Editors of Encyclopaedia Britannica. 2025. "Treaty of Versailles | Definition, Summary, Terms, & Facts." Encyclopedia Britannica. https://www.britannica.com/event/Treaty-of-Versailles-1919.

[7] Bisno, Adam. 2023. "How Hyperinflation Heralded the Fall of German Democracy." Smithsonian Magazine.

https://www.smithsonianmag.com/history/how-hyperinflation-heralded-the-fall-of-german-democracy-180982204/.

[8] Wexler, Ellen. 2023. "Before He Rose to Power, Adolf Hitler Staged a Coup and Went to Prison." Smithsonian Magazine. https://www.smithsonianmag.com/history/adolf-hitler-coup-prison-beer-hall-putsch-180983207/.

[9] Editors of Encyclopaedia Britannica. "Beer Hall Putsch." Encyclopedia Britannica. https://www.britannica.com/event/Beer-Hall-Putsch.

[10] United States Holocaust Memorial Museum. 2023. "Beer Hall Putsch (Munich Putsch)." Holocaust Encyclopedia. https://encyclopedia.ushmm.org/content/en/article/beer-hall-putsch-munich-putsch

[11] Bisno, Adam. 2023. "How Hyperinflation Heralded the Fall of German Democracy." Smithsonian Magazine. https://www.smithsonianmag.com/history/how-hyperinflation-heralded-the-fall-of-german-democracy-180982204/.

[12] Lerner, Eugene M. 1955 "Money, prices, and wages in the Confederacy, 1861-65." Journal of Political Economy 63, no. 1: 20-40.

[13] Federal Reserve Bank of Minneapolis. "Consumer Price Index, 1913- ." https://www.minneapolisfed.org/about-us/monetary-policy/inflation-calculator/consumer-price-index-1913-.

[14] Batten, Dallas S. "Inflation: The cost-push myth." Federal Reserve Bank of St. Louis Review 63, no. 6 (1981): 20-26.

[15] Volmert, Isabella. 2023. "U.S. Egg Producers Conspired to Fix Prices From 2004 to 2008, A Federal Jury Ruled | AP News." AP News. https://apnews.com/article/egg-producers-price-gouging-lawsuit-conspiracy-8cd455003a3a40bab74d0f046d0f2c9d.

[16] Iacurci, Greg. 2023. "Egg Prices Rose 60% in 2022. One Farm Group Claims It's a 'collusive Scheme' by Suppliers." CNBC. https://www.cnbc.com/2023/01/23/high-egg-prices-due-to-a-collusive-scheme-by-suppliers-group-claims.html.

[17] McQuilkin, Hilary, and Meghna Chakrabarti. 2023. "'Greedflation': A Once Fringe Theory of Inflation Gains Momentum | on Point." WBUR. https://www.wbur.org/onpoint/2023/06/02/greedflation-a-once-fringe-theory-of-inflation-gains-momentum.

[18] Lincicome, Scott. 2023. "Three Big Strikes Against Greedflation." Cato Institute. https://www.cato.org/commentary/three-big-strikes-against-greedflation.

[19] The Institute For Public Policy Research. 2023. "Revealed: How Powerful Companies Are Amplifying Inflation Through Their Profit Margins." IPPR. https://www.ippr.org/media-office/revealed-how-powerful-companies-are-amplifying-inflation-through-their-profit-margins.

[20] Glover, Andrew, José Mustre-del-Río, and Alice von Ende-Becker. 2023. "How much have record corporate profits contributed to recent inflation?" Federal Reserve Bank of Kansas City Economic Review 108, no. 1: 1-13.

[21] Conlon, Christopher, Nathan H. Miller, Tsolmon Otgon, and Yi Yao. "Rising markups, rising prices?" In AEA Papers and Proceedings, vol. 113, pp. 279-283. 2014 Broadway, Suite 305, Nashville, TN 37203: American Economic Association, 2023.

[22] Woods, Darian. 2023. "Is Greedflation Really the Villain?" https://www.npr.org/transcripts/1182019025.

[23] Severen, Christopher, and Arthur A. Van Benthem. 2022. "Formative experiences and the price of gasoline." American Economic Journal: Applied Economics 14, no. 2: 256-284.

[24] U.S. Bureau of Labor Statistics, Consumer Price Index for All Urban Consumer, retrieved from FRED, Federal Reserve Bank of St. Louis. https://fred.stlouisfed.org/series/CPIAUCSL.

[25] Nadeem, Reem, and Reem Nadeem. 2024. "Top Problems Facing the U.S." Pew Research Center. https://www.pewresearch.org/politics/2024/05/23/top-problems-facing-the-u-s/.

[26] "Consumer Price Index Historical Tables for U.S. City Average: Mid–Atlantic Information Office: U.S. Bureau of Labor Statistics." 2022. Bureau of Labor Statistics. https://www.bls.gov/regions/mid-atlantic/data/consumerpriceindexhistorical_us_table.htm.

[27] "How The Fed Implements Monetary Policy With Its Tools: In Plain English." https://www.stlouisfed.org/in-plain-english/the-fed-implements-monetary-policy.

[28] "Monetary Policy." Federal Reserve Education. https://www.federalreserveeducation.org/about-the-fed/archive-structure-and-functions/archive-monetary-policy/.

[29] "How Does the Federal Reserve Affect Inflation and Employment?" Board of Governors of the Federal Reserve System. https://www.federalreserve.gov/faqs/money_12856.htm.

[30] "The Federal Funds Rate—Federal Reserve Bank of Chicago." https://www.chicagofed.org/research/dual-mandate/the-federal-funds-rate.

CHAPTER TWO. SAVING AND INVESTING

[1] Alexander, Dan. 2021. "It's Official: Trump Would Be Richer if He Had Just Invested His Inheritance Into the S&P 500." Forbes. https://www.forbes.com/sites/danalexander/2021/10/11/its-official-trump-would-be-richer-if-he-had-just-invested-his-inheritance-into-the-sp500.

[2] Alexander, Dan. 2024. "Here's How Much Donald Trump Is Worth." Forbes. https://www.forbes.com/sites/danalexander/article/the-definitive-networth-of-donaldtrump.

[3] "Total Market Value of U.S. Stock Market." 2025. Siblis Research. https://siblisresearch.com/data/us-stock-market-value/.

[4] Renshaw, Edward F., and Paul J. Feldstein. 1960. "The case for an unmanaged investment company." Financial Analysts Journal 16, no. 1: 43-46.

[5] Jorion, Philippe, and William N. Goetzmann. 1999. "Global stock markets in the twentieth century." The Journal of Finance 54, no. 3: 953-980.

[6] Bogle, John C. 2017. The little book of common sense investing: the only way to guarantee your fair share of stock market returns. John Wiley & Sons.

[7] Lazzara, Craig J., Anu R. Ganti, Davide Di Gioia, Grace Stoddart. 2023. "SPIVA® U.S. Scorecard." S&P Global (2023).

[8] Bogle, John C. The little book of common sense investing: the only way to guarantee your fair share of stock market returns. John Wiley & Sons, 2017.

[9] Li, Yun. 2020. "Buffett on Coronavirus, Airlines and More: Watch the 5 Best Moments From the Berkshire Meeting." CNBC. https://www.cnbc.com/2020/05/04/warren-buffett-berkshire-hathaway-annual-shareholder-meeting-highlights.html.

[10] U.S. Census Bureau, Current Population Survey. 2024. "Region--All People (Both Sexes Combined) by Median and Mean Income: 1974 to 2023." https://www2.census.gov/programs-surveys/cps/tables/time-series/historical-income-people/

[11] "The Power of Dividends: Past, Present, and Future." 2024. Hartford Funds. https://www.hartfordfunds.com/insights/market-perspectives/equity/the-power-of-dividends.html.

[12] TurboTax. 2025. "A Guide to the Capital Gains Tax Rate: Short-term Vs. Long-term Capital Gains Taxes." https://turbotax.intuit.com/tax-tips/investments-and-taxes/guide-to-short-term-vs-long-term-capital-gains-taxes-brokerage-accounts-etc/L7KCu9etn.

[13] The Internal Revenue Service. "Topic no. 409, Capital gains and losses." https://www.irs.gov/taxtopics/tc409

[14] Greenwald, Bruce C., Judd Kahn, Erin Bellissimo, Mark A. Cooper, and Tano Santos. Value investing: from Graham to Buffett and beyond. John Wiley & Sons, 2020.

[15] Graham, Benjamin. 2006. "The Intelligent Investor." HarperBusiness.

[16] Allyn, Bobby. 2022. "Meta Announces Another Drop in Revenue." NPR, October 27, 2022. https://www.npr.org/2022/10/27/1132042031/meta-announces-another-drop-in-revenue.

[17] Damodaran, Aswath. "PE Ratio by Sector (US)." https://pages.stern.nyu.edu/~adamodar/New_Home_Page/datafile/pedata.html

[18] Shiller, Robert J. 2011. "ECON 252: Financial Markets. Lecture 7—Efficient Markets." Open Yale Courses. https://oyc.yale.edu/economics/econ-252-11/lecture-7

[19] Osler, Carol L., and P. H. Chang. 1995. "Head and shoulders: Not just a flaky pattern." Federal Reserve Bank of New York Staff Report No. 4.

[20] Greenspan, Alan. 2008. "The age of turbulence: Adventures in a new world." Penguin.

[21] Hamer, Ashley. 2019. "Tuesday Is No Longer the Best Day to Book a Flight." https://www.discovery.com/exploration/Best-Day-to-Book-a-Flight

[22] Cross, Frank. 1973. "The behavior of stock prices on Fridays and Mondays." Financial Analysts Journal 29, no. 6: 67-69.

[23] French, Kenneth R. 1980. "Stock returns and the weekend effect." Journal of Financial Economics 8, no. 1: 55-69.

[24] Gibbons, Michael R., and Patrick Hess. 1981. "Day of the week effects and asset returns." Journal of Business: 579-596.

[25] Schwert, G. William. 2003. "Anomalies and market efficiency." Handbook of the Economics of Finance 1: 939-974.

[26] Shiller, Robert J. 2016. "Irrational exuberance" Princeton University Press.

[27] Pearce, Douglas K., and V. Vance Roley. 1984. Stock prices and economic news. No. w1296. National bureau of economic research.

[28] Chan, Wesley S. 2003. "Stock price reaction to news and no-news: drift and reversal after headlines." Journal of Financial Economics 70, no. 2: 223-260.

[29] Engelberg, Joseph E., and Christopher A. Parsons. 2011. "The causal impact of media in financial markets." the Journal of Finance 66, no. 1: 67-97.

[30] Shiller, Robert J. 2016. "Irrational exuberance" Princeton University Press.

[31] "Insider Trading." Legal Information Institute. https://www.law.cornell.edu/wex/insider_trading.

[32] Oppel Jr., Richard A. 2001. "Employees' Retirement Plan Is a Victim as Enron Tumbles." The New York Times. https://www.nytimes.com/2001/11/22/business/employees-retirement-plan-is-a-victim-as-enron-tumbles.html.

[33] "401(k) Investors Sue Enron." November 26, 2001. CNN. https://money.cnn.com/2001/11/26/401k/q_retire_enron_re/.

[34] Ziolkowski, Caleb. 2020. "Senators Dumped Stocks Amid Coronavirus Crisis. Here's What We Know about Congress' Financial Self-Interest." https://www.washingtonpost.com/politics/2020/03/25/senators-dumped-stocks-amid-coronavirus-crisis-heres-what-we-know-about-congress-financial-self-interest/.

[35] "More on the Burr FBI Probe." 2022. Politico. https://www.politico.com/minutes/congress/09-6-2022/more-on-the-burr-fbi-probe/

[36] Faturechi, Robert. 2021. "Burr's Brother-in-Law Called Stock Broker, One Minute After Getting Off Phone With Senator." ProPublica. https://www.propublica.org/article/burrs-brother-in-law-called-stock-broker-one-minute-after-getting-off-phone-with-senator.

[37] "Roll Call Vote 112th Congress - 2nd Session. An original bill to prohibit Members of Congress and employees of Congress from using nonpublic information derived from their official positions for personal benefit, and for other purposes." https://www.senate.gov/legislative/LIS/roll_call_votes/vote1122/vote_112_2_00014.htm.

[38] Kelly, Kate, Adam Playford, Alicia Parlapiano, and Ege Uz. 2022. "Stock Trades Reported by Nearly a Fifth of Congress Show Possible Conflicts." The New York

Times. https://www.nytimes.com/interactive/2022/09/13/us/politics/congress-stock-trading-investigation.html.

[39] Wang, Vivian. 2019. "Ex-Rep. Chris Collins Pleads Guilty to Insider Trading Charges." The New York Times. https://www.nytimes.com/2019/10/01/nyregion/chris-collins-guilty-congress.html.

[40] Breuninger, Keving, Dan Mangan, Tucker Higgins. 2020. "Ex-New York congressman Chris Collins sentenced to 26 months for insider-trading tip to son." CNBC. https://www.cnbc.com/2020/01/17/chris-collins-sentenced-to-26-months-for-insider-trading-tip.html.

[41] "President Donald Trump Grants Full Pardon To Former New York Congressman Chris Collins." 2020. CBS News. https://www.cbsnews.com/newyork/news/trump-pardons-chris-collins/.

[42] Kelly, Kate, Adam Playford, Alicia Parlapiano. 2022. "Despite their influence and extensive access to information, members of Congress can buy and sell stocks with few restrictions." https://www.nytimes.com/interactive/2022/09/13/us/politics/congress-stock-trading-investigation.html

[43] "Ending Trading and Holdings In Congressional Stocks (ETHICS) Act." https://www.congress.gov/bill/118th-congress/senate-bill/1171

[44] Dube, Arindrajit, Ethan Kaplan, and Suresh Naidu. "Coups, corporations, and classified information." The Quarterly Journal of Economics 126, no. 3 (2011): 1375-1409.

[45] Ziobrowski, Alan J., Ping Cheng, James W. Boyd, and Brigitte J. Ziobrowski. "Abnormal returns from the common stock investments of the U.S. Senate." Journal of financial and quantitative analysis 39, no. 4 (2004): 661-676.

[46] Ziobrowski, Alan J., James W. Boyd, Ping Cheng, and Brigitte J. Ziobrowski. "Abnormal returns from the common stock investments of members of the U.S. House of Representatives." Business and Politics 13, no. 1 (2011): 1-22.

[47] C. Eggers, Andrew, and Jens Hainmueller. "Capitol losses: The mediocre performance of Congressional stock portfolios." The Journal of Politics 75, no. 2 (2013): 535-551.

[48] Belmont, William, Bruce Sacerdote, Ranjan Sehgal, and Ian Van Hoek. "Do senators and house members beat the stock market? Evidence from the STOCK Act." Journal of Public Economics 207 (2022): 104602.

[49] "Party Division." https://www.senate.gov/history/partydiv.htm.

[50] "Party Divisions of the House of Representatives, 1789 to Present." https://history.house.gov/Institution/Party-Divisions/Party-Divisions/.

[51] Federal Reserve Bank of St. Louis, NBER based Recession Indicators for the United States from the Period following the Peak through the Trough [USREC], retrieved from FRED, Federal Reserve Bank of St. Louis; https://fred.stlouisfed.org/series/USREC.

[52] https://investor.vanguard.com/investor-resources-education/article/how-do-midterm-elections-impact-your-investment-portfolio
[53] Klement, Joachim. 2020. "Republicans or Democrats: Who Is Better for the Economy?" https://blogs.cfainstitute.org/investor/2020/09/08/republicans-or-democrats-who-is-better-for-the-economy/.
[54] Blinder, Alan S., and Mark W. Watson. 2016. "Presidents and the U.S. economy: An econometric exploration." American Economic Review 106, no. 4: 1015-1045.
[55] Kahneman, Daniel, Paul Slovic, and Amos Tversky. 1982. "Judgment under uncertainty: Heuristics and biases." Cambridge university press.
[56] Saunders, Edward M. 1993. "Stock prices and Wall Street weather." The American Economic Review 83, no. 5: 1337-1345.
[57] Wright, William F., and Gordon H. Bower. 1992. "Mood effects on subjective probability assessment." Organizational behavior and human decision processes 52, no. 2: 276-291.
[58] Bagozzi, Richard P., Mahesh Gopinath, and Prashanth U. Nyer. 1999. "The role of emotions in marketing." Journal of the academy of marketing science 27, no. 2: 184-206.
[59] Trombley, Mark A. 1997. "Stock prices and Wall Street weather: Additional evidence." Quarterly Journal of Business and Economics: 11-21.
[60] Hirshleifer, David, and Tyler Shumway. 2003. "Good day sunshine: Stock returns and the weather." The journal of Finance 58, no. 3: 1009-1032.
[61] Mullainathan, Sendhil, Markus Noeth, and Antoinette Schoar. 2012. "The market for financial advice: An audit study." No. w17929. National Bureau of Economic Research.
[62] Zweig, Jason. 2021. "Want to Get Rich Quick? Who Can Stop You?" The Wall Street Journal. https://www.wsj.com/articles/want-to-get-rich-quick-who-can-stop-you-11620399961
[63] Tarver, Jordan. 2024. "What Is A Fiduciary Financial Advisor?" Forbes. https://www.forbes.com/advisor/investing/financial-advisor/what-is-fiduciary-financial-advisor/
[64] Tepper, Taylor. 2024. "How To Choose A Financial Advisor." https://www.forbes.com/advisor/investing/how-to-choose-a-financial-advisor/
[65] Doherty, Jacqueline. 1999. "Amazon.bomb" Barron's.
[66] Lunden, Ingrid. 2018. "Amazon's share of the U.S. e-commerce market is now 49%, or 5% of all retail spend." TechCrunch.
[67] Hetzner, Christiaan. 2022. "You can bet against Jim Cramer with a new ETF from the fund manager who already shorts Cathie Wood's stock picks." Fortune. https://fortune.com/2022/10/06/jim-cramer-short-etf-cnbc-mad-money-sjim-cathie-wood-tuttle/.
[68] "A dozen key dates in the demise of Bear Stearns." 2008. Reuters. https://www.reuters.com/article/us-bearstearns-chronology/timeline-a-dozen-key-dates-in-the-demise-of-bear-stearns-idUSN1724031920080317.

⁶⁹ Egan, Matt. 2018. "The stunning downfall of Bear Stearns and its bridge-playing CEO." CNN. https://www.cnn.com/2018/09/30/investing/bear-stearns-2008-crisis-jimmy-cayne/index.html.

⁷⁰ Jakab, Spencer. 2023. "Betting Against Pundits Is Even Worse Than Listening to Them." The Wall Street Journal. https://www.wsj.com/articles/betting-against-pundits-is-even-worse-than-listening-to-them-3f5f2c1c.

⁷¹ Glassman, James K., and Kevin A. Hassett. 1999. Dow 36,000: The New Strategy for Profiting From the Coming Rise in the Stock Market.

⁷² https://shillerdata.com/.

⁷³ The 700 Club. 2022. "The 700 Club—January 12, 2022" YouTube. https://www.youtube.com/watch?v=x3yeJBpk_ik.

⁷⁴ Akorlie, Christian and Cooper Inveen. 2022. "Ghana to default on most external debt as economic crisis worsens." Reuters. https://www.reuters.com/world/africa/ghana-announces-external-debt-payment-suspension-slipping-into-default-2022-12-19/.

⁷⁵ Bella, Timothy. 2022. "Pat Robertson says Putin was 'compelled by God' to invade Ukraine to fulfill Armageddon prophecy." The Washington Post. https://www.washingtonpost.com/world/2022/03/01/pat-robertson-putin-god-russia-ukraine/.

⁷⁶ "Managing the Crisis: The FDIC and RTC Experience–Chronological Overview." Federal Deposit Insurance Corporation. https://www.fdic.gov/bank/historical/managing/chronological/pre-fdic.html.

⁷⁷ "Bank Failures in Brief–Summary 2001 through 2023." Federal Deposit Insurance Corporation. https://www.fdic.gov/bank/historical/bank/.

⁷⁸ "About Treasury Marketable Securities." https://www.treasurydirect.gov/marketable-securities/.

⁷⁹ Carlson, Kyle, Joshua Kim, Annamaria Lusardi, and Colin F. Camerer. 2015. "Bankruptcy rates among NFL players with short-lived income spikes." American Economic Review 105, no. 5: 381-384.

⁸⁰ "Starting Your Retirement Benefits Early." https://www.ssa.gov/benefits/retirement/planner/agereduction.html.

⁸¹ Sheiner, Louise and Georgia Nabors. 2023. "Social Security: Today's financing challenge is at least double what it was in 1983." The Brookings Institution. https://www.brookings.edu/articles/social-security-todays-financing-challenge-is-at-least-double-what-it-was-in-1983/.

⁸² Ruffing, Kathy. 2012. "Social Security: It's Not 1983." https://www.cbpp.org/blog/social-security-its-not-1983.

⁸³ United States Department of Labor. 2024. "Employee Benefits Security Administration. Private Pension Plan Bulletin Historical Tables and Graphs 1975-2020."

⁸⁴ "Millennials didn't kill the "organization man" after all. Federal data reveals it was the boomers all along." 2024. Fortune. https://fortune.com/2023/09/02/job-hopping-millennials-boomers-switching-careers-disloyalty-organization-man-bls/.

270

[85] Block, H. 2023. "401K and IRA early distribution penalties" H&R block. https://www.hrblock.com/tax-center/irs/tax-responsibilities/ira-rules-and-penalties/.
[86] "Roth IRA vs. Traditional IRA." Charles Schwab. https://www.schwab.com/ira/roth-vs-traditional-ira.
[87] "Which IRA is right for you?" Fidelity. https://www.fidelity.com/retirement-ira/ira-comparison.
[88] "How term life insurance works: The basics." Guardian Life Insurance. https://www.guardianlife.com/life-insurance/how-term-life-works.
[89] "Permanent life insurance: what it is and how it works." Guardian Life Insurance. https://www.guardianlife.com/life-insurance/permanent.
[90] Iervasi, Katia. 2024. "Is Whole Life Insurance a Good Investment in 2025?" NerdWallet. https://www.nerdwallet.com/article/insurance/is-whole-life-insurance-good-investment.

CHAPTER THREE. SPENDING

[1] "Household savings." OECD. https://data.oecd.org/hha/household-savings.htm.
[2] "American Credit Card Debt Hits a New Record—What's Changed Post-Pandemic?" 2023. U.S. Government Accountability Office. https://www.gao.gov/blog/american-credit-card-debt-hits-new-record-whats-changed-post-pandemic.
[3] Phil Rosen. 2023. "The Housing Market Is Historically Unaffordable—but a Record Number of Americans Now Own Their Home without a Mortgage." Business Insider. https://markets.businessinsider.com/news/commodities/housing-market-home-mortgage-unaffordable-rates-fed-prices-investors-finance-2023-11.
[4] "Average U.S. FICO score at 718." 2023. FICO Decisions Blog. https://www.fico.com/blogs/average-us-fico-score-718.
[5] Fried, C. 2022. "What does FICO Score 8 mean?" American Express. https://www.americanexpress.com/en-us/credit-cards/credit-intel/fico-score-8/.
[6] Horymski, C. 2024. "Experian 2023 Consumer Credit Review." Experian. https://www.experian.com/blogs/ask-experian/consumer-credit-review/.
[7] Horymski, C. 2024. "What is the average credit score in the U.S.?" Experian. https://www.experian.com/blogs/ask-experian/what-is-the-average-credit-score-in-the-u-s/.
[8] "What is a 'daily periodic rate' on a credit card?" 2024. Consumer Financial Protection Bureau. https://www.consumerfinance.gov/ask-cfpb/what-is-a-daily-periodic-rate-on-a-credit-card-en-46/.
[9] Kurt, Daniel. 2024. "How is Interest Calculated on Credit Cards?" https://time.com/personal-finance/article/how-is-credit-card-interest-calculated/.
[10] Banker, Sachin, Derek Dunfield, Alex Huang, and Drazen Prelec. 2021 "Neural mechanisms of credit card spending." Scientific Reports 11, no. 1: 4070.
[11] Bermudez, Rene. 2023. "Can You Get a No-Credit-Check Mortgage?" https://www.lendingtree.com/home/mortgage/how-to-get-a-mortgage-with-no-credit-score/.

[12] Ramsey, Dave. "The total money makeover: A proven plan for financial fitness." Thomas Nelson, 2013.
[13] Axelton, Karen. 2024. "What Is an Origination Fee?" Experian. https://www.experian.com/blogs/ask-experian/what-is-an-origination-fee/.
[14] Brozic, Jennifer. 2024. "What Is a Loan Application Fee?" Experian. https://www.experian.com/blogs/ask-experian/what-is-loan-application-fee/.
[15] Egan, John. 2021. "How to Avoid Paying a Prepayment Penalty." Experian. https://www.experian.com/blogs/ask-experian/how-to-avoid-paying-prepayment-penalty/.
[16] "CFPB Bans Excessive Credit Card Late Fees, Lowers Typical Fee from $32 to $8." 2024. Consumer Financial Protection Bureau. https://www.consumerfinance.gov/about-us/newsroom/cfpb-bans-excessive-credit-card-late-fees-lowers-typical-fee-from-32-to-8/.
[17] "What is Gambling Disorder?" American Psychiatric Association. https://www.psychiatry.org/patients-families/gambling-disorder/what-is-gambling-disorder.
[18] "FAQs: What is Problem Gambling?" National Council on Problem Gambling. https://www.ncpgambling.org/help-treatment/faqs-what-is-problem-gambling.
[19] Anselme, Patrick, and Mike JF Robinson. 2013. "What motivates gambling behavior? Insight into dopamine's role." Frontiers in Behavioral Neuroscience 7: 182.
[20] "Ivy League Acceptance Rates for the Class of 2028." 2024. Crimson Education. https://www.crimsoneducation.org/us/blog/ivy-league-acceptance-rates/.
[21] "World Population Prospects 2024." United Nations. https://population.un.org/wpp/.
[22] "Estimated probability of competing in professional athletics." 2024. National Collegiate Athletic Association. https://www.ncaa.org/sports/2015/3/6/estimated-probability-of-competing-in-professional-athletics.aspx.
[23] "What to Know About Male Breast Cancer." Breast Cancer Research Foundation. https://www.bcrf.org/blog/male-breast-cancer-statistics-research.
[24] "Probability of Competing Beyond High School." National Collegiate Athletic Association. https://www.ncaa.org/sports/2013/12/17/probability-of-competing-beyond-high-school.
[25] "How Dangerous is Lightning?" National Weather Service. https://www.weather.gov/safety/lightning-odds.
[26] "Risk of Death. 18 Things More Likely to Kill You Than Sharks." 2022. Florida Museum of Natural History. https://www.floridamuseum.ufl.edu/shark-attacks/odds/compare-risk/death/.
[27] "App Review Guidelines." 2024. Apple. https://developer.apple.com/app-store/review/guidelines/
[28] Frank, Allegra. 2017. "Overwatch loot box probabilities revealed—at least for China." Polygon. https://www.polygon.com/2017/5/5/15558448/overwatch-loot-box-chances-china.

[29] Johnson, Ben. 2019. NPR. "Loot Boxes Are A Lucrative Game Of Chance, But Are They Gambling?" https://www.npr.org/2019/10/10/769044790/loot-boxes-are-a-lucrative-game-of-chance-but-are-they-gambling.

[30] Reilly, Luke. "New Minimum Age Classifications for Gambling, Loot Box Content in Australia." IGN. https://www.ign.com/articles/new-minimum-age-classifications-for-gambling-loot-box-content-in-australia.

[31] "Professional and Amateur Sports Protection Act." 1992. https://journalistsresource.org/wp-content/uploads/2022/10/Senate_Report-102_248.pdf.

[32] Purdum, David. 2018. "Supreme Court strikes down federal law prohibiting sports gambling." ESPN. https://www.espn.com/chalk/story/_/id/23501236/supreme-court-strikes-federal-law-prohibiting-sports-gambling.

[33] Wile, Rob. 2024. "Sports gambling takes a toll on Americans' checkbooks, research shows." NBC News. https://www.nbcnews.com/business/consumer/online-sports-gambling-bankrupting-households-reducing-savings-rcna167235

[34] Haskew, Logan, Ryan Hessling, Rubens Pessanha, Melissa Lanning Trumpower. 2023. "Better Business Bureau Scam Tracker Risk Report." Better Business Bureau. https://bbbfoundation.images.worldnow.com/library/0e107982-0211-43c0-8875-c09f406f25d6.pdf.

[35] "Author of Russia's MMM Pyramid Scheme Who Swindled Millions Dies." 2018. France 24. https://www.france24.com/en/20180326-author-russias-mmm-pyramid-scheme-who-swindled-millions-dies.

[36] Liesman, Steve. 2008. "Mavrodi Charged, Could Face 7 Years in Jail." The Moscow Times. https://www.themoscowtimes.com/archive/mavrodi-charged-could-face-7-years-in-jail.

[37] Archives, Upi. 1994. "Russian Pyramid Victims Hit Government." UPI. https://www.upi.com/amp/Archives/1994/08/28/Russian-pyramid-victims-hit-government/7879778046400/.

[38] Bigg, Claire. 2018. "Jailed for Not Paying a Fine, Ponzi Scheme Founder Plots 'Financial Apocalypse.'" RadioFreeEurope/RadioLiberty. https://www.rferl.org/a/mmm_mavrodi_plots_financial_apocalypse-update/24517183.html.

[39] Witt, Howard. 1994. "Russian Investors Entered Stock Scheme With Eyes Wide Open." Chicago Tribune. https://www.chicagotribune.com/1994/07/31/russian-investors-entered-stock-scheme-with-eyes-wide-open/.

[40] "Inflation, consumer prices (annual %)–Russian Federation." International Monetary Fund. https://data.worldbank.org/indicator/FP.CPI.TOTL.ZG?locations=RU

[41] "Madoff Whistleblower: SEC Failed to Do the Math." 2010. NPR. https://www.npr.org/2010/03/02/124208012/madoff-whistleblower-sec-failed-to-do-the-math.

273

[42] Zarroli, Jim. 2008. "Hedge Fund Maven Madoff Falls Hard." NPR. https://www.npr.org/templates/story/story.php?storyId=98204357.

[43] Gross, Terry. 2024. "'Madoff' takes account of the biggest financial Ponzi scheme in history." NPR. https://www.npr.org/2024/07/10/g-s1-9114/madoff-takes-account-of-the-biggest-financial-ponzi-scheme-in-history.

[44] Zarroli, Jim. 2021. "Bernie Madoff, Whose Ponzi Scheme Bilked Thousands, Dies In Prison." NPR. https://www.npr.org/2021/04/14/987165621/bernie-madoff-whose-ponzi-scheme-bilked-thousands-dies-in-prison.

[45] "Multilevel Marketing: 'The Research, Risks and Rewards.'" AARP. https://www.aarp.org/content/dam/aarp/aarp_foundation/2018/pdf/AARPResearchExecutiveSummaryFINAL101018.pdf.

[46] "Multi-Level Marketing Businesses and Pyramid Schemes." Federal Trade Commission. https://consumer.ftc.gov/articles/multi-level-marketing-businesses-pyramid-schemes.

[47] "Pyramid Schemes." The U.S. Securities and Exchange Commission. https://www.investor.gov/protect-your-investments/fraud/types-fraud/pyramid-schemes.

[48] "Pyramid Schemes / Multi-Level Marketing." State of California Department of Justice. https://oag.ca.gov/consumers/general/pyramid_schemes.

[49] "BBB Tip: Foreign money exchange scams." 2017. Better Business Bureau. https://www.bbb.org/article/news-releases/16915-bbb-tip-foreign-money-exchange-scams.

[50] "Nigerian Money Transfer Scams." North Carolina Attorney General. https://ncdoj.gov/protecting-consumers/sweepstakes-and-prizes/nigerian-money-transfer-scams/.

[51] "Consumer sentinel network data book December 2023." 2023. Federal Trade Commission. https://www.ftc.gov/reports/consumer-sentinel-network-data-book-2023.

[52] "Warning Signs of Investment Fraud." Washington State Department of Financial Institutions. https://dfi.wa.gov/financial-education/information/warning-signs-investment-fraud.

[53] "What to Know About Romance Scams." Federal Trade Commission. https://consumer.ftc.gov/articles/what-know-about-romance-scams.

[54] Fletcher, Emma. 2019. "Romance scams rank number one on total reported losses." Federal Trade Commission. https://www.ftc.gov/news-events/data-visualizations/data-spotlight/2019/02/romance-scams-rank-number-one-total-reported-losses.

[55] "Depreciation Infographic: How Fast Does My New Car Lose Value?" 2010. Edmunds. https://www.edmunds.com/car-buying/how-fast-does-my-new-car-lose-value-infographic.html.

[56] "Consumer Expenditures News Release." 2024. U.S. Bureau of Labor Statistics. https://www.bls.gov/news.release/cesan.htm.

[57] Lukas, Marcel F., and Ray Charles Howard. 2023. "The influence of budgets on consumer spending." Journal of Consumer Research 49, no. 5: 697-720.
[58] Geiger, A.W. 2019. "8 facts about love and marriage in America." Pew Research Center. https://www.pewresearch.org/short-reads/2019/02/13/8-facts-about-love-and-marriage/.
[59] Dew, Jeffrey P., Sonya L. Britt, and Sandra J. Huston. 2012. "Examining the Relationship Between Financial Issues and Divorce." Family Relations 61 (4): 615–28.
[60] Brown, Natalia. 2023. "The Hidden Cost Of Debt." National Debt Relief. https://www.nationaldebtrelief.com/blog/lifestyle/lifestyle-articles/how-debt-affects-your-mental-and-physical-health/.
[61] "Infographic: Love & Money in 2021." 2022. TD Stories. https://stories.td.com/us/en/article/infographic-love-and-money-2021.
[62] Gerson, Emily Starbuck. "When You Get Married, Do You Share Debt?" Experian. https://www.experian.com/blogs/ask-experian/when-you-get-married-do-you-share-debt/.
[63] Fay, Bill. 2025. "Can You Inherit Debt?" https://www.debt.org/advice/inheriting/.
[64] Lino, Mark, Kevin Kuczynski, Nestor Rodriguez, and Tusa Rebecca Schap. 2017. "Expenditures on children by families, 2015."
[65] Ward, Adrian F., and John G. Lynch Jr. 2019. "On a need-to-know basis: How the distribution of responsibility between couples shapes financial literacy and financial outcomes." Journal of Consumer Research 45, no. 5: 1013-1036.
[66] "About Financial Abuse." National Network to End Domestic Violence. https://nnedv.org/content/about-financial-abuse.
[67] "What is Financial Abuse?" National Domestic Violence Hotline. https://www.thehotline.org/resources/financialabuse/.

PART TWO. ECONOMIC LITERACY

CHAPTER FOUR. INTRODUCTION TO ECONOMICS

[1] "The health consequences of smoking—50 years of progress: a report of the Surgeon General." 2014. US Department of Health and Human Services.
[2] Mcguire, Thomas G. 2000. "Chapter 9 Physician Agency." Handbook of Health Economics, 461–536.
[3] Mosley, Tanya. 2024. "Journalist says we're 'basically guinea pigs' for a new form of industrialized food." https://www.npr.org/2024/04/18/1245541903/journalist-says-were-basically-guinea-pigs-for-a-new-form-of-industrialized-food.
[4] Boal, William M. 1995. "Testing for employer monopsony in turn-of-the-century coal mining." The RAND Journal of Economics: 519-536.
[5] Singh, Ayush. 2023. "The Rise and Fall of Company Towns." Federal Reserve Bank of Richmond.

https://www.richmondfed.org/publications/research/econ_focus/2023/q3_economic_history

6 Manning, Alan. 2021. "Monopsony in labor markets: A review." ILR Review 74, no. 1: 3-26.

7 Check out www.tylervigen.com/spurious-correlations for more examples.

CHAPTER FIVE. INCOME

1 "Union Members—2024." 2025. U.S. Bureau of Labor Statistics. https://www.bls.gov/news.release/pdf/union2.pdf

2 Walters, Matthew and Lawrence Mishel. 2023. "How unions help all workers." Economic Policy Institute. https://www.epi.org/publication/briefingpapers_bp143/.

3 U.S. Census Bureau, Real Median Family Income in the United States [MEFAINUSA672N], retrieved from FRED, Federal Reserve Bank of St. Louis; https://fred.stlouisfed.org/series/MEFAINUSA672N

4 Sherman, Arloc, Danilo Trisi, Josephine Cureton. 2024. "A Guide to Statistics on Historical Trends in Income Inequality." Center on Budget and Policy Priorities. https://www.cbpp.org/research/poverty-and-inequality/a-guide-to-statistics-on-historical-trends-in-income-inequality

5 Pazzanese, Christina. 2016. "The costs of inequality: increasingly, it's the rich and the rest." Harvard Gazette.

6 Piketty, Thomas. "Capital in the twenty-first century." 2014. Harvard University Press.

7 Piketty, Thomas. 2015. "About Capital in the Twenty-First Century." American Economic Review, 105 (5): 48-53.

8 "Society at a Glance 2024: OECD Social Indicators." 2024. OECD Publishing. https://doi.org/10.1787/918d8db3-en.

9 US Census Bureau. 2023. "How the Census Bureau Measures Poverty." Census.gov. https://www.census.gov/topics/income-poverty/poverty/guidance/poverty-measures.html.

10 Venator, Joanna, and Richard V. Reeves. 2015. "Measuring Relative Mobility, Part 2." The Brookings Institution. https://www.brookings.edu/articles/measuring-relative-mobility-part-2/.

11 Well-detailed summary of literature is presented in Lovenheim, Michael F., and Jonathan Smith. 2022. "Returns to different postsecondary investments: Institution type, academic programs, and credentials." No. w29933. National Bureau of Economic Research.

12 Carnevale, Anthony P., and Jeff Strohl. 2010. "How Increasing College Access Is Increasing Inequality, and What to Do About It." In "Rewarding Strivers: Helping Low-Income Students Succeed in College." New York, NY: Century Foundation Press.

13 Radwin, D., Conzelmann, J.G., Nunnery, A., Lacy, T.A., Wu, J., Lew, S., Wine, J., and Siegel, P. 2018. "2015–16 National Postsecondary Student Aid Study." U.S.

Department of Education. https://nces.ed.gov/pubs2018/2018466.pdf.

[14] "Quartiles and selected deciles of usual weekly earnings by educational attainment." Bureau of Labor Statistics. https://www.bls.gov/charts/usual-weekly-earnings/usual-weekly-earnings-by-quartiles-and-selected-deciles-by-education.htm.

[15] "Annual Earnings by Educational Attainment." 2024. National Center for Education Statistics. https://nces.ed.gov/programs/coe/indicator/cba/annual-earnings.

[16] Lovenheim, Michael F., and Jonathan Smith. 2022. Returns to different postsecondary investments: Institution type, academic programs, and credentials. No. w29933. National Bureau of Economic Research.

[17] "Labor Market Outcomes of College Graduates by Major." 2025. Federal Reserve Bank of New York. https://www.newyorkfed.org/research/college-labor-market#--:explore:outcomes-by-major.

[18] "Labor Market Outcomes of College Graduates by Major." 2025. Federal Reserve Bank of New York. https://www.newyorkfed.org/research/college-labor-market#--:explore:outcomes-by-major.

[19] Buber, Sinem. "The Most Regretted and Most Loved College Majors." 2022. ZipRecruiter. https://www.ziprecruiter.com/blog/regret-free-college-majors/.

[20] O'Shaughnessy, Thomas. 2023. "Reality Check: Exploring Unrealistic Undergraduate Salary Expectations." Clever Real Estate. https://listwithclever.com/research/college-student-salary-expectations-study/.

[21] "Gen Z Salary Expectations Survey." 2022. Real Estate Witch. https://www.realestatewitch.com/college-graduate-salary-2022/.

[22] Perry, Mark J. 2022. "Chart of the Day . . . or Century?" American Enterprise Institute. https://www.aei.org/carpe-diem/chart-of-the-day-or-century-8/.

[23] Hanson, Melanie. 2025. "Average Private vs Public College Tuition." https://educationdata.org/private-vs-public-college-tuition

[24] "World University Rankings 2024." Times Higher Education. https://www.timeshighereducation.com/world-university-rankings/2024/world-ranking

[25] "International Students." 2023. Open Doors. https://opendoorsdata.org/fast_facts/fast-facts-2023/

[26] "List of U.S. states by population." Encyclopedia Britannica. https://www.britannica.com/topic/largest-U-S-state-by-population

[27] Bennett, William J. 1987. "Our greedy colleges." New York Times 18: A27.

[28] Robinson, Jenna A. 2017. "The Bennett Hypothesis Turns 30." James G. Martin Center for Academic Renewal.

[29] "Postsecondary Institution Revenues." 2023. National Center for Education Statistics. https://nces.ed.gov/programs/coe/indicator/cud.

[30] Korn, Melissa, Andrea Fuller, Jennifer S. Forsyth. 2023. "Colleges Spend Like There's No Tomorrow. 'These Places Are Just Devouring Money.'" The Wall

Street Journey. https://www.wsj.com/articles/state-university-tuition-increase-spending-41a58100.

[31] McGinty, Jo Craven. 2021. "March Madness Is a Moneymaker. Most Schools Still Operate in Red." https://www.wsj.com/articles/march-madness-is-a-moneymaker-most-schools-still-operate-in-red-11615545002

[32] "Postsecondary Institution Revenues." 2023. National Center for Education Statistics. https://nces.ed.gov/programs/coe/indicator/cue.

[33] Yoder, Steven. 2022. "Twilight of income-share agreements to pay for college?" The Hechinger Report. https://hechingerreport.org/twilight-of-income-share-agreements-to-pay-for-college/.

[34] Cameron, Margaux, T. Austin Lacy, Peter Siegel, Joanna Wu, Ashley Wilson, Ruby Johnson, Rachel Burns, and Jennifer Wine. 2021. "2019-20 National Postsecondary Student Aid Study (NPSAS: 20): First Look at the Impact of the Coronavirus (COVID-19) Pandemic on Undergraduate Student Enrollment, Housing, and Finances (Preliminary Data). NCES 2021-456." National Center for Education Statistics. https://nces.ed.gov/pubs2021/2021456_Summary.pdf.

[35] "What is a federal Direct Loan?" 2023. https://www.consumerfinance.gov/ask-cfpb/what-is-a-federal-direct-loan-en-1553/.

[36] "529 savings plans." Fidelity. https://www.fidelity.com/529-plans/overview

[37] "College Student Employment." 2022. National Center for Education Statistics. https://nces.ed.gov/programs/coe/indicator/ssa/college-student-employment.

[38] "The Simple Truth About the Gender Pay Gap." American Association of University Women. https://www.aauw.org/resources/research/simple-truth/.

[39] Wall, Howard J. 2000. "The gender wage gap and wage discrimination: illusion or reality?" The Regional Economist: 10-11.

[40] Wall, Howard J., Alyson Reed. 2001. "How Much of the Gender Wage Gap Is Due to Discrimination?" Federal Reserve Bank of St. Louis. https://www.stlouisfed.org/publications/regional-economist/april-2001/how-much-of-the-gender-wage-gap-is-due-to-discrimination.

[41] Graham, Phil and John F. Early. 2024. "The 'Gender Pay Gap' Is a Myth That Won't Go Away." The Wall Street Journal. https://www.wsj.com/articles/the-gender-pay-gap-is-a-myth-that-wont-go-away-1f0e3841.

[42] Fry, Richard and Carolina Aragão. 2025. "Gender pay gap in U.S. has narrowed slightly over 2 decades." https://www.pewresearch.org/short-reads/2023/03/01/gender-pay-gap-facts/.

[43] Orzack, Steven Hecht, J. William Stubblefield, Viatcheslav R. Akmaev, Pere Colls, Santiago Munné, Thomas Scholl, David Steinsaltz, and James E. Zuckerman. 2015. "The human sex ratio from conception to birth." Proceedings of the National Academy of Sciences 112, no. 16: E2102-E2111.

[44] Larsen Gibby, Ashley, and Kevin JA Thomas. 2019. "Adoption: a strategy to fulfill sex preferences of US Parents." Journal of Marriage and Family 81, no. 2: 531-541.

[45] Baccara, Mariagiovanna, Allan Collard-Wexler, Leonardo Felli, and Leeat Yariv. "Child-adoption matching: Preferences for gender and race." American Economic Journal: Applied Economics 6, no. 3 (2014): 133-158.

[46] "Injuries, Illnesses, and Fatalities." U.S. Bureau of Labor Statistics. https://www.bls.gov/iif/.

[47] Leeth, John D., and John Ruser. 2003. "Compensating wage differentials for fatal and nonfatal injury risk by gender and race." Journal of Risk and Uncertainty 27: 257-277.

[48] "Labor Force Statistics from the Current Population Survey." U.S. Bureau of Labor Statistics. https://www.bls.gov/cps/cpsaat18.htm.

[49] Oaxaca, Ronald. 1973. "Male-female wage differentials in urban labor markets." International economic review: 693-709.

[50] Blinder, Alan S. 1973. "Wage discrimination: reduced form and structural estimates." Journal of Human resources: 436-455.

[51] Babcock, Linda, and Sara Laschever. 2003. "Women don't ask: Negotiation and the gender divide." Princeton University Press.

[52] Kray, Laura, Jessica Kennedy, and Margaret Lee. 2023. "Now, Women Do Ask: A Call to Update Beliefs about the Gender Pay Gap." Academy of Management Discoveries.

[53] Tungodden, Jonas, and Alexander Willén. 2023. "When parents decide: Gender differences in competitiveness." Journal of Political Economy 131, no. 3: 751-801.

[54] Foster, Thomas B., Marta Murray-Close, Liana Christin Landivar, and Mark DeWolf. 2020. "An evaluation of the gender wage gap using linked survey and administrative data." U.S. Census Bureau, Center for Economic Studies.

[55] Blau, Francine D., and Lawrence M. Kahn. 2017. "The gender wage gap: Extent, trends, and explanations." Journal of economic literature 55, no. 3: 789-865.

[56] Sin, Isabelle, Steven Stillman, and Richard Fabling. 2022. "What drives the gender wage gap? Examining the roles of sorting, productivity differences, bargaining, and discrimination." Review of Economics and Statistics 104, no. 4: 636-651.

[57] Shapiro, Ari. 2016. "On Equal Pay Day, Why The Gender Gap Still Exists." NPR. https://www.npr.org/2016/04/12/473992254/on-equal-pay-day-why-the-gender-gap-still-exists.

[58] Lewin, Tamar. 1983. "The quiet allure of Alan Greenspan." The New York Times. https://www.nytimes.com/1983/06/05/business/the-quiet-allure-of-alan-greenspan.html.

[59] Greenspan, Alan. 2008. "The age of turbulence: Adventures in a new world." Penguin.

[60] "State of Residence by Place of Birth Flows." U.S. Census Bureau. https://www.census.gov/data/tables/time-series/demo/geographic-mobility/state-of-residence-place-of-birth-acs.html.

[61] Kerns-D'Amore, Kristin. 2023. "Change in Marital Status Became More Common Reason for Moving from 2021 to 2022, Housing/Neighborhood

Improvement Reasons Declined." U.S. Census Bureau.
https://www.census.gov/library/stories/2023/09/why-people-move.html.
[62] Boustan, Leah Platt, Price V. Fishback, and Shawn Kantor. 2010. "The effect of internal migration on local labor markets: American cities during the Great Depression." Journal of Labor Economics 28, no. 4: 719-746.
[63] "Works Progress Administration (WPA)." History. 2017.
https://www.history.com/topics/great-depression/works-progress-administration.
[64] Molloy, Raven, Christopher L. Smith, and Abigail Wozniak. 2011. "Internal migration in the United States." Journal of Economic perspectives 25, no. 3: 173-196.
[65] Frey, William H. 2023. "Americans' local migration reached a historic low in 2022, but long-distance moves picked up." The Brookings Institution.
https://www.brookings.edu/articles/americans-local-migration-reached-a-historic-low-in-2022-but-long-distance-moves-picked-up/.
[66] Boustan, Leah Platt, Price V. Fishback, and Shawn Kantor. 2010. "The effect of internal migration on local labor markets: American cities during the Great Depression." Journal of Labor Economics 28, no. 4: 719-746.
[67] Paris, Francesca. 2018. "What Migrants Displaced By The Dust Bowl And Climate Events Can Teach Us." NPR.
https://www.npr.org/2018/10/20/659074873/what-migrants-displaced-by-the-dust-bowl-and-climate-events-can-teach-us.
[68] "Edwards v. People of State of California."
https://www.law.cornell.edu/supremecourt/text/314/160.
[69] Jones, Jeffrey M. 2024. "Immigration Surges to Top of Most Important Problem List." https://news.gallup.com/poll/611135/immigration-surges-top-important-problem-list.aspx.
[70] Constant, Amelie F. 2014. "Ethnic identity and work." IZA Discussion Paper.
[71] Orrenius, Pia M., and Madeline Zavodny. 2009. "Do immigrants work in riskier jobs?." Demography 46: 535-551.
[72] Friedberg, Rachel M., and Jennifer Hunt. 1995. "The Impact of Immigrants on Host Country Wages, Employment and Growth." Journal of Economic Perspectives, 9 (2): 23–44.
[73] Albert, Christoph. 2021. "The Labor Market Impact of Immigration: Job Creation versus Job Competition." American Economic Journal: Macroeconomics, 13 (1): 35–78.
[74] Banerjee, Abhijit V., and Esther Duflo. 2019. "Good economics for hard times." PublicAffairs.
[75] Doran, Kirk, Alexander Gelber, and Adam Isen. 2022. "The effects of high-skilled immigration policy on firms: Evidence from visa lotteries." Journal of Political Economy 130, no. 10: 2501-2533.
[76] Cullen, Zoe, and Ricardo Perez-Truglia. 2023. "The old boys' club: Schmoozing and the gender gap." American Economic Review 113, no. 7: 1703-1740.

[77] Mobius, Markus M., and Tanya S. Rosenblat. 2006. "Why beauty matters." *American Economic Review* 96, no. 1: 222-235.

CHAPTER SIX. HOUSING

[1] Ostrowski, Jeff. "73% of aspiring homeowners cite affordability as their primary obstacle." Bankrate. https://www.bankrate.com/mortgages/homeownership-remains-centerpiece-of-american-dream/

[2] Glaeser, Edward L., and Bryce A. Ward. 2009. "The causes and consequences of land use regulation: Evidence from Greater Boston." *Journal of urban Economics* 65, no. 3: 265-278.

[3] Glaeser, Edward L., Joseph Gyourko, and Raven Saks. 2005. "Why is Manhattan so expensive? Regulation and the rise in housing prices." *The Journal of Law and Economics* 48, no. 2: 331-369.

[4] Brand, Madeleine. "Yale Professor Predicts Housing 'Bubble' Will Burst." NPR. https://www.npr.org/2005/06/03/4679264/yale-professor-predicts-housing-bubble-will-burst.

[5] https://shillerdata.com/.

[6] Majerovitz, J. 2023. Can economists predict recessions? Saint Louis Fed. https://www.stlouisfed.org/on-the-economy/2023/sep/can-economists-predict-recessions.

[7] "Selected Housing Characteristics." U.S. Census Bureau. https://data.census.gov/table/ACSDP5Y2022.DP04.

[8] "The Down Payment Report." 2017. Down Payment Resource. https://downpaymentresource.com/wp-content/uploads/2017/11/Down-Payment-Report.Nov2017.FINAL_.pdf.

[9] "When is an adjustable rate mortgage a good idea?" Fortune. https://fortune.com/recommends/mortgages/when-is-an-adjustable-rate-mortgage-a-good-idea/.

[10] McArthur, Colin and Sarah Edelman. 2017. "The 2008 Housing Crisis. Don't Blame Federal Housing Programs for Wall Street's Recklessness." Center for American Progress. https://www.americanprogress.org/article/2008-housing-crisis/.

[11] "Selected Housing Characteristics." U.S. Census Bureau. https://data.census.gov/table/ACSDP5Y2022.DP04.

[12] "Impact of Institutional Buyers on Home Sales and Single-Family Rentals." 2022. The National Association of Realtors. https://www.nar.realtor/sites/default/files/documents/2022-impact-of-institutional-buyers-on-home-sales-and-single-family-rentals-05-12-2022.pdf

[13] Levi, Ari. 2021. "Zillow says it's closing homebuying business, cutting 25% of workforce; earnings miss estimates." https://www.cnbc.com/2021/11/02/zillow-shares-plunge-after-announcing-it-will-close-home-buying-business.html.

[14] Brooks, Khristopher J. 2022. "Redfin lays off 862 employees as housing market cools." CBS News. https://www.cbsnews.com/news/redfin-layoff-hundreds-of-workers-zillow/

[15] Vogell, Heather, Haru Coryne, and Ryan Little. 2022. "Rent Going Up? One Company's Algorithm Could Be Why." ProPublica. https://www.propublica.org/article/yieldstar-rent-increase-realpage-rent

[16] Vogell, Heather. 2022. "Company That Makes Rent-Setting Software for Apartments Accused of Collusion, Lawsuit Says." ProPublica. https://www.propublica.org/article/realpage-accused-of-collusion-in-new-lawsuit

[17] Vogell, Heather. 2023. "DOJ Backs Tenants in Case Alleging Price-Fixing by Big Landlords and a Real Estate Tech Company." ProPublica. https://www.propublica.org/article/doj-backs-tenants-price-fixing-case-big-landlords-real-estate-tech.

[18] "End Hedge Fund Control of American Homes Act." https://www.congress.gov/bill/118th-congress/senate-bill/3402/text

[19] "Stop Wall Street Landlords Act of 2022." https://www.congress.gov/bill/117th-congress/house-bill/9246/text?q=%7B%22search%22%3A%22stop+Wall+Street+landlords%22%7D

CHAPTER SEVEN. HEALTHCARE

[1] Sable-Smith, Bram. 2018. "Insulin's High Cost Leads To Lethal Rationing." NPR. https://www.npr.org/sections/health-shots/2018/09/01/641615877/insulins-high-cost-leads-to-lethal-rationing.

[2] Popli, Nik. 2023. "Here's How the Other Major Insulin Makers Are Responding after Eli Lilly's Price Cap." Time. https://time.com/6259974/insulin-eli-lilly-cost-cap-sanofi-novo-nordisk/.

[3] Pierson, Brendan. 2023. "States Cry Foul at Lilly's $13.5 M Insulin Class Action Settlement." Reuters. https://www.reuters.com/legal/litigation/states-cry-foul-lillys-135-mln-insulin-class-action-settlement-2023-08-16/.

[4] Wall, Barbra. 2014. "History of Hospitals." Upenn.edu. https://www.nursing.upenn.edu/nhhc/nurses-institutions-caring/history-of-hospitals/.

[5] Thomasson, Melissa. 2017. "The history and current reality of the U.S healthcare system." Committee on Homeland Security and Governmental Affairs, One Hundred Fifteenth Congress.

[6] "Consolidated Omnibus Budget Reconciliation Act (COBRA)." https://www.law.cornell.edu/wex/consolidated_omnibus_budget_reconciliation_act_(cobra).

[7] Keisler-Starkey, Katherine, and Lisa N. Bunch. 2011. "Health insurance coverage in the United States" U.S. Census Bureau.

[8] "Medical Expenditure Panel Survey (MEPS) Insurance Component (IC)." https://datatools.ahrq.gov/meps-ic?tab=private-sector-state&dash=27.

[9] Branham, D. Keith, Christie Peters, Nancy De Lew, and Benjamin D. Sommers. 2022. "Health Insurance Deductibles Among HealthCare. Gov Enrollees, 2017-2021." U.S. Department of Health and Human Services.

[10] "National Health Expenditures 2021 Highlights" National Health Expenditure Data. https://www.cms.gov/files/document/highlights.pdf.

[11] "Civilian noninstitutional population by age, sex, race, and ethnicity." https://www.bls.gov/emp/tables/civilian-noninstitutional-population.htm.

[12] Benz, Jennifer, J. Titus, T. Tompson, and S. Leitz. 2020. "Americans' views of healthcare costs, coverage, and policy."

[13] Brent D. Fulton, Daniel R. Arnold, and Richard M. Scheffler. 2018. "Market Concentration Variation of Healthcare Providers and Health Insurers in the United States." The Commonwealth Fund. https://www.commonwealthfund.org/blog/2018/variation-healthcare-provider-and-health-insurer-market-concentration.

[14] Lopez, Eric and Gretchen Jacobson. 2020. "How Much More than Medicare Do Private Insurers Pay? A Review of the Literature." KFF. https://www.kff.org/medicare/issue-brief/how-much-more-than-medicare-do-private-insurers-pay-a-review-of-the-literature/.

[15] "Enforcement Actions." Centers for Medicare & Medicaid Services. https://www.cms.gov/priorities/key-initiatives/hospital-price-transparency/enforcement-actions.

[16] Amin, Krutika, Karen Pollitz, Gary Claxton, Matthew Rae, and Cynthia Cox. "Ground Ambulance Rides and Potential for Surprise Billing." 2021. Peterson-KFF Health System Tracker. https://www.healthsystemtracker.org/brief/ground-ambulance-rides-and-potential-for-surprise-billing/.

[17] Cutler, David. 2020. "The World's Costliest Healthcare…and what America might do about it" Harvard Magazine. https://www.harvardmagazine.com/2020/04/feature-forum-costliest-health-care.

[18] "David Cutler: Can the U.S. Healthcare System Be Fixed?" 2020. Harvard Magazine. https://www.harvardmagazine.com/2020/03/david-cutler.

[19] Bates, Laurie J., and Rexford E. Santerre. 2013. "Does the U.S. healthcare sector suffer from Baumol's cost disease? Evidence from the 50 states." Journal of Health Economics 32, no. 2: 386-391.

[20] Hartwig, Jochen. 2008. "What drives healthcare expenditure?—Baumol's model of 'unbalanced growth' revisited." Journal of Health Economics 27, no. 3: 603-623.

[21] Colombier, Carsten. 2012. "Drivers of healthcare expenditure: Does Baumol's cost disease loom large?".

[22] Brook, Robert H. 2006. "The Health Insurance Experiment: A Classic RAND Study Speaks to the Current Healthcare Reform Debate." RAND. https://www.rand.org/pubs/research_briefs/RB9174.html.

[23] "APM Measurement: Progress of Alternative Payment Models." 2019. Healthcare Payment Learning & Action Network.

[24] Finkelstein, Amy. 2007. "The aggregate effects of health insurance: Evidence from the introduction of Medicare." The quarterly journal of economics 122, no. 1: 1-37.

[25] Kochhar, Rakesh, and Stella Sechopoulos. 2022. "How the American Middle Class Has Changed in the Past Five Decades." Pew Research Center. https://www.pewresearch.org/short-reads/2022/04/20/how-the-american-middle-class-has-changed-in-the-past-five-decades/.

[26] Ortaliza, Jared, Giorlando Ramirez, Venkatesh Satheeskumar, and Krutika Amin. 2021. "How Does U.S. Life Expectancy Compare to Other Countries? - Peterson-Kaiser Health System Tracker." Peterson-Kaiser Health System Tracker. https://www.healthsystemtracker.org/chart-collection/u-s-life-expectancy-compare-countries/.

[27] "World Development Indicators." 2023. The World Bank. http://data.worldbank.org/data-catalog/world-development-indicators

[28] "Tableaux récapitulatifs des taux de remboursement." 2025. https://www.ameli.fr/haute-saone/assure/remboursements/rembourse/tableau-recapitulatif-taux-remboursement

[29] "Take out a private health insurance policy known as a 'mutuelle.'" 2023. https://www.womenforwomenfrance.org/en/our-resources/physical-sexual-and-mental-health/paying-health-costs/take-out-a-private-health-insurance-policy-known-as-a-mutuelle

[30] "U.S. Health Care from a Global Perspective, 2022: Accelerating Spending, Worsening Outcomes." 2023. The Commonwealth Fund. https://www.commonwealthfund.org/publications/issue-briefs/2023/jan/us-health-care-global-perspective-2022.

[31] "U.S. Health Care from a Global Perspective, 2022: Accelerating Spending, Worsening Outcomes." 2023. The Commonwealth Fund. https://www.commonwealthfund.org/publications/issue-briefs/2023/jan/us-health-care-global-perspective-2022.

[32] "Waiting Times for Health Services: Next in Line." 2020. OECD. https://doi.org/10.1787/242e3c8c-en.

[33] "How Canada Compares: Results From the Commonwealth Fund's 2016 International Health Policy Survey of Adults in 11 Countries—Accessible Report." 2017. Canadian Institute for Health Information.. https://www.cihi.ca/sites/default/files/document/text-alternative-version-2016-cmwf-en-web.pdf.

[34] Schneider, Eric C., Arnav Shah, Michelle M. Doty, Roosa Tikkanen, Katharine Fields, Reginald Williams, and Mirror Mirror II. 2021. "Reflecting poorly: healthcare in the U.S. compared to other high-income countries." The Commonwealth Fund.

CHAPTER EIGHT. TAXES AND PUBLIC DEBT

[1] Hendricks, Christy. 2010. "Fire Chief Responds to Questions After Home Left to Burn." KVFS12. https://www.kfvs12.com/story/13281481/fire-chief-responds-to-burning-questions-after-home-left-to-burn/.

[2] "No Pay, No Spray: Firefighters Let Home Burn." 2010. NBC News. https://www.nbcnews.com/id/wbna39516346.

[3] Gura, David. 2010. "They Didn't Pay the Fee: Firefighters Watch Tennessee Family's House Burn." NPR. https://www.npr.org/sections/thetwo-way/2010/10/08/130436382/they-didn-t-pay-the-fee-firefighters-watch-tennessee-family-s-house-burn.

[4] Lampe, Chad. 2012. "Tenn. Town Fights Fire With Money." NPR. https://www.npr.org/2012/03/18/148858042/tenn-town-fights-fire-with-money.

[5] "Fighting back against the crash tax." 2011. CLM Magazine. https://www.theclm.org/Magazine/articles/fighting-back-against-the-crash-tax-trend/311.

[6] DeSilver, Drew. 2024. "Who Pays, and Doesn't Pay, Federal Income Taxes in the U.S.?" Pew Research Center. https://www.pewresearch.org/short-reads/2023/04/18/who-pays-and-doesnt-pay-federal-income-taxes-in-the-us/.

[7] "Tax Deduction." Tax Foundation. https://taxfoundation.org/taxedu/glossary/tax-deduction/.

[8] "Standard Deduction." Tax Foundation. https://taxfoundation.org/taxedu/glossary/standard-deduction/.

[9] Mengle, Rocky. 2024. "20 Common Tax Deductions: Examples for Your Next Tax Return." TurboTax. https://turbotax.intuit.com/tax-tips/fun-facts/9-things-you-didnt-know-were-tax-deductions/L6M1dynSH.

[10] "Social Security: Current Facts and Figures." 2023. Alliance For Retired Americans. https://retiredamericans.org/wp-content/uploads/2023/06/Social-Security-Figures-Fact-Sheet-Update-2.pdf.

[11] "Military Expenditure (% of GDP) | Data." 2019. The World Bank. https://data.worldbank.org/indicator/MS.MIL.XPND.GD.ZS.

[12] "An Update to the Budget Outlook: 2023 to 2033." 2023. Congressional Budget Office. https://www.cbo.gov/publication/59159.

[13] "What Is the National Debt Costing Us?" 2024. Peter G. Peterson Foundation. https://www.pgpf.org/blog/2024/02/what-is-the-national-debt-costing-us.

[14] Saenz, Matt. 2021. "Research Note: Economic Security Programs Significantly Reduce Poverty in Every State." Center on Budget and Policy Priorities. https://www.cbpp.org/research/poverty-and-inequality/economic-security-programs-significantly-reduce-poverty-in-every.

[15] "Spending on Veterans in the Budget." 2024. Peter G. Peterson Foundation. https://www.pgpf.org/blog/2024/04/spending-on-veterans-in-the-budget

[16] "Policy Basics: Where Do Our Federal Tax Dollars Go?" 2024. Center on Budget Policies and Priorities.

[17] "Poll: Americans Have Inflated View of Foreign Aid." 2010. PBS. https://www.pbs.org/newshour/politics/foreign-ai.

[18] "Foreign Aid 101: A quick and easy guide to understanding US foreign aid." 2021. Oxfam. https://www.oxfamamerica.org/explore/research-publications/foreign-aid-101/.

[19] "The 0.7% aid target." 2024. House of Commons Library. https://commonslibrary.parliament.uk/research-briefings/sn03714/.

[20] "Official Development Assistance (ODA)." ONE Data. https://data.one.org/topics/official-development-assistance/.

[21] "The Lusitania Disaster." Library of Congress. https://www.loc.gov/collections/world-war-i-rotogravures/articles-and-essays/the-lusitania-disaster/.

[22] "U.S. Enters the War." https://www.theworldwar.org/learn/about-wwi/us-enters-war.

[23] "Zimmermann Telegram." https://www.theworldwar.org/learn/about-wwi/zimmermann-telegram.

[24] "Your Guide to America's Finances." 2023. Fiscal Data. https://fiscaldata.treasury.gov/americas-finance-guide/.

[25] "Debt Limit." U.S. Department of the Treasury. https://home.treasury.gov/policy-issues/financial-markets-financial-institutions-and-fiscal-service/debt-limit

[26] Reagan, Ronald. "Inaugural Address 1981." Ronald Reagan Presidential Library & Museum. https://www.reaganlibrary.gov/archives/speech/inaugural-address-1981

[27] "The Reagan Presidency." Ronald Reagan Presidential Library & Museum. https://www.reaganlibrary.gov/reagans/reagan-administration/reagan-presidency

[28] "Why did the national debt in the hands of the public increase from approximately $700 billion to over $2,400 billion during the 1980s?" 2000. https://www.frbsf.org/research-and-insights/publications/doctor-econ/2000/11/national-debt-80s.

[29] "Budget Basics: National Defense." 2024. Peter G. Peterson Foundation. https://www.pgpf.org/budget-basics/budget-explainer-national-defense.

[30] Stevenson, Richard W. 2001. "Surplus Estimate Hits $5.6 Trillion." New York Times. https://www.nytimes.com/2001/01/31/us/surplus-estimate-hits-5.6-trillion.html.

[31] "The History of the Debt." TreasuryDirect. https://www.treasurydirect.gov/government/historical-debt-outstanding/.

[32] "When Does Federal Debt Reach Unsustainable Levels?" 2023. https://budgetmodel.wharton.upenn.edu/issues/2023/10/6/when-does-federal-debt-reach-unsustainable-levels.

[33] Caner, Mehmet, Thomas J. Grennes, and Friederike Fritzi N. Köhler-Geib. 2010. "Finding the tipping point-when sovereign debt turns bad." World Bank.

https://documents1.worldbank.org/curated/en/509771468337915456/pdf/WPS5391.pdf.

[34] Reinhart, Carmen M., and Kenneth S. Rogoff. 2010. "Growth in a Time of Debt." American Economic Review 100, no. 2: 573-578.

[35] Wong, Wailin, Adrian Ma. 2023. "This obscure program lets Americans donate to help pay off the national debt." https://www.npr.org/2023/05/26/1178507752/this-obscure-program-lets-americans-donate-to-help-pay-off-the-national-debt.

[36] "Debt Limit." U.S. Department of the Treasury. https://home.treasury.gov/policy-issues/financial-markets-financial-institutions-and-fiscal-service/debt-limit.

[37] "The Debt Ceiling: An Explainer." 2021. The White House. https://www.whitehouse.gov/cea/written-materials/2021/10/06/the-debt-ceiling-an-explainer/

CONCLUDING REMARKS

[1] Kaiser, Tim, Annamaria Lusardi, Lukas Menkhoff, and Carly Urban. 2022. "Financial education affects financial knowledge and downstream behaviors." Journal of Financial Economics 145, no. 2: 255-272.

[2] "Junior Achievement." Encyclopaedia Britannica. https://www.britannica.com/topic/Junior-Achievement.

[3] Hastings, Justine S., Brigitte C. Madrian, and William L. Skimmyhorn. 2013. "Financial literacy, financial education, and economic outcomes." Annu. Rev. Econ. 5, no. 1: 347-373.

[4] Consumer Financial Protection Bureau. 2023. "Financial Literacy Annual Report." https://files.consumerfinance.gov/f/documents/cfpb_financial-literacy-fy-2022_annual-report_2023-03.pdf.

[5] "2024 Survey of the States." Council for Economic Education. https://www.councilforeconed.org/policy-advocacy/survey-of-the-states/

[6] "S&P Global FinLit Survey." Global Financial Literacy Excellence Center. https://gflec.org/initiatives/sp-global-finlit-survey/